Current Issues in American Democracy

Current Issues in American Democracy

(Revised 1977)

GERSON ANTELL & WALTER HARRIS

Dedicated to serving

AMSCO

our nation's youth

When ordering this book, please specify:
either **R 21 P** or CURRENT ISSUES IN AMERICAN DEMOCRACY

Amsco School Publications, Inc.
315 Hudson Street   New York, N.Y. 10013

309.173
A627c
1977

ISBN 0–87720–605–8

PREFACE

CURRENT ISSUES IN AMERICAN DEMOCRACY explores some of the most perplexing problems of our time: among them, inflation, drug use and abuse, crime and criminal justice, poverty, and pollution. While these and the other problems and issues discussed in this book have not been oversimplified, every effort has been made to present them in terms that secondary school students can understand, and in a style that is lively, poignant, and interesting.

Issues such as how to achieve racial integration and how to define criminal acts are controversial topics that are capable of arousing passionate debate among partisans. These issues, which defy easy solutions, must still be raised, and this book does not shy away from them. For teachers who seek to provide their students with the tools they will need to understand the society in which they live and to meet their responsibilities as citizens, *Current Issues in American Democracy* should prove a valuable aid.

The treatment of each issue provides enough information to allow the teacher to use a variety of teaching strategies. In addition to the discussion lesson, the teacher may wish to employ inquiry and discovery techniques, individualized or small-group activities, or one of the role-playing alternatives. The text has been so organized that each chapter may be presented as a separate lesson, thereby freeing the teacher to select only those that are appropriate to the needs and interests of the class.

The authors, who have spent many years in the classroom, have provided for individual differences with a variety of supplementary readings and exercises. Moreover, the photographs, charts, cartoons, and readings will afford numerous opportunities for the development of both social studies and language skills. Thus the classroom teacher will find ample material to maintain a high level of student interest through a judicious combination of reading, discussion, and exercise activities.

Acknowledgments

Grateful acknowledgment is made to the following sources for permission to use copyrighted materials, which appear on the pages indicated:

Harcourt Brace Jovanovich, Inc., *page 269*, from "Four Preludes on Playthings of the Wind" from SMOKE AND STEEL by Carl Sandburg, copyright, 1920, by Harcourt Brace Jovanovich, Inc., renewed, 1948, by Carl Sandburg, reprinted by permission of the publisher.

Harper and Row, Publishers, *pages 215–216*, from *Dark Ghetto*, by Kenneth Clark, reprinted by permission of Harper and Row.

Holt, Rinehart and Winston, Inc., *page 48*, from "The Road Not Taken" from THE POETRY OF ROBERT FROST edited by Edward Connery Lathem, copyright 1916, © 1969 by Holt, Rinehart and Winston, Inc., copyright 1944 by Robert Frost, reprinted by permission of Holt, Rinehart and Winston, Inc.

Tom Lehrer, *pages 296–297*. "Pollution," © 1965 by Tom Lehrer, used by permission.

The illustrations in this book were supplied through the courtesy of:

Malcolm Arth: 59 (left). The (Buffalo, New York) *Bennett Beacon:* 28, 333. Black Star: Michael Abramson, 182; Matt Herron, 210 (left); D. & A. Pellegrino, 293 (bottom); Steven Shames, 104 (left), 253; Oscar Suitrago, 163 (top); Bob Towers, 66. Magnum: Rene Burri, 59 (right); Bruce Davidson, 301; Charles Gatewood, 171; Roger Malloch, 170 (right); Burk Uzzle, 170 (left).

The New York *Daily News:* Warren King, 263. *The New York Times:* John Soto, 38. Photo Researchers, Inc.: Van Bucher, 162; Ron Engh, 72; Rhoda Galyn, 44; Barbara Pfeffer, 190. Publishers-Hall Syndicate: Walt Kelly, 296. Rapho Guillumette: Christa Armstrong, 259 (left); Esaias Baitel, 79; Bob Combs, 221; Robert de Gast, 274; Geoffrey Gove, 245 (top); Esther Henderson, 299; Hanna Schreiber, 55; Paul E. Sequeira, 130, 154.

"The Tennessean": Tom Little, 91, 98. United Press International: 210 (right), 245 (bottom). Wide World Photos: 65, 104 (top), 119, 130, 156, 163 (bottom), 174, 189, 259 (right), 267, 293 (top and right). Will-Jo Associates, Inc., and Bill Mauldin: 137.

CONTENTS

Unit V   Health

Unit VI   Minorities

Unit VII   Criminal Justice

Unit VIII   Dissent

Unit IX   Metropolitan Areas

Unit X The Environment

Unit XI World Affairs

Unit I   Today's Problems

Chapter 1   How We See Things

Sammy Spears walked quickly into the youth lounge at the John F. Kennedy Neighborhood Center. As always, Sammy carried a clipboard stuffed with papers. As always, a few papers escaped from the jaws of the metal clip and glided to the floor. Sammy, a bit annoyed, bent down to pick them up. He wasn't prepared for what he saw as he raised his head and looked around the room.

Billy and Tommy were standing face to face, eyes blazing. A crowd of young people surrounded Billy and Tommy.

"What's going on here?" Sammy shouted. Ten people tried to answer all at once. They were not any help.

"OK," Sammy said, as he separated Billy and Tommy. "What's it all about?"

Tommy told his story.

Billy told his story.

Know the Whole Story

Sammy Spears has worked at neighborhood centers for many years. He knows that if he were to ask each person in the lounge, one at a time, to tell what happened, each one might tell a different story. In the present

1

situation the problem is made even more difficult because Billy is black and Tommy is white. Even though each person *thinks* he is telling the truth, Sammy knows that the story each tells is really only a part of the truth. Why is this so? The answer is that each person sees only a part of the whole story.

Look quickly at the drawing. What do you see? Look up for a while.

Now look at the drawing again. Do you still see the same thing?

Some of you will see a vase.

Some of you will see two faces.

Some may see both a *vase* and *two faces* (but not at the same time, of course).

The vase is *always* in the picture, even if you do not see it.

The faces are *always* in the picture, even if you do not see them.

In the same way, some of the people in the lounge see only Tommy's side of the story. Others see only Billy's side of the story. Both sides are there, but people are often "blind" to the *other* side of the story.

DO YOU SEE ALL OR ONLY PART OF THE WHOLE?   You probably know the story of the blind men and the elephant. (If you don't, look at page 16.) The story is a *fable* (a story that was made up to teach us a lesson). The elephant in this fable can be thought of as the world around us. The blind men are all the people in the world. The lesson the fable teaches us is that we all have blind spots in our views. That is, all of us look at the world in different ways. We think or feel in different ways.

Regarding the argument between Billy and Tommy, some of the people in the lounge sided with the person who was the same race that they were. This was wrong, of course, but even if the original argument had not been caused by racial conflict, some people would have sided with the person of their own race.

Perhaps we will understand that people *see* things in different ways if we examine some extreme examples.

Perhaps you have read about an African tribe that fattens up the wives of the chief. The fatter the women are, the more attractive they are supposed to be. On the other hand, some American women will go without meals to get thin. The thinner they are—they think—the more beautiful they are.

Moslems and Orthodox Jews will eat beef but will not eat pork. On the other hand, a Hindu will not slaughter a cow (which is the source of beef) for food even if he is starving.

Some adult Americans place their aged parents in homes for old people. On the other hand, in Eskimo groups, old people used to go out into the freezing cold to wait for death. This was expected of them. This does not mean that the Eskimos did not love and respect old people. It means that the Eskimos thought of life and death in different ways from the average American.

You may think that long hair is just fine for a young man. On the other hand, a billboard in a suburban town urged, "Students! Beautify America—get your hair cut!"

Some of our *blind spots,* then, are caused by religious differences. Sometimes blind spots result from *cultural* differences, and, often, from age differences (or what we call the *generation gap*). For example, Jill thinks that Bobby's long hair is "darling." But Jill's father does not want "longhaired hippies" dating his daughter.

In the fable of the blind men and the elephant, each man was sure he was right, and, in his own way, each *was* right. Yet they all were wrong. Why? Because each man knew only part of the story. No one knew the whole story.

Most of us are like the blind men in the story. We see the world only from a certain angle. Not everyone else sees the world in the same way we do. We shall try to find out why we all look at the world so differently.

Forces That Shape Our Views

Steve is a teenager. His father is chief surgeon at Mount Airy Hospital. Steve's mother, who used to teach school before she was married, sometimes goes into the local high school as a substitute teacher. Steve has his own room, a stereo set, color television, and a minibike. His father has promised that, if Steve's grades are good, he will buy him a small sports car.

Leslie is also a teenager. She lives in a rundown apartment in a poor

Forces that shape our views of the world

section of the city. Leslie shares her room with three younger sisters. Her mother is always tired from cleaning, doing the wash, cooking, and taking care of the kids. Leslie's father works hard, but he doesn't earn enough to give the kids spending money.

Do you think Leslie and Steve see the world in the same way?

Surely they do not. No matter who you are, the way you look at the world around you is going to be shaped by (1) your parents, (2) your friends, (3) your *environment,* and (4) the experiences you have had in life. Let us look at these forces more closely.

PARENTS Both of Steve's parents are college graduates, and both came from well-to-do families. Leslie's parents do not have much education or money. The problems Leslie's parents had to face—growing up poor—were much different from the problems Steve's parents faced. Steve's mother is very upset if Steve goes to school with shoes that need a shine or a shirt that needs pressing. Leslie's mother is more concerned that Leslie has a pair of shoes and a decent outfit to wear to school.

The first people we know and the first people we trust are our parents. It is natural, therefore, that it is our parents who first tell us what is right and what is wrong, and if something is good or bad. Our parents are the first to tell us what is pretty and what is ugly. To win our parents' love, we try to imitate them and to accept whatever they accept as the way we should look at the world.

FRIENDS As we grow older, we begin to have friends of our own age. You may have heard of a *peer group.* A peer is your equal—a person your age, who goes to the same school or lives in the same neighborhood. Just as we once tried so hard to please Mom and Dad, now we try hard to please our peers. We want to be part of the peer group—to belong. We do what the rest do. We dress alike, talk alike, act alike, and often think alike. Oh, not completely, but we can tell right away when someone does not belong. Often it is our so-called friends who get us started doing dangerous or illegal things. But no one likes to be left out of whatever the group is doing.

ENVIRONMENT Our environment is the third force that shapes the way we look at the world. Just what environment is may be more difficult to understand. (We shall have more to say about environment in a later unit.) Part of Steve's environment is his private room and all the things his parents have bought for him. Part of Leslie's environment is a crowded room in a rundown building in a poor area.

These different environments have given Steve and Leslie widely different experiences in life. Steve and Leslie have each seen things and met people who would seem quite strange to the other person.

When Steve walks out of his home, he sees trees and grass and attractive homes. This is his environment too. When Leslie walks out of her home, she sees decaying buildings, illness, and violence. This is her environment too.

NATIONALITY   Steve and Leslie do, however, have in common many things that are the result of their nationality. Both live in the United States. Our country's government, laws, schools, sports, and entertainment give Steve and Leslie more in common with each other than with teenagers in other parts of the world. In other words, if by chance Steve and Leslie were to meet in Tibet, they would find that they knew many of the same things. Neither Steve nor Leslie would have much in common with teenagers in Tibet. Once back home, however, Steve and Leslie might think that they did not have very much in common with each other.

Summary   Things are not always what they first seem to us to be. This is true because most people have blind spots. Therefore, few people really see the whole picture and know the whole story. The reason most people see things so differently is that all of us have different parents and friends. We are raised in different environments. If Sammy Spears wants to find out what really happened between Billy and Tommy, he cannot just accept the stories that the boys tell him. He will have to find out for himself. This is not an easy thing to do.

Looking Ahead   In the next chapter, we shall learn how to go about finding out for ourselves.

EXERCISES

MATCHING QUESTIONS   Match each term in Column A with its definition in Column B.

Column A

1. environment
2. peer group
3. to "belong"
4. "blind spot"

Column B

(*a*) to see the world in only one way
(*b*) surroundings, family, friends
(*c*) your friends or people of the same age
(*d*) to be part of the group

MULTIPLE-CHOICE QUESTIONS   For each question, write the letter of the best answer.

1. The main idea of this chapter is that (*a*) things are not always what they seem to be (*b*) your first guess is usually right (*c*) young people should not listen to their friends (*d*) Steve and Leslie do not come from the same kind of environment.

2. The illustration on page 2, a vase and two faces, was used to show that (*a*) most pictures are really tricks (*b*) a vase is easier to see than faces (*c*) if people examine the same object they must all see the same things in that object (*d*) different people often reach different conclusions even when they look at the same object or events.

3. The *main* point in the fable of the blind men and the elephant is that (*a*) all people think differently (*b*) to know the truth you must know the whole story (*c*) each one of the blind men was wrong (*d*) all people think alike.

4. The way that an individual "sees" the world is shaped by (*a*) parents only (*b*) friends only (*c*) environment only (*d*) all three—parents, friends, and environment.

5. The conclusion to be reached from this chapter is that if you want to find out what really happened in any situation, you should (*a*) trust your own instincts (*b*) ask, or read the report of, one of the people involved in the situation (*c*) ask, or read the report of, an eyewitness (*d*) try to get the whole story from many different sources.

6. Which statement about Leslie would be most difficult to prove either true or false? (*a*) Leslie is a teenager. (*b*) Leslie lives in a poor section of the city. (*c*) Leslie shares her room with three sisters. (*d*) Leslie does not see the world in the same way that Steve does.

SHARPENING SKILLS   What do you see? Examine the following illustration. Then describe what you see.

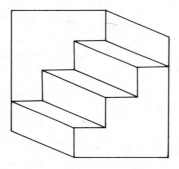

Chapter 2 Controversial Issues

Tempers were at the boiling point in the boys' locker room. Ross Baker was red with rage. Glenn Perry had just said that poor people are too lazy to work.

Another argument was going on across the hall. Ronnie Morris said that marijuana was not harmful, and anyone who wanted to buy and smoke it should be able to do so. Carol Lewis said she had dated a young man who had become a heroin addict. The young man had started smoking marijuana and then went on to the "harder stuff."

At work, in school, or at play, on any day of the week, these and other controversial subjects may come up. People often take sides about these subjects. Usually, they feel very strongly about the sides they have taken. Therefore, whenever a controversial subject comes up for discussion, people will have different opinions and strong views. Discussion will often be very *emotional* (full of feeling).

Ross is convinced that poverty is like a trap. He believes that it is very difficult for anyone born into a poor family to get out of poverty without help from outside. Glenn is just as strongly convinced that each individual shapes his or her own life. Glenn believes that people would not be poor if they really wanted to work. Minutes before this argument, Ross and Glenn had been good friends. Now they are ready to have a fight. Can Ross and Glenn discuss the poverty issue intelligently at this moment? Probably not! Neither Ross nor Glenn is ready to listen to reason. Does this mean that controversial subjects should not be discussed? Consider the case of the ostrich.

Once upon a time, an ostrich lived in a barnyard with many other animals. One day, a fight broke out between the cows and the pigs. Two sides were formed, and all the animals except the ostrich joined either the cows or the pigs. The ostrich said that the problem was not his, and he refused to take a side. He stuck his head in the sand. He thought that, if he could not see the problem, it would go away. But the ostrich was right in the middle of the warring groups. The cows charged. The pigs charged. The ostrich never saw what happened because he was trampled to death by the charging cows and pigs.

The Need to Discuss Problems

The story of the ostrich teaches us that problems do not disappear just because we do not see them (stick our heads in the sand). The wise thing to do is to face up to whatever it is that troubles us and try to work out our problems.

America has many problems that will not just go away even if we ignore them. In the United States each individual can work to bring about change and help to make our society better than it was before.

Throughout this book you will read about some of the problems that Americans face today. There is an urgent need to get these problems out in the open and discuss them freely. You will have a role to play, whether you like it or not. Don't be like the ostrich. Learn about and take a stand on such issues as the generation gap, Women's Liberation, racism, pollution, poverty, and conformity.

The issues you will discuss are sensitive ones. Students will often be emotional, one-sided, and keep their minds closed to other views. Does it pay to discuss such issues? We believe that the answer to this question is definitely yes for the following reasons:

Discussion keeps open the channels of communication. Ross and Glenn were having an argument, but they were talking—and as long as they continue to talk there is a chance that they will be able to agree on some things. Once they stop talking, they either start fighting or close off any chances of reaching an understanding about anything.

We learn to appreciate different opinions and values. Glenn really is a sympathetic person. Ross thinks that Glenn is unsympathetic. Perhaps as tempers cool and talk continues, both young men will understand each other's views and feelings. It is possible that they really agree on most issues but are getting emotional about issues and slogans that neither understands very well.

If Ross and Glenn, and each one of us, are to share the same room—or country—or world, we have to learn to accept one another's opinions and values.

We learn how to discuss controversial issues. Perhaps Ross will be able to outshout Glenn. He will not accomplish anything. Shouting is not discussion. Discussion is based upon mutual respect. Ross and Glenn must first of all respect each other as individuals. They must respect each other's rights as individuals to a wide variety of opinions and values. They must be willing to accept a give and take in their discussions.

How to Find Out

FACTS OR OPINIONS   A fact is something that can be proved true or false. For example, if a friend says to you, "It's raining," you can prove this by going outside or by walking to the window and sticking your hand out. An opinion, on the other hand, is something that cannot be proved true or false. For example, if a friend returns from a trip and says, "The people in Country A are friendly, but the people in Country B are unfriendly," this is an opinion. You have no way of proving or disproving this statement.

You may have heard that each person has the right to his or her own opinions or beliefs. At first this may sound right, but if you think a bit, you realize that all opinions are not *valid* (correct).

VALUES   Glenn says that poor people are lazy. Ross says this is not true. (Actually, both rich and poor people may be lazy.) Neither Glenn nor Ross is making a statement of fact. Both are voicing their opinions. Also, in this issue, their opinions are based upon their own *values* (sense of what is or is not important). Ross and Glenn were unable to solve their differences.

Suppose someone voices the opinion that people of one race are *inferior* to (not as good as) people of another race. This is an opinion that is not based

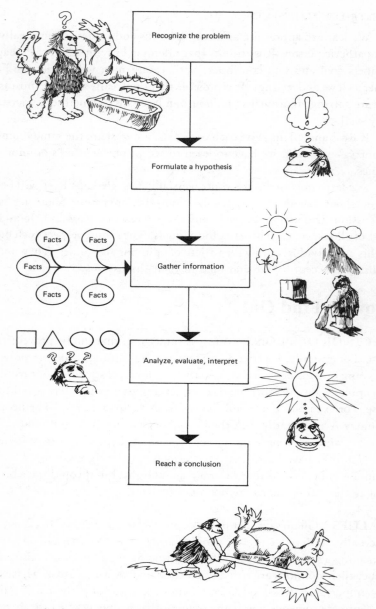

What steps in the inquiry method did the caveman use to solve his problem?

upon fact. Moreover, it is an opinion that has caused a great many people to lose their freedom and their rights as individuals. Therefore, even though we cannot stop a person from thinking this way, the opinion is not based upon sound thinking.

INQUIRY METHOD   An opinion, we have said, may prove to be right or wrong. Yet we all have opinions, and many times in our lives, how we act or speak is based on our opinions, whether they are right or wrong. But there *is* a way to find out whether our opinions are reasonable. In your science classes the method is called the *scientific method* of observation. We shall call it the method of *inquiry* (asking a question to find an answer).

Suppose that Ronnie says marijuana should be legalized and Carol says it should not be legalized. How can we decide this issue for ourselves? To do this we must keep our minds open for a time (this is called *suspending judgment*). Now we can follow these steps:

Recognize the problem. Ronnie and Carol agree that a problem exists. The problem, in this case, has to do with the *legalization* (to make something lawful) of the sale of marijuana.

Formulate a hypothesis. A *hypothesis* is a statement, or—perhaps better still—an argument, that is put forward for further discussion or investigation. Ronnie and Carol might agree to accept the hypothesis that marijuana should *not* be legalized. This is just a starting point. Now they have to prove whether it is right or wrong.

Gather information. Ronnie and Carol will now have to look for books and magazine and newspaper articles that deal with the topic. They should interview several experts in the field. Of course, they must always keep a record of their readings and interviews. (Can you explain why?)

Analyze, evaluate, and interpret the information. If Ronnie and Carol make an honest effort, they will examine very critically the information they have found. If, however, they look only for articles that back up their point of view and talk only to people with views like theirs, they will not get a true picture or the whole story. With open minds, Ronnie and Carol will at least have a more complete picture (to know the whole truth you have to know the whole story).

Reach a conclusion. Now Ronnie and Carol can reach a conclusion. They can agree with their hypothesis (marijuana should not be legalized), or they can disagree with it. Whichever decision they reach, they must still keep open minds. If new information becomes available, they must analyze, evaluate, and interpret it.

Summary   America's problems today are controversial. They are sensitive issues that cause people to become emotional. As citizens in a democracy, we must take a stand on controversial issues. The intelligent way to reach an opinion is to keep an open mind, respect the views and opinions of others, and examine the facts before reaching a conclusion.

Looking Ahead   In the next chapter, we shall examine the forces that shape public opinion in America.

EXERCISES

MATCHING QUESTIONS   Match each term in Column A with its definition in Column B.

Column A

1. emotions
2. controversy
3. fact
4. opinion
5. valid
6. values
7. inferior
8. scientific method
9. hypothesis
10. inquiry

Column B

(*a*) not equal to or as good as something or someone else
(*b*) sense of what is or is not important
(*c*) asking a question to find an answer
(*d*) a statement put forward for further discussion or investigation
(*e*) a step-by-step procedure for finding the truth
(*f*) feelings
(*g*) a statement that can be proved true or false
(*h*) a subject about which people tend to take opposing sides
(*i*) correct or true
(*j*) a statement that cannot be proved true or false

FACT OR OPINION?   Indicate whether the statements below are facts (F) or opinions (O).

1. The good side always wins the war.
2. School should teach you only the things that most people believe are right.
3. Nonwhites often suffer from discrimination in housing and jobs.
4. People should be able to buy and sell anything they want to.
5. There are more automobiles in the United States today than there were ten years ago.
6. A woman's place is in the home.
7. If you ignore a problem, it usually goes away.

SELECT THE BEST SOURCE OF INFORMATION   Three possible sources of information are given for each topic or issue listed below. Select the letter representing the *best* source of information for the topic.

1. Legalization of Marijuana
   (*a*) Report of a two-year study by the Surgeon General of the United States on the effects of marijuana smoking on health
   (*b*) Editorial in a leading newspaper opposing legalization of marijuana
   (*c*) Statement by a well-known rock and roll singer challenging the editorial on the values of marijuana
2. How Young People Feel About School
   (*a*) Editorials in school newspapers
   (*b*) Report prepared by school principals
   (*c*) Interviews with students
3. How Minority Groups Are Treated in the United States
   (*a*) Articles written by a Russian writer during a visit to the United States for the Communist newspaper *Pravda*
   (*b*) Article written by a black writer for *Jet*
   (*c*) Articles prepared by its reporters for the *New York Times*

ANALYZING, EVALUATING, AND INTERPRETING INFORMATION   Read the statements on page 16. You will find some that are based on emotion and others that are based on careful thought. For each statement, tell whether it is based on emotion (E) or thought (T).

1. We've lived in this community for 20 years. We don't want those people here. We know what will happen to our community if they move in.

2. We don't care if we have to keep our children out of school all year. We don't want any kids bussed into our neighborhood school.

3. Fluoridation of our nation's water supply is part of a Communist attempt to destroy America.

4. If democracy in America is to survive, we must solve the problems of racism and discrimination.

5. I don't want to see women competing against men in sports because it would hurt me to see a woman defeat a male player.

KNOW THE WHOLE STORY   The fable of the blind men and the elephant tells of six blind men from India who set off on a long trip. One day, in a forest, they came across a huge animal that they had never heard of before. Each man examined one part of the animal. From this examination, each thought that he knew what the animal was like.

Look at the cartoon. Based on your reading of this chapter and on the cartoon, tell (1) what each blind man thought the elephant was like, and (2) what the blind men should have done with the information they had.

Chapter 3   Public Opinion

Ronnie Morris is a senior at Central High. She was curious about how the students at Central feel about the new rule that all students must carry a program card. Students must show their cards if asked to do so by a school authority. Miss Billoti, Ronnie's social studies teacher, suggested that Ronnie make a survey of the school on this issue.

Question sheet in hand, Ronnie walked into the school cafeteria. She was shocked at the answers she received to her questions. At the first table, one student said, "Who cares? Nobody's going to pay any attention to your poll." Another said, "Even if everybody hates the rule, they still won't change it."

The next day, Ronnie reported her experiences to the class. "Miss Billoti," Ronnie asked, "is it true that no one pays attention to public opinion polls? Doesn't what people think really count?"

Public Opinion and Democracy

Miss Billoti thought for a while. Then she answered, "Certainly, what you and others think counts. After all, if democracy is to work, a government must either have or win the support of the people. You are the people."

Miss Billoti and the class then went on to discuss the importance of public opinion in a democracy. She said that public opinion is the belief, or idea, most of the people have on some issue of political or social importance.

Carol Lewis said, "Do you mean that public opinion is something like air pressure? You can't see it but it is always there." Ronnie said, "You can't measure public opinion as accurately as you can measure air pressure."

Miss Billoti said, "You're right, Ronnie. In fact, it's not often that most of the American people hold the same belief at one time. Actually, I would think that it would be more correct if we spoke of many kinds of public opinion when discussing any issue of importance to the American people."

At this point, Ross Baker joined in. "The people—who are the American people? When a politician says that the people support this or that, he really means that some group supports whatever he is supporting."

Miss Billoti agreed that the term *the people* is not very clear. She pointed out that the people change their minds—that is, *public opinion changes.* She

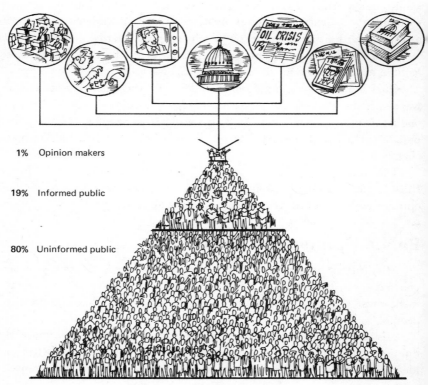

1%   Opinion makers

19%   Informed public

80%   Uninformed public

Opinion makers in our society

gave as an example of this the results of polls taken on the attitude of Americans to the war in Vietnam. "In 1965," Miss Billoti said, "most Americans supported the war, but by 1968, most Americans wanted the United States to end the war or pull out."

Ronnie wanted to know, "What makes the American people think one way or the other?" Carol added, "Yes, what makes Americans willing to fight and die, or carry picket signs and join protest marches?"

WHO MAKES PUBLIC OPINION?   Miss Billoti drew a pyramid on the chalkboard. "At the base," she said, "or about 80 percent of the total area, are the uninformed public. A smaller middle area, or about 19 percent of the total, is made up of the informed public. These are Americans who are concerned with and talk about issues. At the top of the pyramid are the remaining one percent. These are the opinion makers of our society."

Miss Billoti asked the class who they thought belonged in the top one percent of the pyramid. The class made up a list that included the President of the United States, senators and representatives and other government officials, some newspapers, newspaper columnists, and television newscasters. Since the class period was now over, Miss Billoti asked everyone to come to the next day's class prepared to discuss how opinion makers can shape public opinion.

HOW OPINIONS ARE SHAPED   When the class met the following day, they saw that Miss Billoti had placed the following list on the chalkboard:

Forces Shaping Public Opinion

1. Media   2. Pressure Groups
   a.   a.
   b.   b.
   c.   c.

Miss Billoti asked the class to fill in the blank spaces. The class supplied the information that newspapers, radio, and television are the major sources of information for most people. One student suggested that movies are also important in shaping public opinion. Another student added that books and magazines influence a smaller group, but they are also examples of the media. Glenn Perry asked the meaning of the word *media*.

Several students explained that media are such things as books, newspapers, and television. They are the pipelines through which people communicate with each other on a *mass* (large) scale. If an event were not reported in the papers or on television, we would not know that it had happened. For most of us, therefore, it would be as if the event had never taken place.

Glenn realized that the way an event is reported and the amount of coverage it receives can influence public opinion. He pointed out that the local newspaper often prints stories about the bad things that take place at Central High School. But the paper does not often print stories about the many good things that take place at Central. As a result, many people get the wrong impression of Central.

Propaganda

At this point, Ronnie spoke up. "Why can't we start a *propaganda* campaign to change the *image* of Central High School?"

"Propaganda?" Glenn asked. "Isn't that telling lies?"

"No," Ronnie replied. "Propaganda means that a group—that's us —spreads its ideas in a planned way."

Miss Billoti joined in. "Most people think that propaganda twists the truth, or is a lie, but Ronnie is correct. Propaganda can be the truth."

"OK," Glenn said, "I'm for it. How do we spread our propaganda?"

Miss Billoti asked the class to think of ways in which they have been influenced by a propaganda technique. These are the ways the class suggested:

NAME CALLING   Calling someone a racist, a Communist, or almost any other name often ends intelligent discussion. If the name sticks in other people's minds, then the person who was called a name is thought of unfavorably by others.

GLITTERING GENERALITIES   Central High School was a victim of this device because newspapers often told of "problems" at Central without really getting to the heart of these so-called problems. Then people in the community would say, "Oh, Central—that's where they had those problems."

IDENTIFICATION Central could, however, point out a well-known person who had graduated from the school. People would then identify that person with Central. Then they might think that if so-and-so made it at Central, so could they.

CARD STACKING Card stacking is like going into a card game with the deck stacked so that you get all the aces. When using this device, you tell all the bad things about the opposition. Then you point out all the good things about something you favor (for example, Central High School).

BANDWAGON "Everybody's doing it." If people can be made to believe that most of the crowd will go to Central, few students would want to be "left out." They too will want to go to Central High School.

TRANSFER Transfer uses a person's loyalty to one thing to make that person loyal to something else. For example, if you can convince someone that all loyal Americans favor one idea, then the individual might think that to be against this idea is to be un-American. You can see how this device can cut off all thinking. Any group, whether it is a nation, a racial or ethnic group, a community, or Central High School, can convince many or most of its members that being against a particular point of view is being disloyal to the group.

Summary *Public opinion* is important in any democratic society, whether that society is a nation or a school. Most people do not have the same opinions, and public opinion is really made by small groups of people—either *pressure groups* or the people who control the *media* (channels of communication). Propaganda devices can be used to sway people to accept an idea that the group wants or favors.

Looking Ahead The term *democracy* was used many times during the class discussion. In the next chapter, we shall consider more fully the meaning of democracy.

EXERCISES

ESSAY QUESTION   Write a short paragraph that includes each of the following terms: public opinion   opinion makers   media   propaganda   pressure group.

RECOGNIZING PROPAGANDA DEVICES   Match each propaganda device in Column A with an example of the device in Column B.

Column A

1. name calling
2. glittering generalities
3. identification
4. card stacking
5. bandwagon
6. transfer

Column B

(*a*) Everybody's wearing "Gillie's Slacks."
(*b*) All loyal Americans are in favor of prayers in the schools.
(*c*) He's a racist imperialist pig.
(*d*) Top tennis stars use No-Net tennis balls.
(*e*) We all know that Central High School has had its problems.
(*f*) Tired of dark, cold, snowy winter? Come to our warm, sunny island.

CONDUCTING A PUBLIC OPINION POLL   Public opinion polls have become an important source of information about the way people think. Some people go as far as to say that public opinion polls actually influence the way people think. What really is being said is that public opinion polls can create a *bandwagon* effect.

1. Ask 25 students *at random* (without making a careful choice): *"Do you favor giving just 'Pass' or 'Fail' grades instead of marks in all subjects?"* Then list the answers in 3 columns, as follows: *Yes   No   Don't Know.*
2. Find percentage figures for each category. Make the total in each category into a fraction of 25 and convert the fraction into a percent. For example, if 5 students said "No," this is 5/25, or 20 percent.
3. After you have found your percentages, conduct a *second* poll. This time,

change the question slightly by saying: *"Eighty percent of the students polled at this school favor changing the grading system in all subjects from marks to 'Pass' or 'Fail.' What is your opinion?"* Once again, select 25 students at random and record the number answering *Yes, No,* and *Don't Know.*

4. Compare these results with your first poll. What conclusions can you draw from your results?

CHECK THE NEWSPAPER   Do you read your daily newspaper with a critical eye? Some people charge that newspapers deliberately slant or distort the news they report. For a week, select a few articles every day from your favorite newspaper to prove or disprove each of the following charges:

1. Only one political viewpoint—the publisher's—is presented.
2. Crime, sex, and sports are given the greatest coverage, even though other, more important events happened in the world.
3. A reporter's opinion is often presented as if it were a fact.
4. Certain news stories are placed up front and are given big headlines and more space so that they seem more important than stories with small headlines and limited space that are buried in the back pages.
5. Newsmen often cite "anonymous" or unnamed sources which the reader has no way of checking up on.
6. When the paper makes an error of fact, the correction is given far less space than the original error.
7. The paper does not print anything that might offend an important advertiser.
8. Reporters are more interested in making their stories entertaining or exciting than in presenting them accurately.

Chapter 4   Dealing With Problems in a Democracy

A crowd was gathering outside the entrance of the school. Mary Somers tried to find out what was going on. She saw that Mrs. Rodriguez, a physics teacher, was arguing with a student who was handing out leaflets. The student was saying, "Power to the people." Other students were joining in, saying, "Right on!" The student was telling Mrs. Rodriguez that the United States is an imperialist fascist country. Mrs. Rodriguez was saying that the United States is a democracy.

She asked the student, "If you don't think the United States is a democracy, what country do you think is?"

The student replied, "The People's Republic of China."

Mary hurried into school. All day, what she had seen and heard remained in her mind. Her last class was in problems of American democracy. As soon as the class started, Mary raised her hand and told Mr. Weber, her teacher, what she had seen.

"Mr. Weber, what *is* democracy?" she asked.

Mary's question is not easy to answer. Many countries call themselves democracies. The United States considers itself a democracy, yet the nations that we call Communist all say that they are democratic people's republics. Mr. Weber and the class decided to spend the period discussing the meaning of democracy. Here are some of the ideas they discussed.

First, the class discussed democracy as a *political* system. This involves how the country is governed.

Second, the class discussed democracy as a *way of life.* That is, they discussed the *social* and *economic features* of American society. For example, they talked about the schools, homes, jobs, unions, and the rights of individuals in our society.

Democracy as a Political System

The word *democracy* comes from two Greek words, *demos* and *kraten,* meaning "rule of the people." Abraham Lincoln, as you know, said that democracy was a "government of the people, by the people, and for the people." In the political sense, democracy is a way of governing in which the government is elected and controlled by the people of the country.

WHY GOVERNMENTS ARE NEEDED   People do not live alone. We live in groups (we call these groups *societies*). If we are to continue to live in societies, rules are needed. The rules may be made up by all of the members in a society. Or the rules may be made up by a small group for everyone else to follow.

In a democratic society, the rules are made either directly by all adult citizens (*direct democracy*), or indirectly (*representative democracy*) by people chosen by the citizens. When a democracy does not have many members, as was true of ancient Athens and colonial New England, all of the citizens could get together and vote on most issues that came up. (In ancient Athens and in colonial New England, not all adults were citizens, however.) In the United States today, it would be impossible for millions of Americans to vote on every issue that comes up. Therefore, citizens choose people (assemblymen, senators, and congressmen) to *represent* them, to act in their name, on most issues. If Americans do not think their representatives are doing a good job, they can replace them in the next election.

In a totalitarian or authoritarian society, all power is in the hands of one person or a small group of people. Another name for this type of society is dictatorship. The word "totalitarian" is based on the word "total." This means that all of the people in a society and all of the resources of the society have one goal—to serve the state or the dictator or group that controls the state. All political parties but one are illegal. In the Soviet Union and the People's Republic of China, a small group within the Communist party sets the rules for everyone else to follow.

In some of the new nations of Africa, Asia, and Latin America, small groups of military leaders make the rules for the people. In these countries the dictatorships may not be as complete, or *total,* as in Russia and China. We usually call such societies *authoritarian* rather than totalitarian.

If we made a scale of all countries in the world today and placed them according to who rules, we would find that at one end of the scale would be some countries where only a few people rule and at the other end of the scale would be countries where the majority of the people rule. No country, probably, is completely democratic and no country, probably, is completely totalitarian.

The scale shows how countries today might look if measured according to who rules. You may disagree with the placement, and you might want to add other countries to the scale.

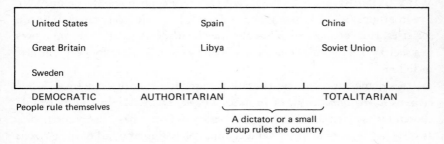

DEMOCRACY AND REPUBLIC   A country may be a democracy with a republican *form* of government, or it may be a democracy with a form of government known as a monarchy, as in Great Britain. A republican form of government is one in which there is no *hereditary* ruler such as a king or queen. Some countries are republics—such as the Soviet Union—but they are not democracies. Therefore, the important thing to remember is that the form of the government is not as important as the degree to which the people actually control it.

Majority Rule   As long as mankind lives in groups, rules will be needed. What is not easy to answer is the question of how to make the rules and enforce them once they are made. Somehow or other, a balance has to be reached between no rules at all (complete freedom) and no freedom at all. In a totalitarian society people are forced to do what they are told. In some societies, tradition makes people do things in the same way as their ancestors did. For example, the caste system in India set up a system of rules so that Hindus know what they can and cannot do. How could you get people to follow the rules in a democracy?

When you stop to think about it, a society is really made up of many different groups. For example, there are farmers' groups, business groups, women's groups, labor unions, church groups, veterans' groups, professional groups (such as the American Medical Association), and civil rights groups. Each group has its own special interests. In a democracy, the trick is to get these groups to take part in the workings of the government.

People can belong to more than one group at a time. In a democracy, political parties such as our Democratic and Republican parties may bring together the interests of many groups. By belonging to a political party, a group is able to present its points of view and special interests. Through discussion and compromise, various groups reach a common basis of agreement or consent.

In a democracy the majority rules. However, a democracy must balance the rights of the majority and the rights of the minority. Too much emphasis on the rights of the majority could lead to totalitarianism. Too much emphasis on the rights of a minority could lead to no government at all. The minority must accept the majority decisions *knowing that they can have their say and another chance to become the majority next time.* The majority must respect the rights of the minority.

Democracy as a Way of Life

Are only governments democratic or undemocratic? Can a school be democratic? Can an individual be democratic? Democracy is more than just a form of government—it is also a way of life. Therefore, the answer to these questions is yes, a school, an individual, or a family may or may not be democratic, even though the individual or group is living in a democratic country.

Democracy as a way of life has to do with *liberty* and *equality*. For example: Are all people free and equal before the law? Do all citizens have equal educational opportunities in free public schools? Are all individuals protected against discrimination? Can workers join labor unions and can a person enter any occupation or business that he or she chooses?

The United States was a political democracy long before all its people were granted equal rights by law. We are still working to improve our social and economic practices.

LIBERTY   Liberty means freedom, but how much freedom can the individual have in a democracy? To return to Mary's class, Mr. Weber reminded them that people live in groups. Groups may both give and take away liberty from the individual. Mr. Weber walked up close to Mary and swung his arm until his fist stopped just short of Mary's nose. He asked, "Can I do whatever I please? Can I swing at you if that is what I want to do?" Mary answered, "You have no right to hit me. Your right to swing your fist stops before your fist reaches my nose."

Liberty is not *absolute* (complete); it is always *relative* (depends on the situation). Mr. Weber asked, "Can the group actually increase freedom by *restricting* (withholding) freedom?" No one in the class could answer, so Mr. Weber asked another question. "Suppose Tommy always talked out in class and tried to answer every question I asked. Would I be increasing or decreasing freedom if I refused to call on Tommy all the time and made him talk only when called upon?" Sally answered, "Well, you would be taking

Discussing problems in a democratic society

some freedom from Tommy but giving the rest of us more freedom to take part in class." Tommy raised his hand and said, "Isn't that like limiting the number of fish you can catch? Doesn't that increase the freedom of more people to fish?"

Mr. Weber agreed that it did. As long as people live in society, democracy has to try to reach a happy medium between individual freedom and the needs of the society as a whole.

EQUALITY Mary's thoughts went back to the incident in front of school. She remembered reading a sign that one student was holding. The sign said, "All men are created equal—except!" Mary asked, "In a democracy, are all people really equal?"

Someone said, "No, some people are born smarter than others. And a rich person's children have a head start on a poor man's children."

Mr. Weber replied, "Of course, each individual is different. We admire a famous athlete and a great scientist, but their achievements do not give them special privileges. We are all equal before the law. If rich or famous people park in front of a fire hydrant, they should be ticketed just like the rest of us. Each person should be treated with dignity and judged on the basis of his or her own merit and ability."

Mary said, "Very nice, but we know that things don't always work that way in this country. Just because we have rights on paper doesn't mean we really have them. I know that it's illegal not to rent an apartment to anyone because of race, but landlords find ways to break the law. I also know that everyone is entitled to a fair trial—but can a poor person afford a high-priced lawyer? No, the most a poor person gets is a court-appointed lawyer, who may be just out of law school."

Tommy joined in, "Wait a minute, I'm on the track team. In a track meet we all start at the same time. We run the same distance and we follow the same rules. But some finish ahead of others. We all had an equal chance to finish first. *Equality also means the right to be unequal.*"

Mr. Weber said, "The test of any system is whether it meets the needs of the people. People will turn away from a system that they think has failed them. They *will* adopt a system that they think will offer some improvement. Since 1776 we have been convinced that democracy is the best system for us."

Mary jumped up and said, "That isn't enough. Young people today won't accept a way of life that's based only on past glories. We're living now!"

Summary   Mr. Weber summed it up. "Democracy must continue to change if it is to survive. American democracy is *dynamic*. That means that it changes all the time to meet the needs of the American people."

Looking Ahead   In the ten units of this book, we shall examine some of America's problems and learn how our society is trying to solve them.

EXERCISES

MATCHING QUESTIONS   Match each term in Column A with its definition in Column B.

Column A

1. democracy
2. society
3. totalitarian
4. direct democracy
5. representative democracy
6. liberty
7. dynamic
8. republic

Column B

(*a*) a group of people living together
(*b*) a government ruled by a small group of people
(*c*) always changing
(*d*) a government in which the people rule
(*e*) a form of government in which there is no hereditary ruler, such as a king or emperor
(*f*) freedom
(*g*) rules of the society are made by people chosen by its citizens
(*h*) rules of the society are made by all of its citizens

INTERPRETING A CARTOON   In this chapter, we have said that democracy in America is dynamic—it changes all the time to meet the needs of the people. However, people disagree as to where America should be headed. Some want to go back to "the good old days"; others like things as they are; and others want to change things quickly.

The cartoon expresses the artist's point of view about where America is headed. Study the cartoon and do the following:

1. In a few words, describe each person in the cartoon.
2. Tell what the artist's point of view is. Do you agree with it?
3. Write a short paragraph telling where *you* think America should be heading.

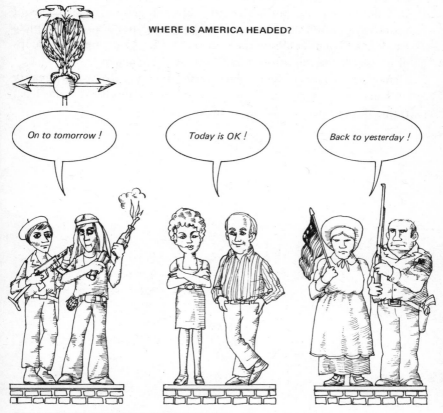

WHERE IS AMERICA HEADED?

MULTIPLE-CHOICE QUESTIONS   For each question, write the letter of the best answer.

1. The main idea of this chapter is that (*a*) the United States is a democracy (*b*) not all countries are democracies (*c*) democracy is both a form of government and a way of life (*d*) a republic is not a democracy.

2. An example of *political* democracy is to (*a*) place all power in the hands
   of one political party (*b*) allow citizens to choose their representatives in
   Congress (*c*) allow a well-organized minority to rule (*d*) allow everyone
   to do whatever they want to do.
3. In a *republican* form of government (*a*) the party in power is called the
   Republican party (*b*) there is no hereditary ruler, such as a king (*c*)
   there is also a democratic political system (*d*) there is majority rule.
4. In a democracy (*a*) political parties bring together the demands of
   various groups (*b*) there is no need to keep a balance between complete
   freedom and none at all (*c*) there are no conflicting or opposing groups
   of ideas (*d*) the minority cannot become the majority.
5. Democracy *as a way of life* involves questions of (*a*) liberty and equality
   (*b*) balancing the rights of the majority and minority (*c*) the legal
   rights of poor people (*d*) all of these.

Unit II   Youth

Chapter 1   The Role of
Young Adults

Jimmy Green was excited when he got home from school today. He had been elected vice-president of his class at Central High School and was anxious to tell his mother all about it.

Mrs. Green and two women neighbors were talking and drinking coffee in the kitchen when Jimmy burst in. "I won! I won!" Jimmy shouted. The ladies seemed startled. The talking stopped. For a moment, Jimmy forgot what was on his mind and a little anger could be heard in his voice as he said, "Every time I'm around, you people stop talking!" Mrs. Willis, an older lady who lives on the third floor, replied, "Now, Jimmy. Be quiet. You know that children should be seen but not heard."

Perhaps you have had your own *humiliating* (shaming) experiences at the hands of adults. For example, how many times have you been told to think for yourself? Probably a great many times. But, when you do, an adult—a teacher, parent, or neighbor—tells you that what you think is silly. Or you are told that it's about time you had a sense of responsibility—and then you are told that you cannot do this, that, or the other thing.

Who Are Young Adults?

Jimmy Green is 15 years old. He is a young adult, not a child, as Mrs. Willis thinks. When does a *child* become a *young adult?* According to some

33

adults, never. According to some young people, right now. Of course the answer is somewhere in between. Some people *mature* (grow up emotionally) faster than others, and some people never seem to grow up. Young adults are people between the ages of 14 and 24 years. Physically, they are adults. But in this world, it is the parents, teachers, and lawmakers who decide when to accept an individual into the adult world. How does a young adult know when he or she is accepted? The answer is: When he or she is allowed to make decisions and do the things that other adults are allowed to do, an individual has been accepted as an adult.

Jimmy Green was taught in school that everyone in a democracy has the right to speak out. As vice-president of his class, Jimmy will have a lot to say. Jimmy knows that there is nothing in the United States Constitution, or in the constitution of any state, that says only adults are allowed to speak.

Jimmy is not satisfied just because he is allowed to speak. Like most young people, Jimmy wants to be listened to when he talks. He wants to be taken seriously. When he is "allowed" to speak in class, or as the representative of all his classmates at school, Jimmy does not want his ideas *put down* (rejected) by teachers with "You don't understand" or "It can't be done."

Young people in America are being listened to. The influence of American youth is growing. Here is why:

There are more young people than ever before. In 1960 the Bureau of the Census counted some 27 million individuals—or about 15 percent of the total population—between the ages of 14 and 24. In 1970 the number had leaped to 40 million, or 20 percent of the population. What is more, the number of young adults is increasing at a faster rate than the total population of the United States.

Young people know more. Young Americans today know more about what is going on in the world than their parents and grandparents did when they were young adults. Why do young Americans know more? The answer is that they have read more, are better educated, and have traveled more widely than was possible when their parents and grandparents were young.

Young people buy more. Young adults between the ages of 14 and 24 earned nearly $45 billion in 1971. They also influenced the spending of another $135 billion. It is estimated that young adults will spend one out of every three dollars spent in the United States by 1980.

Young people are more involved. It was youth who led the cry to end the war in Vietnam. It is American youth that is calling for racial justice and asking us to save our environment. Moreover, many young adults are voting. Eighteen-year-olds have been granted the vote.

Jimmy Green, like every other teenager, has heard, all too often, these words from adults: "When I was your age . . ." Times are changing. They always have and probably always will. Each *generation* (the people born at about the same time) has its "own thing," its own way of looking at the world. Grandpa cannot understand Dad's generation. Dad cannot understand your generation. As far as you are concerned, Dad is only a little bit less out-of-date than Grandpa. We call the differences in attitudes and ways of thinking between the generations the *generation gap*.

The Generation Gap

Actually, young people of Mom and Dad's generation were also involved in what was going on around them at the time. Your parents, for example, might have been inspired by the fight against social injustice in the United States during the 1950s.

The changes in the way we live have helped to bring about the generation gap. Today, more and more people live in the cities. Even though the houses in rural areas may have been far apart, everybody seemed to know everyone else's business. A hundred families may live in one city apartment building, yet it is quite possible for a person not to know the name of the next-door neighbor. So, while they are crowded together in cities, young people are often really more alone and on their own than they would be in a rural area.

NEW LIFE-STYLES   In the city, particularly in high school, young people are likely to meet many different kinds of people. The people that the young person meets might have *life-styles* (attitudes and ways of doing things) completely different from those of anyone at home. Thus, while parents are saying that to do this or that is bad, new friends are saying just the opposite.

Teenagers today have many more *options* (choices) than their parents did. There are many new kinds of jobs. The workday and the workweek are shorter, leaving more time to do as one pleases. More products, such as cars

Generation gap

and television sets, are available. People have more money with which to buy these products. It is no longer necessary for most youngsters to go to work full time while in their mid-teens. In fact, the law does not allow you to work at all until you are a certain age. You must stay in school. So, even if you want to, you are not able to do as adults often say they did when they were young: "I was earning my own living when I was your age."

The Problem of Roles

Few of us really know what is expected of us. (This is as true of adults as it is of teenagers.) You see, whenever we speak of the role of youth, we are also speaking of the role of older adults, such as parents, teachers, and other "authority figures." In some older societies, there is no problem about the role of youth. Each boy becomes a man and each girl becomes a woman at an early age. They marry and have their own families at an early age. Each knows what is expected of the other. But American youth today spend a long period of time under the control of their parents. Teenagers have fewer responsibilities, even though they are told to be more responsible.

Young people and their parents therefore are in a fix. Parents want to be democratic, but they do not know how far to go in setting rules and limits to what young people can or should do. For example, who should decide how late is too late to come home? How much money should a teenager have? How much schoolwork should be done, and when? Which friends are good for you? What should our standards of *morality* (what is right and what is wrong) be?

One thing is certain—young people are becoming an increasingly more important economic and political force. They are speaking out, and they are being heard. Older adults would be wise to listen to them.

YOUTH IN ACTION   Mr. Stone, a middle-aged biology teacher at a local high school, said to his young colleague Ms. Ramirez, "Youth is a disease that all people get, but fortunately they outgrow it." Ms. Ramirez did not think the remark was funny. She pointed out to Mr. Stone that today there are many things wrong in our world and in our country. Young people could stay on the sidelines (as Mr. Stone did when he was young). Young people could show their anger by throwing stones at the *system* (our society or way of life). Ms. Ramirez said it is wonderful that young people today are working within the system to help change it.

Young people of all ages are interested in their community and their environment. In one large city, for example, students from a local junior high school decided that they wanted to clean up the *graffiti* (painted writings on public walls) that made the walls of their park playground ugly. With the help of people in the community, the students attacked the walls like an army. Armed with buckets of sudsy water and cans of spray paint remover, the teenagers and their allies battled the paint for five hours. While they could not remove all the graffiti from the walls, the young people did show the community that an attractive community is the concern of people of all ages.

This student showed his concern for the environment by cleaning out a polluted pond

In another large city, a college student was saddened to watch the pond in the park near his home become a dumping ground for old tires, empty bottles, and all sorts of trash. He remembered how he used to catch fish in the pond's clear waters. Now the water was slimy and greenish. The young man did something about this. He began to clear out the trash. He made plans to drain the 4.5 million gallons of greenish water, clean it, and return it to the pond. Other young people from the neighborhood joined him. Now there is a clean, clear pond for all to enjoy—thanks to these young people.

Summary Young people are a very visible group. Older adults see them coming out of high school. They also see them at political conventions. Young people are vocal. Older adults hear them on the buses, in classrooms, and in the dining room. Do older adults understand what they see, and are they really listening to what the young people are saying?

Looking Ahead In the next chapter, we shall examine the ways in which young people's life-styles differ from the life-styles of their parents.

EXERCISES

MATCHING QUESTIONS   Match each term in Column A with its definition in Column B.

Column A

1. adult
2. generation
3. generation gap
4. morality
5. the system
6. life-styles

Column B

(*a*) people born at about the same time
(*b*) attitudes and ways of doing things
(*c*) ideas of what is right and wrong
(*d*) differences in the ways of acting and thinking between young adults and older adults
(*e*) a mature person
(*f*) our society and our way of life

MULTIPLE-CHOICE QUESTIONS   For each question, write the letter of the best answer.

1. The *main* idea of this chapter is that (*a*) children should be seen but not heard (*b*) all 15-year-olds are adults (*c*) young people are playing an increasingly important role in society (*d*) young people generally have no responsibilities.

2. One of the major complaints young people make of adults is that the adults (*a*) do not really listen to them (*b*) give them too much freedom (*c*) are usually uneducated (*d*) do nothing for them.

3. One reason why the influence of young Americans is growing is that they (*a*) have decreased in number (*b*) are leaving school at an earlier age (*c*) are buying more goods and services (*d*) do not get involved in politics.

4. Which statement would be the most difficult to prove true or false? (*a*) The population of the cities is growing more rapidly than the population of rural areas. (*b*) The workweek is shorter today than it was 50 years ago. (*c*) A generation gap exists between teenagers and their parents. (*d*) Some states do not allow teenagers under 16 years of age to work at many types of jobs.

5. Which of the following would be a fair conclusion to reach after reading this chapter? (*a*) It is more fun to be young than old. (*b*) It is more fun to be old than young. (*c*) Parents and teachers should not tell young adults what to do or not to do. (*d*) Parents and teachers should listen carefully to young adults.

DEVELOPING A POSITION PAPER Many parents and teachers complain that teenagers today are irresponsible—they do not behave in a mature, adult way. On the other hand, teenagers complain that parents and teachers do not give them a chance to grow up. In this exercise, you are asked to develop a position paper on the issue of teenagers' responsibility for behaving in a mature way. To help you prepare your paper, the exercise is in three parts.

1. Prepare a list showing what you think the *rights* and *responsibilities* of an average teenager should be at home and in school. For example:

	Rights	*Responsibilities*
At Home:	1. Decide own clothes	1. Help pay for clothes
	2.	2.
In School:	1. Choose own classes	1. Attend classes regularly
	2.	2.

2. Prepare a chart showing how parents and teachers can encourage or discourage teenagers from growing up. For example:

	Encouragement	*Discouragement*
Parents:	1. Allow teenager to decide when and where to do homework	1. Force teenager to take music lessons
	2.	2.
Teachers:	1. Give students a voice in planning studies	1. Do not allow teenagers to choose their courses
	2.	2.

3. Using the information that you have prepared in answering the first two parts of this question, write your position paper. Develop one of two positions: (*a*) *Parents and Teachers Do Not Allow Teenagers to Play an Active Role in Life,* or (*b*) *Teenagers Do Have the Opportunity to Play an Active Role in Life.*

Chapter 2   Youth Culture

Mrs. O'Neil was worried. It was past midnight and Judy O'Neil still had not come home. Mr. O'Neil was trying to calm his wife, but he too was upset. "Judy is a big girl," Mr. O'Neil said. "She's only 16," replied Mrs. O'Neil. "I told her to be in by midnight. I just can't understand young people today. They are so irresponsible. So many are headed for trouble."

Mr. O'Neil trusts Judy. Yet he does agree with his wife that many young people today are "headed for trouble." For example, Mr. O'Neil was thinking of Judy's friend, Millie Jameson. Millie is strange, Mr. O'Neil thinks. She wears her hair very long and straight. Her clothes are different from those of the other girls. What's more, Millie often comes to the O'Neil house with her guitar or, even worse, with loud rock records. Mr. O'Neil is sure that Millie is a bad influence on Judy.

Not all parents are alike. Millie's parents do not think that their daughter is a bad influence on anyone. In fact, they are very proud of her. They do not object to the way she dresses and think that the music Millie listens to makes more sense than some of the things they listened to at her age. The Jamesons trust Millie to come home at a sensible hour. They have often said that "whatever she will do at 1 A.M. she will do at midnight." Of course, the Jamesons do want Millie to come home at a reasonable hour.

The Problem of the Generations

Judy and Millie (and their parents) face the same problems faced by families all over the United States. As long as there are teenagers at home, differences of one kind or another are going to come up between the young people and their parents. As you saw in the families of Judy and Millie, not all young people are alike and not all parents are alike. Yet there are a number of ways in which youth and the older generation tend to be different. Usually these differences result in conflict between adults and teenagers.

The following table lists the major ways in which young people differ from their parents. The table *generalizes* (states what is true in most cases). Therefore, you must not think that every young or every mature person fits each description below. What the generalizations tell us is that young people or their parents tend to be as we are describing them. Thus, not all young people are liberal and not all parents are conservative. What is more, your parents, for example, might be liberal about some things, such as the time you must come home Saturday night, and conservative about other things, such as the clothes you wear.

Youth	*Parents*
Liberal:	Conservative:
1. Experiment with new things and ideas	1. Prefer tried and true to change and the unknown
2. Willing to break with tradition and accepted standards	2. Want to preserve family, self-interest, and accepted values
3. Expect and look for change in everything	3. Want to settle down; have sampled different things in their youth
4. Want independence from parents	4. Try to hold on to children
Daring:	Cautious:
1. Eager to learn by trying new things	1. Have experienced pain and failure in the past
2. Have not faced as many difficulties or had as many failures	2. Try to avoid failure and pain for themselves and their children
Group-Centered:	Family-Centered:
1. Concerned with the whole of society	1. Place family first
2. Influenced by friends in dress, music, language	2. Expect to keep parental authority role

Mr. and Mrs. O'Neil seem to think that young people are all alike —irresponsible and headed for trouble. Like many adults, the O'Neils think of young people as a group. Well, young people today, in many ways, are a group, but it was older people who forced them into this position.

In the previous chapter we learned that in the United States today young people are prevented from entering the adult world long after they are physically mature. We learned, for example, that:

1. In school the rules and the curriculum are decided upon by teachers and administrators.
2. At home parents provide food, clothing, and spending money.
3. In the outside world, parents and other adults make the rules that all people, including teenagers, are expected to follow.

Like it or not, then, young people are kept out of the "adult" world. Young people are forced to be a group.

What Is Youth Culture?

A *culture* is the way of life of a people. Culture has to do with habits, religious practices, arts, skills, music, and dress. So when people speak of a life-style, they are really speaking of culture. If we examine the life-style of young people today, we can see that it is not the same as the life-style of their elders.

Mr. Jameson accepts the fact that Millie belongs to a culture that is not the same as his own. Mr. O'Neil cannot accept what is called the *youth culture*. Judy and Millie accept it. Actually most young people do think of themselves as a group. Almost 80 percent of the teenagers questioned in one survey said that they were the same as others their own age. Perhaps even more important, young people take pride in their generation. Mrs. O'Neil might think that today's youth are irresponsible, but Judy O'Neil and her friends sincerely believe that the values young people have are far better than the values of their parents and other adults.

THE DOUBLE STANDARD   One way in which the life-style of young people today differs from the life-style of the older generation is the absence of the *double standard*. This term was used to describe a code of behavior that held it was all right for men to behave in ways that were forbidden to women. For example, Mr. O'Neil would not have been so worried if Judy were a boy instead of a girl. If he had a son, Mr. O'Neil would possibly admire and brag about his son's freedom to do what he pleases. But Judy is a girl, and Mr. O'Neil doesn't want anyone talking about her in a bad way.

Young people today challenge the double standard. Judy and Millie believe that they should be free to do whatever boys can do. They do not believe that men are the protectors of women. Judy wants to be a doctor. Millie wants to go into politics. Both agree that women can compete as equals of men in professions, business, politics, and sports.

Young adults today are so much alike that some adults often scornfully remark that you can't tell the boys from the girls. Young men wear their hair long. Girls wear slacks and blue jeans. Men have their hair styled. Both sexes often wear outfits that are interchangeable.

EXPRESSING FEELINGS   Teenagers seem to listen to rock music for hours. To many adults, rock is just loud noise. To young people, however, rock is the major form of music. Parents often complain that they cannot understand their children's language. The important thing is that young people do understand this language. To young people, rock music has more to say about what is going on in society, both good and bad, than all the books and discussions at school.

Beware of exaggerations, however. Just because a youth culture exists does not mean that American youth are completely different from their parents and other adults. Family training and public education are such that most young people share many of the same attitudes, values, and political beliefs of the older generation. Moreover, young people must naturally grow older, and most will join the mainstream of American life. It must not be forgotten that juvenile delinquents, "hippies" (people who adopt a life-style completely different from and in protest against the way of life of the country), and radicals are a minority of the population of young people. Most young adults do not get into trouble. The vast majority of young people are not drug addicts.

Summary   A youth culture exists today. It is a culture that reflects the new life-style of many young people. This culture is expressed in music, dress, language, and values.

Looking Ahead   In the next chapter, we shall take a look at how young people handle the problem of being members of a group and still maintain their individuality.

EXERCISES

MATCHING QUESTIONS   Match each term in Column A with its definition in Column B.

Column A

1. culture
2. double standard
3. youth culture
4. generalize
5. tradition
6. rock

Column B

(*a*) a life-style adopted by young people
(*b*) to state what is true in most cases
(*c*) the music of most young people
(*d*) belief that men can do things that women are not allowed to do
(*e*) the arts, skills, habits, and way of life of a people
(*f*) old, accepted ways of doing things

MULTIPLE-CHOICE QUESTIONS   For each question, write the letter of the best answer.

1. The main idea of this chapter is that young people (*a*) are headed for trouble (*b*) are accepted as adults at an early age in America (*c*) have a culture of their own (*d*) enjoy rock music.

2. According to the chapter (*a*) all young people are alike (*b*) all parents are alike (*c*) young people today are ashamed of their generation (*d*) adult society discriminates against young people.

3. Youth expresses itself in many ways. Which of the following is *not* an example of youth expressing itself? (*a*) styles of dress (*b*) making the rules for society (*c*) "hip" talk (*d*) rock music

4. Which of the following beliefs is most widely accepted by young people today? (*a*) The values of youth are better than the values of their elders. (*b*) Men should not wear their hair long, and women should not wear their hair short. (*c*) It is always better to stick to the old ways of doing things. (*d*) Women should not be allowed to do all the things that men do.

5. According to this chapter (*a*) a youth culture does not exist (*b*) young people look at life the same way their parents do (*c*) youth culture is bad (*d*) youth culture reflects the life-style of young people.

WRITE AN EDITORIAL   Prepare an editorial on the topic *youth culture* for your school newspaper. Use the information in this chapter. Your editorial should answer the following four questions:

1. Is there a youth culture? Prove your answer.
2. Why did American youth develop a separate culture?
3. What are some of the major features of the youth culture?
4. How has the youth culture been exaggerated?

Chapter 3 Youth, Individuality, and Conformity

Steve wanted to be a member of the Daring Dukes. Most of the guys he knew were already in the club. Bobby invited Steve to the clubhouse and, for the first time, Steve sat in on the Dukes' "rapping."

"Black Benjie" thought the Dukes' girls should wear special sweaters to "show the colors" (the emblem and special colors that members of the Dukes wear).

"Spanish Mike" said the whole gang should go to the dance that the YSA (Youth Services Agency) was giving in the park.

"Pete the Professor" cornered Steve and started to tell Steve what a regular guy should be like, act like, and think like.

Steve tossed and turned in bed that night. Sure, he still wanted to be a Duke, but now he had some doubts. Steve likes to wear a shirt and tie. He thinks that by doing so, he is a little different, and he enjoys being different. Suppose, Steve was thinking, he does not want to wear the Dukes' jacket? What if he does not feel like going to the park dance? In a nutshell, what bothered Steve was this question: Did he have to give up being Steve to become one of the group?

The Less Traveled Road

The great American poet Robert Frost wrote a poem about a journey he once made. He told how he arrived at a spot where the road he was traveling

What do the two roads in the illustration stand for?

on split off into two different directions. Frost took the road that was less traveled; that is, most people would have taken the other road.

> Two roads diverged in a wood, and I—
> I took the one less traveled by,
> And that has made all the difference.

We must make choices at many many times in our lives. At some times the choice is to do what most other people do; at others, we choose to do what we want to do even if it means doing it alone. Taking the less traveled road is to do what most other people would not do. Young people today often use the expression "do your own thing." Is this like taking the less traveled road?

Another way of expressing this is to say that a person is an *individualist*. An individualist lives in his or her own way and does not worry about what other people think. The opposite of an individualist in society is a *conformist*. Unlike the individualist, the conformist does what other persons do. He or she is part of the group, and it is the group, not the individual member of the group, that decides such things as clothing styles, "hip" talk, and even standards of *morality* (what is right and wrong).

Individuality in American Life

Our country was founded on the theory that "the less government we have, the better." This means that Americans wanted to be left alone and free from government interference in whatever they did. Later on, this same *concept* (idea or way of thinking) was used by the big business firms, which demanded that the government practice "laissez-faire" (keep their hands off business).

When America had a large frontier and when each person or individual had a chance to do well or reach the top, individualism made a lot of sense. Democracy, as you know, is based on the idea that every individual will have a chance to reach the highest possible point of development for himself and herself. Thus any action by government or other individuals or groups that prevents individuals from reaching their full capacity is undemocratic.

Young people have greater freedom to do as they please and more time to do the things they want to do. They no longer work long hours in the fields, factories, or mines, as they did into the 20th century. Young people have more spending money. Even though adults still make many important decisions (and some minor ones too), it is fairly well accepted that a young adult should have a greater say in school and in the community. As a result, many young people are demanding, and receiving, a greater say at home.

Attitudes in all areas of life have changed. Ideas about how people should behave are changing. The standards of our grandparents' day are passing away. For example, sex is no longer discussed behind closed doors—it is discussed openly. Young people are experimenting—often with very sad results—in sex before marriage. Birth control pills have made some young people think that it is "safe" to have intercourse before marriage. The rising rate of venereal disease and premarital pregnancies among teenagers should make young people pause and think. Abortion laws are being repealed, however, making it easier for young women to avoid unwanted pregnancies. Many adults have complained that society is becoming too *permissive*. These adults think that young people should not be allowed to do as they please.

Conformity in American Life

Americans have never been complete individualists. They have always worked in groups. Sometimes the group was a religious one, as in colonial New England settlements. Sometimes the group was a community, as in the frontier towns of the 1870s and 1880s. Sometimes the group was an *ethnic* (based on nationality and culture) one—such as the Irish immigrants in Boston and black Americans in southern communities after the Civil War.

The hardy pioneer wanted the government's help in taking land from the Indians. Big business wanted the government's help in keeping foreign competition out and in building railroads across the country.

So, if Americans have always been both individualists *and* conformists, why is there such fuss today? Today, the pressure to conform, particularly among young adults, has increased. Here is why:

Everything is big today. Cities are big and people are crowded together on buses, in trains, and in schools. The individual becomes just a part of the crowd. As part of the crowd, the individual must punch a time card, start and end a lesson with the sound of a bell or chimes, move on the green light and stop at the red light, and so on.

Life has become *routinized* (made to follow a set pattern) by the machine. Modern technology requires that individuals do what the machine demands, not what the individual wants to do. Just to give one example, think of an individual on an assembly line whose only job is to tighten bolts on the fender of an automobile. Suppose that while the line is moving, the individual decides to leave the machine. The fenders would keep moving, but no one would tighten the bolts.

New ideas stress the group rather than the individual. Some young people are convinced that group living is better than the life of their parents. These young people are attracted by the ideas of Fidel Castro in Cuba and Mao Tse-tung in China. Groups in middle-class white communities are all telling young people that the individual should sacrifice himself to the interests of the group. These groups are *radical* (want fast, extreme changes). But even *moderates* (who want slow change) are demanding more group involvement and community control. They are saying that the individual should work as part of the community in the interest of the community.

Young adults are a group. There is no question that a "youth culture" exists today. It is difficult for a youth to be left out of this culture. Young people are kept together in places called schools. They meet and listen to rock music. They talk the same language. They wear the same kinds of clothes. Long hair, once worn only by far-out types, is acceptable for both sexes.

Nonconformity has become a *fad* (something that people are interested in only for a while). It is popular among young people to do the opposite of what their elders are doing. It is popular to be *antiestablishment* (against the ideas of those who are in control—that is, adults). When large numbers of young people are doing the same things at the same time—even though they may be doing the opposite of what their elders want them to—they are actually being conformists. That is, if everybody is "doing his or her own thing," but it turns out that everyone is doing just about the same thing, then the group pressure has merely been shifted. The youth world is setting the pace and others are following the same road.

Summary   Modern life has made it very difficult to be a complete individualist. However, even though there is conformity among youth today, there is also greater opportunity to be free to "do your own thing"—to be yourself, and to be an individual if that is what you choose.

EXERCISES

MULTIPLE-CHOICE QUESTIONS   For each question, write the letter of the best answer.

1. The main idea of this chapter is that (*a*) Steve wanted to join the Daring Dukes (*b*) early Americans were individualists (*c*) government has an important role to play in American life (*d*) even though there is a great deal of conformity today, young people can still be individualists.

2. An individualist would most likely (*a*) wear the same clothes and styles his or her friends wear (*b*) do one thing even if the rest of the crowd does something else (*c*) be active in clubs and community work (*d*) take up every new fad that comes along.

3. A conformist is a person who would most likely (*a*) join every group, club, and community activity (*b*) wear clothing styles that please him or her even if others are wearing the latest style (*c*) do those things that

please him or her even if by doing so the group is displeased (*d*) choose what most other people would not choose.

4. A factor contributing to individualism among youth today is (*a*) the tradition of individualism in American life (*b*) the tradition of working together in groups (*c*) the bigness of everything today (*d*) new ideas that stress the importance of the community.

5. A factor contributing to conformity among youth today is (*a*) youth has greater freedom today (*b*) young people can experiment more today than before (*c*) individuals often get lost in the crowd of modern society (*d*) it is easier to make it on your own today.

MATCHING QUESTIONS   Match each term in Column A with its definition in Column B.

Column A	*Column B*
1. conformist	(*a*) an idea or way of thinking
2. concept	(*b*) an individual who wants quick changes
3. radical	(*c*) something that temporarily interests people
4. moderate	(*d*) an individual who does what others do
5. fad	(*e*) an individual who is against those in power
6. antiestablishment	(*f*) a person who lives life as he or she pleases
7. individualist	(*g*) a person who favors slow change

Unit III   The Family

Chapter 1   Why Are There Families?

The Reverend Edwin Turner asked Tom Morgan if he would take Sally Williams to be his wife. Tommy said, "I do." A new cycle had begun. Sally's mother, eyes swollen with tears, remembered her own marriage to Sally's father. Mrs. Williams also remembered the joys and pains, the laughs and sorrows—giving birth to Sally and watching Sally grow, cut her first tooth, start school, and date Tom Morgan. Sally will have many of the same experiences her mother had. Sally will have a family and the cycle will be renewed.

What Is a Family?

A family, of some type or other, is found in every society. More than 92 percent of Americans live in families. Yet, it is not easy to say exactly what a family is. Most people would say that a family is "all the people living in the same house," or "a group made up of the two parents and their children," or "two or more adults living together and cooperating in the rearing of their own or adopted children." Of course, these explanations are correct—but a family is more than that, and less than that, too. If there is little love at home, then the family is just a collection of strangers who have been brought together only by chance. As the poet Charles Swain has said,

> What is home with none to meet,
> None to welcome, none to greet us?
> Home is sweet, and only sweet,
> When there's one we love to meet us.

Functions of the Family

SOCIAL UNIT   A *social unit* is a group of people who are brought together for a special purpose. For example, a city, town, or village is a social unit. It provides people with, among other things, police protection and fire and sanitation services. A school is a social unit that provides education. A church, a temple, or a synagogue is a unit that is a place for worship or meditation. The family, however, is the oldest social unit known to mankind. The family keeps the larger social units (town, city, state, nation) alive by handing down cultural traditions. The family develops our loyalties to the larger social units. Families exist in every country in every part of the globe. Like all social units, the family exists because it performs important functions for its members and fills deep-seated needs.

We are what our families are. There is an old saying, "The apple doesn't fall far from the tree." This means that the kind of fruit is determined by the tree that bore it. An individual, in much the same way, is what he or she is because of *hereditary factors.* What we are like physically is determined first by our parents and then by our *environment.* Some examples of hereditary factors include the color of our skin, eyes, and hair, our height and physique, and, to some degree, our intelligence. Some examples of environmental influences that make us what we are include the physical conditions (the neighborhood we live in, the schools we go to) and psychological conditions in our family life. For example, are our parents tense or relaxed, are they strict with us or are they *permissive* (let us do as we please)? Then again, if our parents have had a great deal of education, their influence on us will be different from what it would have been if they had had very little.

The family serves the material and emotional needs of its individual members. How does it do this?

ECONOMIC UNIT   The family of 75 years ago was likely to be a big one. Every family member had a job to do. The more workers there were in a family, the better off the family would be. (This was just as true of the city family as it was of the farm family.) Today, it is no longer necessary for every family member to work. However, it is necessary for one or more family members to work to support the rest of the family. Having a big family today is no longer an economic necessity. In fact, a big family is a hardship to many people. This is one reason that the average family is smaller today than it used to be. We will discuss this and other reasons why the family is smaller in a later chapter.

SECURITY UNIT   In early days the family provided all the protection an individual had against outside attack. Today, the family still provides the individual members with a sense of belonging, a place to hold on to.

EDUCATIONAL UNIT   Children learn to speak at home. They learn society's *values* (what is considered right and what is considered wrong), as well as their parents'. Children learn religious values from their families. In days gone by, the family often taught the children an occupation or a trade, whether it was that of farming for boys, or homemaking for girls. What children did not learn at home they learned on the job. Vocational training and career education did not exist in early days.

What personal needs are being met by the family in this picture?

RECREATIONAL UNIT   Before the days of radio and television, the family would sit around the dining room table or near the fire to tell stories, sing songs, or look at pictures. Modern families go to beaches or parks, the movies, or to family gatherings (such as birthdays and weddings) together.

How Are Families Organized?

We have said that a family may be thought of as all the people living in the same house. Years ago, this family might have included parents, six or eight children, grandparents, and perhaps even an aunt, uncle, and some cousins. (We call this type of family an *extended* family because it extends over several generations.) Another definition of a family was that it is made up of two parents and their children. (This is called the *nuclear* family.) Today the number of children in the family would probably be two or three, perhaps four.

THE FAMILIES IN DIFFERENT SOCIETIES   Families, as we have said, exist in every society all over the world. However, the organization, or makeup, of the family is not the same in every society. Thus the definitions we gave for a family fit the type of families we are used to in our society, that is, societies of the Western world. In contrast to the traditional United States or European family, which is usually made up of a father, mother, and one or more children, there are families in other societies that are made up of one father, several wives, and several children from each of his wives. In a few rare cases, there have been societies where one woman had more than one husband at a time. She might then have children from each of her husbands.

THE FAMILY VARIES WITHIN A SOCIETY   In the United States the so-called *typical* family is made up of a husband and wife and their children. However, many other family arrangements exist in this country. For example, there may be only one parent, usually the mother, because of separation, divorce, or death. In other families, children live with grandparents, aunts and uncles, or with guardians. Once more we can see that the typical family organization of two parents and their children had to be changed to meet special needs.

There are today some people who are not happy with any of the traditional family setups. These people are organizing and experimenting with a family unit called a *commune*. A commune is really a small community. It is a variation of the family unit. Different kinds of communes have been organized. One kind is made up of men, women, and children living together as one large family or community. The children who are born into the commune are additional family members. In some cases, they are not considered "the" children of any two members of the commune. The commune, therefore, is an example of a deliberately planned change in the makeup of the traditional family in American society.

Family Breakup

When a young man asked Socrates whether or not he should get married, the Greek philosopher replied, "Either way, you'll regret it." What Socrates was saying is that being single may be difficult, but a marriage is not an easy relationship to hold together successfully. In fact, almost three out of every ten marriages in the United States end up in divorce. On the other hand, most of the people who get divorced will later marry someone else. Perhaps this indicates that these people were unhappy with their marriage partner, not with the marriage relationship.

Whenever a marriage breaks up (and if there are children in that marriage), the family breaks up, because the unit made up of husband, wife, and children has been dissolved. Now if either, or both, parents remarry, a new family unit (or units) must be organized. For example, if Mr. and Mrs. Jones get a divorce and Mr. Jones marries Peggy Smith while Mrs. Jones marries Tom Worth, we have (at least) two new family units —the new Jones family and the new Worth family.

The death of one parent will also break up the traditional family in much the same way (although for different reasons) as when a divorce or separation takes place. Remarriage will once again result in a new family unit. In this case one plus one equals one.

Summary   The family in some form or other exists in every society. In most cases, the basic family unit is made up of a man and woman and their children. Families exist because they serve to meet the basic needs of all people. Children are born and must be cared for. All people need protection, security, and love. Young people need help until they can stand on their own feet and become part of a new family unit.

Looking Ahead   As society changes, the family must adjust to these changes. In the next chapter, we shall discuss how the family tries to adjust to changes taking place in our society.

EXERCISES

MATCHING QUESTIONS   Match each term in Column A with its definition in Column B.

Column A

1. family
2. social unit
3. functions
4. hereditary influences
5. environmental influences
6. extended family
7. nuclear family

Column B

(*a*) duties
(*b*) physical and psychological conditions at home, in school, and in your neighborhood
(*c*) two parents and their children
(*d*) parents, children, grandparents, and relatives all living together
(*e*) a group of people joined together for special purposes
(*f*) mankind's oldest social unit
(*g*) physical characteristics, such as the color of skin, hair, and eyes

MULTIPLE-CHOICE QUESTIONS   For each question, write the letter of the best answer.

1. The family is (*a*) found only in Western societies (*b*) an American institution only (*c*) any group of people (*d*) the oldest social unit known to man.
2. The main idea of this chapter is that families (*a*) perform important physical and emotional duties (*b*) are breaking up very fast in the United States (*c*) have always existed (*d*) are larger than ever.
3. Which of the following is an example of a social unit that provides police protection to its members? (*a*) church (*b*) school (*c*) city (*d*) family
4. Which of the following would not be considered a usual function of the family today? (*a*) provide security (*b*) teach values (*c*) train for a job (*d*) give economic support

5. A family that is made up of husband, wife, and one or two children is called (*a*) a nuclear family (*b*) an extended family (*c*) a commune (*d*) a small family.

6. Which statement is true? (*a*) In no society may a man or woman have more than one marriage partner. (*b*) A typical family unit in the United States is two parents, five children, and one or two relatives, all living together. (*c*) Two family units may break up and then reorganize into new ones. (*d*) Families are the same all over the world.

7. Which of the following statements would be the most difficult to prove either true or false? (*a*) The family is an ancient social unit. (*b*) Some type of family is found in every society. (*c*) The size of the average American family is getting smaller. (*d*) The best type of family consists of two parents and one or two children.

INTERPRETING PHOTOGRAPHS   Look at the photographs below and answer the questions that follow:

Chinese family   Nigerian family

1. What do these pictures have in common with each other?
2. What would be a good title for this group of photographs?
3. What information in the chapter you have just read supports or gives additional evidence of the ideas suggested in these pictures?
4. What types of family unit are shown in these pictures—nuclear, extended, or one-parent families?
5. What additional information do you need to determine whether or not the scenes shown are *typical* of the societies they seem to represent?

Chapter 2 The Family in a Changing Society

Grandpa Bailey was complaining as usual that "the family just isn't what it used to be." Ray and Marguerite were not listening. Every time Grandpa came to the house he was always telling them how good things were when he was young. Grandpa finished off by saying that things used to be better in the "good old days."

"Gramps," Marguerite said, "everything is changing. These are changing times."

Grandpa Bailey's eyes lit up as he went into his favorite topic. "You bet your sweet life things are different today. Why, in my day, your Dad wouldn't have been shopping in the supermarket or doing the dishes after dinner. And another thing, your Ma wouldn't be running around to all those meetings either. She'd be staying home to make sure you kids weren't getting too fresh."

Ray laughed, not out of disrespect, but because he and Marguerite both like Grandpa. Ray knows that Grandpa is just "out of touch." His generation has had its day and times have passed him by. Ray knows from memory, he has heard the story so many times, how Grandpa came from a family of eight children. Ray remembers Grandpa telling how his own grandfather, and an aunt who never married, lived with the family. Everybody who worked brought their earnings to Grandpa's mother. She put aside some for rent, some for food, and some for clothing, and then gave each person a small bit of what was left over for spending money.

Ray and Marguerite like Grandpa to come over once in a while to visit with them, but they would not want him to live with them. Then, too, they are glad that Aunt Mary, who never married, is not living with them. Marguerite, most of all, is happy that once her Dad had enough money the family moved into its own home so that she could have her own room. Marguerite can't imagine how all of Grandpa's brothers and sisters lived so close to one another.

The Family Has Changed

After Joe and Sarah Bailey were married (they are Ray and Marguerite's parents), they lived with Grandpa for a few years. Ray, in fact, was born while they were still living with his father's parents. Until the end of World War II, in 1945, many married couples did not live in their own households. But the percentage of married couples without their own households has declined steadily since 1946—from 10 percent to less than one percent. It is not surprising, therefore, that most young people today are not used to living with their grandparents, aunts, uncles, or other family members.

SMALLER SIZE The family is getting smaller. Today's families are smaller than they once were. One reason for the decrease in the size of the family has already been discussed. As you have seen, families in the past were made up of grandparents, parents, and children all living together. (Today, the family most probably consists of a couple and one or more children.) This brings us to a second reason why today's families are smaller than they once were. Today's families have fewer children. In 1850, for example, the size of the average United States family was 5.6 persons. Today, the average is fewer than 4 persons. This means that the average American family is made up of parents and one or two children today, whereas years ago the American family as a rule had more than two children.

CHANGING FUNCTIONS Grandpa Bailey was right when he said that families are not what they used to be. So, too, were Ray and Marguerite, who explain that changing times cause their differences with Grandpa and his ways.

You will recall that the family is a social unit that exists to perform some very special functions, or duties, for its members. For example, the family is society's way of bringing new members into it. The family also provides security and, one hopes, love for its members. The family is an economic unit, an educational unit, and a recreational unit. In many ways, many of the functions that were once performed mostly by the family as a unit are now being performed by other institutions in our society. Let us examine some of the changes that have taken place.

In years gone by, the family was *self-sufficient*. This means that all that was needed was produced by the family itself. The more workers in the family (that is, children, grandparents, aunts, or uncles) the more that could be produced by the family. Today production is done away from the home, in a factory. Individual family members leave the family home for a part of the day to work in a *producing unit* (factory or store). What does this mean to the family as a unit? For one thing, fewer family members are needed as producers. (This partly explains why the size of families in the United States has become smaller.) Factories produce food and clothing and these are bought in stores. Dad, and often Mom, leave the family household for part of the day to go to work. Food, clothing, and shelter are then bought with the money they earn.

When the family worked together as a unit, Dad taught the boys and Mom taught the girls. Most of the waking hours of the children were spent at the side of their parents. In this way, the parents taught the children not only how to plow a field or cook a roast but what was right and wrong, what was good and bad as they saw it. Young people today spend much of their time in school. Therefore, the schools today share the responsibility for preparing a child for life. Almost as important, if not *as* important as the school, is the influence of young people of the same age, who give values that once were the sole responsibility of the family.

Other Institutions Fill Family Roles

Today, there are a number of *institutions* (social units such as schools and churches) that provide security to individual family members in addition to the security provided by the family.

Furthermore, young people get together with one another and share experiences. Many young people, for example, confide more in each other than they do in their parents. It is their friends who give them the feeling of belonging to a group and, therefore, a sense of well-being and security. Schools protect youngsters and regulate their activities for a good part of the day. Often, a young person will find a teacher or a guidance counselor who will, in many ways, act as a parental substitute. Government, through the police and fire departments, of course, provides many of the basic protections the family once did. Government also acts as a substitute provider when the family head cannot support the family. For example, a family may receive welfare payments, social security payments, free hospital and medical care, and a variety of other types of assistance in time of need.

Few teenagers today depend much upon their families for entertainment. Furthermore, television, radio, stereo sets, or tape recorders give young people hours of entertainment without any help from other family members.

The family is still important in modern life, of course. Long before a youngster attends school and begins to make friends, it is the family that performs the functions it has always performed. It is still the family that the young person comes home to and it is the family that, even after it brings the individual into the world, provides the atmosphere that may very well determine the kind of person that individual will turn out to be. It is still largely true that home life is responsible for emotional well-being or emotional illness. The family can still provide love, a feeling of belonging, and a warm and welcome atmosphere in which an individual can grow into a healthy and stable adult. Or it can do the opposite.

Place of the Aged

In a way, Grandpa Bailey is lucky. He doesn't have to live with his son and his son's family. Over the years, Grandpa Bailey put money in the bank and made some good investments. In addition, once a month he receives a social security check and a small pension check from the firm he had worked for until he retired five years ago.

Not all elderly people are so lucky. Many old people cannot afford to live where and how they please. Many need help. Of course, social security is some help, and so is medicare, which pays for most medical expenses, but these are not enough. And, then again, there is the loneliness of old age. Money alone can't help take away those long lonely nights.

In the old days, the elderly were always part of the family, and, more than likely, Grandpa Bailey would have been the head of a big family. In those days, it was the old people who knew the family's history and passed it

TIM HUTCHINS' STORY: OLD AND FORGOTTEN

Tim Hutchins is 79 years old. For as long as he can remember, he worked. Tim never earned much money, but he did raise two fine boys. Both Tim, Jr., and Bob are married and have families of their own.

Tim could never put aside a dime. For some 50-odd years, by working wherever he could—in fields and in factories—Tim just about made ends meet. His last job was as a doorman. Seven years ago, Tim finally retired. He does not want Bob and Tim, Jr., to support him. They have enough expenses of their own. Anyway, one boy is living in California and the other is in Iowa. Tim does not expect them to come all the way to Boston, where Tim has lived for the last 15 years, just for his sake. Tim has not seen Bob for almost 20 years. Tim has never met Bob's wife and has seen only pictures of Bob's kids. Tim's wife, Mary, died 14 years ago. Hers was not an easy life, but as Tim thinks back every so often, it was a good life. There is nothing to regret, he always says.

Living on social security is not easy. It worked out for a while. But with prices rising all the time, no matter how carefully Tim spends his social security check, there just is not enough money. One of the fellows that Tim meets on the park bench, John Maloney, persuaded Tim to apply for welfare. Welfare helps, but add it all up and there is not enough left for a movie at the end of the week.

The kids on the block call Tim "Old Man Hutchins." He doesn't mind. He does not have much but, as he often says jokingly, he is not going to any parties. His apartment is small, the furniture old and broken-down. The radio and the television set have been with Tim since the days when he worked. Tim hopes they will last as long as he does. Sitting in the park on nice days and listening to the radio or watching television are about the only pleasures Tim has left in life.

A park bench is the only meeting place for many elderly persons

on to the next generation. The old were respected for their wisdom. It was the duty of the family to take care of all its members from birth to death, from infancy to old age. All members of the family were taught to respect their elders. Of course, in those days, few people lived to be very old. A child born around 1900 had an average life expectancy of less than 50 years. Today, however, the chances are that a newborn child will live to be about 70 years old.

Just as it is true that the number of young people in this country is increasing, it is also true that the number of older people in this country is increasing. Therefore, what is to become of people when they get old is a serious problem.

CARE FOR THE AGED Who are the aged? This is not easy to answer. To a teenager, anyone over 30 may seem aged. To a young adult, retired persons may seem aged, yet more people are retiring before age 65 than was true in the past. *Retirement communities* are springing up fast, particularly along the east and west coasts of Florida, in Arizona, and in southern California. These communities have social and recreational centers, security systems, and health services to meet the needs of mature adults.

Community activities in a senior citizens housing unit include group singing

In new public housing developments, a certain portion of the apartments are set aside for the aged. Here too, advance planning provides services that older adults will need, particularly medical services and recreation.

Older people are sometimes too ill or feeble to care for themselves. Perhaps it is this group that is often thought of as "the aged." Private and public nursing homes provide medical care as well as shelter for these individuals. Retirement hotels exist for elderly people who do not need medical care but who cannot live alone.

Summary   The American family is changing. Families are smaller, usually just parents and one or two children. The functions of the family have also changed. The government and the schools have taken over many of the jobs the family once performed. The changes that have taken place have occurred because American society itself has been changed by modern technology. America has become urbanized. Parents rarely train their children for lifetime careers, as they once did. People are living longer today. Therefore, the number of older people in our society is increasing.

Since the family unit is less likely to include the aged, the problem of caring for the increasing number of older people in our society is becoming serious.

Looking Ahead In the next chapter, we shall consider the future of the family as it faces the problems of change. We shall ask ourselves whether or not the family as we know it might disappear.

EXERCISES

MATCHING QUESTIONS   Match each term in Column A with its definition in Column B.

Column A	*Column B*
1. family functions	(*a*) able to produce all that it needs
2. self-sufficient	(*b*) a factory or store
3. producing unit	(*c*) an organization such as a church or school
4. institution	(*d*) housing centers for the elderly
5. retirement communities	(*e*) to provide security, food, education, recreation

MULTIPLE-CHOICE QUESTIONS   For each question, write the letter of the best answer.

1. The main idea of this chapter is that (*a*) the duties of the family are changing because society is changing (*b*) families are not as close knit as they used to be (*c*) family life was better in "the good old days" (*d*) more mothers go to work today.

2. According to this chapter (*a*) the makeup of the family has not changed much over the years (*b*) an increasing percentage of young married couples live in their own households (*c*) married couples are having larger families (*d*) family functions have not changed much.

3. A major reason why families are smaller today is that (*a*) fewer family members are needed as producers (*b*) most religious groups are in favor of small families (*c*) small families receive tax benefits (*d*) landlords will not rent apartments to large families.

4. An example of new institutions taking over functions once performed by the family is (*a*) mother and daughter discuss how the daughter should act on a date (*b*) father and son play baseball together (*c*) grandfather lives in the furnished basement of the family home (*d*) son learns auto mechanics at school.

5. According to this chapter, the family is (*a*) no longer important (*b*) still important (*c*) more important than ever (*d*) being replaced by government.

6. One reason why the problem of the aged exists in our society is that (*a*) the aged expect more today (*b*) there are more aged people than ever before (*c*) nothing is being done to help the aged (*d*) only a few people live into old age today.

7. Which of the following statements is an opinion, not a fact? (*a*) A higher percentage of married couples lived with their parents in 1936 than in 1970. (*b*) The average life expectancy today is greater than it was 50 years ago. (*c*) Many of the functions that were once performed mostly by the family as a unit are now being performed by other institutions in our society. (*d*) A person should not be forced to take care of elderly parents.

Chapter 3   Will the Family Disappear?

Tom and Mary wrote their own marriage vows. They pledged to be faithful to one another and to work together for peace, justice, and the love of all humanity.

Bill and Jane decided to share an apartment. They think they can live together on good terms, and even date other people if they choose.

Sid and Franny are members of the Harmonious Living Commune. All members are considered brothers and sisters. They raise their food *organically* (without chemical fertilizers). They also weave rugs and make small leather goods, which they sell. The members of the commune do not believe in individual ownership of property. They look down on marriage as a kind of "property ownership," in which one human being owns another. Therefore, commune members do not marry. Nevertheless, some "partnerships" last longer than others.

Rose and Marty have been married for 15 years. Now they are getting a divorce. Rose has for some time secretly resented getting married as young as she did. She remembers what she now considers her fairy-tale dreams of dinner by candlelight and romantic vacations. How quickly those dreams were shattered when she had to do the dishes and wash diapers! Marty did not find marriage all it was supposed to be, either. Once the babies arrived, Marty and Rose were stuck in the house. All the extra work around the house was no fun either, and meeting all of those bills—well, if Rose wants a divorce, Marty thinks, she can have it.

What Has Happened to the Family?

The cases described above may make you wonder whether the family or, for that matter, the nation, is falling apart. Actually, we do know that family breakups, or divorces, have been increasing in the United States.

The stories of Tom and Mary, Bill and Jane, and Sid and Franny tell us something else too. Many young people today are experimenting with new life-styles. These young people are rejecting the traditional institutions of marriage and family. Some people are living together without getting married. Others are living in communes. And still others change "roommates" as often as some people might change clothes.

With so many families breaking up and with new life-styles encouraging different forms of human relationships, can we reach the conclusion that the family *as we know it* is doomed? Before you try to answer this question, let us first examine the evidence.

MARRIAGES AND DIVORCES   Fewer than 3 million people got married during the depression year of 1936. The number of divorces in that year was also low—about 250,000. But what happened just after World War II? In 1946 over 4 million Americans got married. However, the number of divorces was over a half million—more than twice that in 1936. The number of marriages and divorces in 1956 was smaller than in 1946 but larger than in 1936. It seems, then, that the figures for 1936 (a depression year) and 1946 (a year when millions of soldiers came home from war) are exceptions.

How can we explain why the number of both marriages and divorces has risen in the following years? For one thing, the population of the United States has grown. Fewer people lived in the United States in 1936 than in 1971. The marriage *rate* was higher in 1936 than in 1971, but the actual *number* of marriages was lower in 1936 than in 1971. The marriage rate jumped after World War II, fell rapidly, and leveled off. Both marriage and divorce rates, however, have been rising since the mid-1960s, but the divorce rate has risen much faster.

The chance for success in marriage is low for teenagers, particularly for young women. Those who marry young are twice as likely to get divorced as couples who get married when they are older. Perhaps, like Rose and Marty, many teenagers see the romance but do not see the drudgery and responsibility that go along with marriage.

FAMILY UNITS AND FAMILY SIZE   There are more family units in the United States than ever before (over 52 million), probably because there are more people in this country than before (over 210 million). But the size of the family unit has been declining slowly but steadily, as we learned in the previous chapter.

Why Has the Family Changed?

We have examined the statistics. We have found that the divorce rate has been rising, while the size of the family has been shrinking. Yet we still cannot say whether or not the family is doomed to disappear. But we can now try to explain why American families are having problems today and hope that you will reach your own conclusions.

INDUSTRIALIZATION   You have already learned that the major function of the family was to serve as an economic unit. Husband, wife, and as many children as possible grew and made the food, clothing, and shelter that the family needed for survival. The industrial revolution has changed this. With the increased use of machines and large-scale factory production, the family is no longer self-sufficient. The family, therefore, is no longer an economic unit. The man (or woman) goes to work and supports the family on earned income. Women and children are not needed to produce the food, clothing, and shelter that the family needs. Thus, their roles have changed too. The industrial revolution has done more than this. Children have been made dependent upon their parents for a longer period of time. Parents often support their children through many years of school.

Washing machines, dishwashers, and all sorts of electric appliances have freed the wife from much of the drudgery of housework. This, and fewer children to care for, no longer makes it necessary for the wife to be tied down at home. In addition, more and more women are receiving the opportunity to get the same education and training that men have had.

Thus we can see that the industrial revolution has (1) changed a major function of the family, and (2) changed the relationships among the members of the family. Let us examine the second item more closely.

ROLES OF FATHER AND MOTHER   In the past, the father went to work. He was boss. Mother did not work outside the house, but she did do all of the housework (with some help from the children or hired "girls"). She did what Dad said. This is no longer true today. Our roles are not so clear-cut. Mom may be working and earning as much as, if not more than, Dad.

Children may not know what is expected of them at home, nor are parents sure as to what to expect of their children. When we do not know our role in life, we become confused. In day-to-day living, this results in family squabbles. You hear it in terms of who should go to the store, take out the garbage, or what time you are to come home. Should Dad decide your allowance and should Mom pick your friends? As Dad's role as boss becomes less clear, it is difficult to answer these and endless other questions.

What might happen to this family if the mother had to go to work?

MOBILITY OF POPULATION   Americans seem to be a people always on the move. As industries grew in the nineteenth century, people moved from farms to cities. Now, people change jobs and locations quite often. Moreover, as more families become *affluent* (have good incomes) they move from the central cities to the suburbs. Because people move around more and more, many families do not seem to "belong" anywhere. They are far away from relatives and old friends. They meet new people and make new friends, but it is not the same. Often, people do not work in the same community in which they live.

Lacking strong roots in a community and trusted relatives and old friends to go to when problems arise, many families seem to be lost. They are bored with the sameness of suburban living and feel trapped in a life that has little meaning for them.

CHANGING SOCIAL ATTITUDES   We have seen that the number of divorces as well as the divorce rate has been increasing. There are two basic reasons for this.

First, society's attitude toward divorce has changed. Millions of people were once taught that their religions considered divorce sinful. Legal separations were sometimes granted, but the couple could never get married again. Many others feared that their friends and neighbors would reject them if they were divorced. Many couples stayed together because they were afraid that a "broken" family would hurt their children. But more people today are willing to ignore or set aside religious teachings. Divorced people are no longer considered "different." More people believe that personal happiness is more important than the responsibility of marriage. The myth of perfect love is recognized today for what it is—a myth. Many young people learn—too late—that a successful marriage requires hard work by both partners. In the past, people lived with their mistakes. But today, the attitude is that if a mistake was made, it can be corrected. The easiest way is to break up the marriage. It is more difficult to find ways to save a marriage that is shaky.

Second, because of society's changing attitudes, divorces are easier to get. Until recently, many states would permit divorce only when one partner's unfaithfulness could be proved. Today, many of these same states will permit divorce for such reasons as desertion and physical or mental cruelty.

NEW LIFE-STYLES   Changing attitudes toward marriage have affected the life-styles of a great many people in our society. The *Pill* (taken to prevent pregnancy) has changed, perhaps forever, the roles of men and women in sexual relationships. Couples can live together without getting married; they no longer need to fear they will have a child.

Some young people are showing an interest in communal living. Of course, some have joined communes to escape from reality, perhaps through drugs. Most communes, however, are made up of persons who are seriously concerned with establishing new values or rediscovering old ones. Very often, these communes are *antimaterialistic*. They are concerned with religion, ecology, and natural living. Often the communes are seeking ways in which people can live together in peace and love and yet develop independently.

Summary   We have been concerned with the question of whether or not the family as we know it will disappear. We have seen that family breakups, or divorces, have been increasing. On the other hand, most people who get divorced marry someone else. We have also noted that a marriage is less likely to be successful when the woman is a teenager at the time of marriage. Finally, we have seen that the number of families in the United States is increasing, although families have been getting smaller in size.

In trying to understand these changes, we have noted the importance of the industrial revolution and modern technology. We have also observed that the mobility of the average American family, and our changing attitudes toward marriage, divorce, and sex have exerted pressures on the traditional family structure.

After considering all of these factors, some people have come to the conclusion that the American family is indeed doomed. They believe that other social forms will take over all of the functions of the family. But others disagree. They believe that the family will never disappear. Regardless of what changes take place in society, the family will adjust to these changes and continue to function. What do you think?

Looking Ahead   The role of women in society is also being questioned. It is unlikely that women will ever again think that their major role in life is to stay home, have children, and do housework. Technology has *liberated* (freed) them from most of the drudgery of housework. Many women are now demanding liberation from any activity or role that places them in a position that is inferior to that of men. They are demanding the same salaries as men who do the same jobs. Not only does this affect the traditional father-mother role, but it also suggests that women have the right to the same personal freedoms that men have considered only theirs. We shall discuss the liberated woman in the next chapter.

EXERCISES

MATCHING QUESTIONS   Match each term in Column A with its definition in Column B.

Column A

1. commune
2. industrialization
3. mobility
4. affluent
5. liberated

Column B

(*a*) freed
(*b*) having a good income
(*c*) a group of people living together as a family
(*d*) wide use of machines
(*e*) freedom to move about

MULTIPLE-CHOICE QUESTIONS   For each question, write the letter of the best answer.

1. The main idea of this chapter is that (*a*) the family will disappear (*b*) the traditional family is under increasing pressures (*c*) it is no longer necessary to marry (*d*) marriage is fun.
2. According to the chapter (*a*) all young people are trying new life-styles (*b*) most young people are rejecting the traditional marriage-family institution (*c*) some young people are experimenting with new life-styles (*d*) new life-styles are better than traditional ways.
3. According to the chapter (*a*) the divorce rate was highest during the depression years (*b*) the divorce rate has increased in the last ten years (*c*) fewer people are getting married today than ever before (*d*) more people get divorced each year than get married.

4. According to the chapter (*a*) more male teenagers than female teenagers get married (*b*) more female teenagers have successful marriages than male teenagers (*c*) more male teenagers than female teenagers get divorced (*d*) teenagers' chances for success in marriage are low.

5. Increased industrialization in the United States has (*a*) made children less dependent on their parents (*b*) changed major functions of the family (*c*) forced women to stay at home (*d*) kept the family together as an economic-work unit.

6. The roles of father and mother today are (*a*) no longer as clearcut as they used to be (*b*) the same as they always were (*c*) simple—Dad is the boss (*d*) reversed—Mom is now the boss.

7. Americans today tend to (*a*) move more than ever before (*b*) stay where they were born (*c*) plant strong roots in one community (*d*) resist changing the place in which they live or their attitudes.

8. Two major reasons for the increase in the divorce rate in the United States are that divorces are easier to get and (*a*) attitudes toward marriage and divorce are changing (*b*) marriages are doomed (*c*) people are marrying too young (*d*) divorced people often get remarried to new husbands or wives.

9. The conclusion reached in this chapter is that (*a*) the family is doomed (*b*) the family is not doomed (*c*) the family no longer serves any useful function (*d*) it is not clear what role the family will play in the future.

Chapter 4   The New Woman: Mrs., Miss, or Ms.?

Mrs. Joan Chu is married, loves her husband and three children, and attends a Women's Liberation meeting every Tuesday night.

Miss Sally Jones is 23, single, and dates a lot of men, but she isn't serious about any one at this time. Sally is a member of Joan's Tuesday night group.

Ms. Jo Grant also belongs to the same Women's Liberation group as Joan and Sally. Jo, who shares an apartment with a girlfriend, thinks that all men are *male chauvinist pigs* (men who exploit and dominate women).

Women's Liberation

To *liberate* means to set free. Joan, Sally, and Jo are three *liberated* (free) women. They share many of the same ideas. Yet they differ greatly in their idea of what a liberated woman should be. Our culture (society) has set up an image (picture) for each of us of what a woman is or should be. Women today are challenging that image because they believe that the image is untrue and places women in an *inferior* (lower) position to men. The Women's Liberation movement is a movement to change this image—to *free* women in both the legal and *psychological* (mental) senses.

Images are hard to shatter, however. We are told in the Bible that woman (Eve) was created from man (Adam's rib). When we study the past, we learn *his*tory (*his* story) rather than *her*story (*her* story). The princess in distress is always rescued by the handsome prince, never the other way around.

WOMEN ARE THE MAJORITY Women have been discriminated against in much the same way as any racial or religious minority group. Actually, however, women are the majority (51 percent) of the American population. Often called the weaker sex, women are actually stronger than men, if average *life span* (how long people live) is any standard. The average life span is 73 years for a woman but only 70 years for a man.

Yet, when a woman marries, she drops her own last name and takes the name of her husband. Many people in our society still look down on an unmarried woman. They think that marriage is the final goal of all women. Of course, this is not true.

Betty Friedan, a leader in the Women's Liberation movement, claims that many women are unhappy as housewives. What is more, Ms. Friedan says that women are not being used to their fullest capacity as long as they are forced to stay at home.

Members of the Women's Liberation movement often use Ms. instead of Mrs. or Miss before their names. What is the difference, they ask, if a woman is or is not married?

Ask a girl or a young woman what she wants to be when she grows up. The expected answer used to be a housewife, teacher, or nurse. But young women today are saying that they want to be whatever they are capable of being—without any restrictions on them because they are women.

Fight for Equality

Women in America have been fighting for equality for a long time. In the 19th century, the Grimke sisters, Angelina and Sarah, worked to *abolish* (end) slavery in America. Even then, these women were aware that white women, too, were not equal to white men. Harriet Tubman and Sojourner Truth, ex-slaves, also were leading *abolitionists* (people who worked to end slavery). Susan B. Anthony was a leader in the struggle for voting rights for women. It was not until 1920 (when the 19th Amend-

What are these women demanding?

ment to the Constitution was passed) that women were first allowed to vote in a national election in this country.

The Civil Rights Act of 1964 bans discrimination because of sex. So does the Equal Pay Act of 1963. Yet women in America tend to hold jobs that have lower status than the jobs that men hold. Moreover, even when women hold the same kinds of jobs as men, they tend to be paid less. The chances are that your teacher in elementary school was a woman—85 percent of all elementary school teachers are women. However, the school principal was probably a man—78 percent of all elementary school principals are men. In high school, the odds of your having a male principal are even greater—96 percent of all secondary school principals are men.

In 1972 Congress passed and sent to the states for ratification the Equal Rights Amendment. This amendment prohibits discrimination of any kind based on sex. If the amendment becomes part of our Constitution, we will have to do some rethinking about some of our most cherished ideas. For example, in time of war would women be drafted along with men? Would they have to fight alongside men in battle? In civilian life, in case of a divorce, the mother is usually awarded custody of the children. Will fathers be given the equal rights to custody of the children? Will a man be able to ask his divorced wife to pay him alimony—instead of the other way around?

Joan Chu, Sally Jones, and Jo Grant are all in Women's Liberation. Yet they do not think alike on all issues. What they do agree on, though, is that every woman should have the chance to choose whatever life she wishes to lead. If Joan Chu wants to be a housewife, that is fine. At the same time, if Sally Jones enjoys dating different men and does or does not want to get married, that is her business. And if Jo Grant would rather live with another woman than with a man, that too is her right.

The right to choose goes beyond the issue of marriage. There are many choices of life-style open to American women today. For one thing, women can more easily prevent, or plan, pregnancies. "The Pill," as it is called, has brought about a revolution in attitudes toward sexual behavior. A woman's right to choose also has been extended to mean the legal right to have an *abortion* (removal of the fetus—to stop the pregnancy). In fact, the United States Supreme Court has held that laws prohibiting abortions are unconstitutional.

Our ideas about a woman's role are changing. Women are demanding and getting the same place in society as men. The *double standard* (which permitted men to do things women were forbidden to do) is being chipped away. Women reject their role as "breeders" who left to men the role as leaders.

Attitudes Change Slowly

In spite of all that we have said, most Americans, male and female, still regard women in a way that would upset the leaders of the Women's Liberation movement. For one thing, three out of four women, according to a recent poll, reject the claim of the Women's Liberation movement that women are treated as second-class citizens. And while most agreed that women should have equal job opportunities and equal pay for equal work, they also felt that a man should hold a door for a woman, that a woman's place is still in the home, and that a wife should not be the family breadwinner even if she can earn more money than her husband. However, while most women said that men should not judge a woman on the basis of beauty and sex appeal, the men questioned still thought that beauty and sex appeal were important in judging a woman.

HOW WOULD YOU FEEL?   Each day, at home, in school, and at work, you are faced with many decisions and situations that require you to play a role as a man or a woman. For example, the guys are getting together a team to play baseball. How would you feel if you are left out because you are a woman? Some women like to play baseball and play it very well. Suppose the teacher needs someone to carry a film projector. How would you feel if you are chosen because you are a man? Some women are physically stronger than many men. Would it make any difference to you if you are a man or a woman if people said that you were not athletic—or that you were delicate? How would you feel if someone called you a "tomboy" or a "sissy"? Do you think that boys should not hit girls? How would you feel if you are known as the brightest girl in the class? Would you rather be known as the prettiest?

A NORMAL, "HEALTHY" INDIVIDUAL   In some ways, our ideas as to what is and what is not healthy and normal in men and women are quite strange. If you are a man, most people would say that you are normal and healthy if you are aggressive, independent, competitive, adventurous. In your relationships with women, you would not be considered "unhealthy" if you "played the field"—that is, if you went from one woman to the next.

If you are a woman, you would probably be considered normal if you were submissive, emotional, excitable in minor crises, and if your feelings were easily hurt. You would probably be considered "sick" if you were tough, aggressive, and had one boyfriend after another. A woman is expected to be faithful to, or involved with, only one man. The man is often expected to be unfaithful. (This is especially true for married couples.)

Suppose that you are not anything like the picture of a man or woman described above. Is anything wrong with you? Certainly not! Today, thanks in large part to Women's Liberation, men and women alike have been liberated from the strange images of normal life that we have created for ourselves. Liberation has given both men and women the freedom to do the things that they really want to do (within limits of course) without fear of being considered sick.

Summary   The Women's Liberation movement tries to gain equality for women on both the social and personal levels. The movement has worked to have laws passed to prevent any kind of discrimination based on sex. In trying to free women from the stereotyped roles of housewife and mother, the movement has also liberated many men. Our society is moving closer to the view that all human beings should be able to do as they wish, within reason, without being ashamed of themselves or worrying about their *self-image* (that is, whether they are being masculine or feminine, whether they are doing "men's work" or "women's work").

EXERCISES

MATCHING QUESTIONS   Match each term in Column A with its definition in Column B.

Column A	*Column B*
1. Ms.	(*a*) believes in the ideas of writers like Betty Friedan
2. liberate	
3. male chauvinist pig	(*b*) people who worked to end slavery
4. abolitionist	(*c*) to set free
5. Women's Liberation	(*d*) a man who believes men are superior to women
6. abortion	
	(*e*) a title used instead of Miss or Mrs. (or, a title used to mean a woman)
	(*f*) end of a pregnancy

NUMBERS TELL A STORY   The tables on page 83 tell us (1) the percentages of women who hold jobs in over a dozen professional, technical, and service fields, and (2) the average incomes that women and men receive for doing the same jobs. Look at the tables and tell whether the statements that follow are true or false. If they are opinions, write O. Remember that 50 percent of the high school graduates and nearly 45 percent of the college graduates in this country are women.

Women in Selected Occupations, 1973

Occupation	Percent Women	Occupation	Percent Women
Private household workers	98	Factory workers	39
Dieticians	92	College teachers	24
Elementary school teachers	84	Managers	18
Librarians	82	Photographers	14
Dancers	81	Scientists	14
Clerical workers	76	Pharmacists	12
Therapists	64	Doctors	9
Social workers	63	Lawyers, judges	5
Service workers (restaurants,		Clergy	3
beauty parlors)	63	Engineers	2

Average Earnings of Women and Men, by Occupational Group, 1973

Occupation	Women	Men
Professional, technical	$8,744	$13,542
Managers	7,024	13,486
Clerical workers	6,054	9,716
Crafts workers	5,545	10,413
Factory workers	5,004	8,747
Service workers	4,483	7,630

1. Men and women earn equal pay for doing the same work.
2. Women are better at housework and teaching children than men.
3. Most librarians are women.
4. Women are not good at mathematics and science, so they do not enter the occupations that require skill in those areas.
5. Clerical workers earn more than technical workers.
6. Women technical and professional workers earn about one-third less than men who do the same jobs.
7. There are no women judges or lawyers.
8. Most women doctors treat infants and children.

WHAT DO YOU THINK?   Tell whether you agree, disagree, or have no opinion about each of the statements that follow. Compare your answers with those of your classmates. Then use the results as the basis for a class discussion.

	Agree	*Disagree*	*No Opinion*

1. A woman's place is in the home.
2. "Miss" and "Mrs." should be replaced by "Ms."
3. Women who work should receive the same pay as men who do the same job.
4. It is all right for a woman to ask a man for a date.
5. If women must stay at home, they should be paid a salary for doing housework and raising children.
6. If a wife can earn a lot more money than her husband, he should stay home to take care of the house and raise the children.
7. All school athletic teams should be open to men and women alike.
8. A woman should keep her maiden name when she gets married.

Unit IV   The Economy

Chapter 1   Taxes

Have you ever had a job? If you have and the job paid $50 or $60 a week, one thing was certain—you didn't get all of the $50 or $60 when you got your paycheck at the end of the week. Some of the money you earned was *deducted* from (taken out of) your salary to pay taxes. You received the difference.

Even if you have never had a job, you still have paid taxes. You paid sales taxes when you bought things in a local store. You paid taxes when you bought a movie ticket, cosmetics, gasoline, and imported goods. You have been paying taxes ever since you were old enough to spend money.

Throughout history governments have used taxes as a way to obtain the income they need to pay for their functions. The United States is no exception. Our federal, state, and local governments all require us to pay some kind of tax. And, in recent years, these taxes have increased greatly.

Government Costs

Back in 1890 the total cost of operating all the governments in the United States was only $850 million. But 86 years later, in 1976, the total cost was $550 billion—an increase of nearly 400 times! How do we account for this? Here are some of the more important reasons.

WARS AND DEFENSE   National defense costs have skyrocketed. In 1890 the total federal budget for national defense amounted to less than $67 million. In 1977 the defense budget was $101 billion—more than the total federal budget for 1961, only 16 years earlier. The war in Vietnam, nuclear weapons, and the desire to keep adequate armed forces even in peacetime have all combined to make defense the single most expensive item in our national budget.

Past wars still cost us money today. Since 1917, the United States has fought two world wars and undeclared wars in Korea and Southeast Asia. The nation had to borrow billions of dollars to pay for these wars. Now the money must be repaid, with interest. We must also care for the veterans of these wars. If we add to these costs the expenses for space exploration (which also has a bearing on national defense) and foreign aid programs, we find that these items cost the government an additional $29 billion in 1977.

National defense, past wars, foreign aid, and space exploration took 33 cents out of every dollar that the government spent in 1977.

GROWING POPULATION, NEEDS, AND EXPECTATIONS
Our growing population has also added to the cost of government. In 1890 there were 63 million Americans. By 1975 the population had more than tripled—to more than 211 million persons. Furthermore, the population itself had also changed. In 1930, for example, only 5 percent of the population was over 65 years of age. By 1975 this figure had doubled to 10 percent. This, of course, was a result of advances in science and medicine, which now enable more people to live longer. Longer life has added to the cost of government—in the form of social security payments and medical care for those over 65.

We expect government to do more for us today. At one time it was thought that governments should stay out of the affairs of private citizens. "That government is best which governs least" was a slogan most Americans would have agreed with before the Great Depression of the 1930s. Today, however, we look to the government to deal with many of the problems we once expected individuals to solve for themselves. In many communities welfare payments to needy people account for the largest single item in the budget. We also expect the government to solve the problems created by pollution. This expense was almost nonexistent 15 years ago.

Not only do we expect more from government, we also expect things done better or on a larger scale than in the past. Through the years, as the American standard of living has risen, the services that government has provided have had to improve. For example, government has had to replace the old-fashioned schoolhouse with modern buildings that contain the latest books and teaching machinery and cafeterias and gyms.

Sometimes progress has its drawbacks, however. For example, as more and more Americans bought cars, the two-lane highways of the past had to be replaced with four- and six-lane expressways. But these in turn added to our problems of ecology. More highways destroy the landscape; exhaust fumes from auto engines poison the trees and foliage; heavy traffic burns up gasoline that can never be replaced; and cars kill thousands of wild animals every year.

INFLATION   Like everyone else, the government has also been affected by inflation. Almost everything costs more today than it did five or ten years ago. So running the government becomes more and more costly.

Almost everyone would agree that the government has to collect taxes in order to meet the expenses we have described above. But who should pay these taxes? How should they be collected? Should there be a limit to the amount of tax that the government may collect from us? Can the power to tax be used for any other purpose than just paying the cost of government? To understand these questions better, let us take a closer look at what taxes do for us.

What Taxes Do for Us

In addition to paying the cost of government that we described above, taxes also *redistribute income*. That is, they take income from some people and give it to others. One of the most famous legends of medieval England was that of Robin Hood. It was said of Robin Hood that he "stole from the rich and gave to the poor." People who criticize our tax system call certain taxes "Robin Hood taxes" because they take money from the rich and give it to the poor. On the other hand, others say this makes good sense, because taxes are paid by those who can afford to pay. When the government spends money to help certain groups of people, such as the aged and the poor, it does, in effect, give them the money it took from others.

Taxes are used to help certain industries sell more goods. In 1971, for example, the government *repealed* (did away with) a tax on new American cars and levied a new tax on all foreign-made cars coming into the country. This was done to help American car makers sell more cars. American cars become less expensive than they had been, and foreign cars became more expensive.

To use another example, the federal government has for many years granted a special tax break to oil-producing companies. This tax break, called the oil *depletion allowance,* frees from any taxes a certain percentage of oil company income. Its purpose is to encourage oil companies to explore for new sources of oil so that the price of oil will remain at a reasonable level.

Taxes may be used to regulate the amount of money spent by individuals and by businesses. Taxes take money out of our pockets. The moneys that we give Uncle Sam and our state and local governments are moneys that we will never spend. The same is true of businesses. Knowing this, the government will use its power to tax to affect the total economy. We shall discuss this in our chapter on inflation.

The Taxes We Pay

There are several ways to describe taxes. One is to classify taxes according to the items that are taxed. For example:

Income taxes are paid according to the amount of money a person or a business earns. The personal income tax also depends on how many people must be fed, clothed, and housed on this income.

Excise taxes are paid on particular goods or services. Taxes on a bottle of perfume and on a movie ticket are examples of excise taxes.

Property taxes are paid by people who own homes and other property.

Sales taxes are paid by consumers when they make purchases in retail stores. Food is not taxed, but restaurant meals, clothing, and most other products are taxed.

Taxes are also classified according to the income of those who have to pay them. For example, a *progressive tax* is designed to take a larger and larger percentage of a person's income as that income increases. This tax takes a higher percentage of a rich person's income than a poor person's income.

On the other hand, a *regressive tax* does just the opposite. This tax takes a larger percentage of a poor person's income than it does of a rich person's income.

Taxes may be classified by the manner in which they are collected. For example, *direct taxes* are paid by the taxpayer to the government or to someone who collects the money for the government. A taxpayer who pays a direct tax knows it. An *indirect tax* is sometimes called a hidden tax. This is a tax that is paid by an individual or a business that can then pass the tax along to someone else. Although the landlord of an apartment house pays a property tax on the building and land, the tax is passed on to the tenants in their rent. So it is the tenants who really pay the tax. To the tenant, therefore, the property tax is an indirect tax, but to the owner of a private house, the property tax is a direct tax because it is paid directly to the government.

INCOME TAXES An *income tax* is collected by the federal government and by most of the states. The income tax is a progressive tax because the percentage one must pay increases with one's income. For example, a married couple with $3,000 in taxable income in 1973 had to pay about 15 percent of $3,000 for federal income taxes. If their income had been $10,000, the tax rate would have been 18 percent. With $50,000 of taxable income, the rate was 34 percent, and with $100,000, they would have had to pay 50 percent in taxes.

The income tax is also a direct tax. It is paid by the taxpayer directly to the government at the end of the year or it is withheld from salary and forwarded to the government by the taxpayer's employer. In either case, the taxpayer is well aware of the tax.

Critics of the income tax rate structure say that the present tax rates are too high. They also say that tax laws favor a few rich people who are able to take advantage of *tax "loopholes."* Loopholes allow large deductions for charitable donations, business losses, and special kinds of income. Reformers want to close these loopholes. One proposal would eliminate (get rid of) most of the deductions that are allowed at present. This would allow a lowering of the tax rate, which now ranges from 14 to 50 percent, to between 12 and 35 percent of taxable income.

Supporters of the present system claim that deductions and special

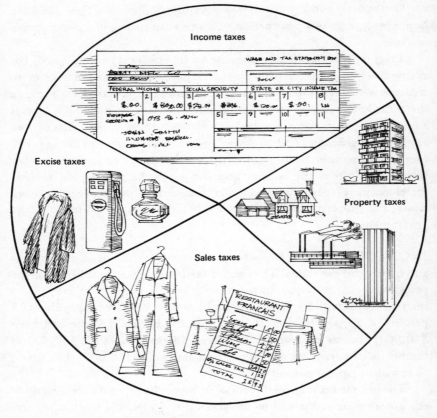

Taxes that Americans pay

privileges were put into the tax laws for good reasons. For example, when a business is helped because of special tax privileges, this benefits its employees and the public as well as the owners of the business.

EXCISE TAXES   About 10 cents of every tax dollar collected by the federal government come from excise taxes. These are taxes on particular goods and services, as we said above. Excise taxes are usually paid directly to the government by the manufacturer. Then the manufacturer adds the excise tax to the sale price of the product. The next buyer, who may be a wholesaler, will then pass the tax on to the retailer, who, of course, will pass it on to the consumer.

Excise taxes have the advantage of being relatively easy to collect. The government does not have to listen to many complaints because the people who finally pay these taxes are usually unaware that they are doing so.

Excise taxes are called regressive because the people who really pay them are not the original producers but the final consumers. These consumers are frequently the people who are least able to afford to pay the taxes. Suppose, for example, that the federal government placed an $80 excise tax on every new car sold. To a person earning $8,000, $80 is 1 percent of total income. To a person earning $40,000, $80 is only one-fifth of 1 percent of total income. The $80 excise tax is a minor annoyance to a $40,000-a-year person, but it is a good slice of the income of an $8,000-a-year person.

PROPERTY TAXES   The major source of income for most local governments is the property tax. Home owners as well as businesses pay a tax on the value of their homes and land or business property (such as a factory or a store). One of the major advantages of the property tax is that the government can predict in advance exactly how much money will be collected. Income tax collections depend upon how much people earn, and sales taxes depend upon how much they spend. But the value of the real estate in a community is set by its government.

Local governments favor the property tax because it is less noticeable than income taxes and sales taxes. Governments are afraid that a sales tax

What is the cartoonist's view of the citizen's tax burden?

Tom Little in "The Tennessean"

will cause people to do their shopping in a different community, and that an income tax will make them move away.

Property taxes have also been called regressive. That is, the amount of tax one pays depends on the value of one's property, not on one's income. It is likely that people in lower income brackets pay a larger percentage of their income for property taxes than people in higher income tax brackets.

SALES TAXES   The biggest moneymaker for state governments is the sales tax. Unlike the income tax, with its deductions and exemptions, everyone must pay the same rate of sales tax. The 6 or 7 percent does not amount to very much. But the sales tax has also been called regressive because poor people spend a larger percentage of their income on taxable purchases than well-to-do people.

Taxes are perhaps the oldest of mankind's "current issues." Thousands of years ago, riots broke out in the streets of Ancient Rome over taxes. American colonists rallied to the cry, "Taxation without representation is tyranny." Governments have been overthrown because they levied unjust taxes on their people.

Who should bear the heaviest burden of taxes is also an ever-present problem. In 1973 it was revealed that President Nixon's federal income tax payments had been only $793 in 1970 and $878 in 1971. This was equal to the amount paid by the average American family of three with an income between $7,500 and $8,500 a year. But the President's salary was $200,000 a year, and he had other income as well. Why did he pay so little? The reason was that tax loopholes allowed him to take certain deductions that the average taxpayer could not take.

We have seen that tax deductions or loopholes were provided to help certain business activities. Is this fair? The question is still being debated. What do you think?

Summary   In recent years, the taxes that Americans have had to pay have increased greatly. We all have had to share the costs of increasing social insurance for the aged and the helpless, of wars and defense expenditures, and of government intervention in all areas of American life.

Looking Ahead   In the next chapter, we shall look at another current economic problem: the problem of inflation.

EXERCISES

MATCHING QUESTIONS   Match each term in Column A with its definition in Column B.

Column A

1. income tax
2. excise tax
3. sales tax
4. property tax
5. progressive tax
6. regressive tax
7. direct tax
8. indirect tax

Column B

(a) a tax that the taxpayer cannot pass along to someone else
(b) a hidden tax
(c) a tax that takes a larger percentage of a poor person's income than of a wealthy person's income
(d) a tax that takes a larger percentage of a wealthy person's income than of a poor person's income
(e) a tax on a particular good or service
(f) a tax paid by consumers for a wide range of goods or services
(g) a tax paid by home owners
(h) a direct, progressive tax levied by the federal government and most state governments

WHICH TAX DO YOU PREFER?   Pretend that your state or local government has decided to raise taxes to meet rising expenses. In each case there is more than one tax proposal under consideration. Each tax proposal would raise as much money as is needed. The only question to be decided is which proposal to accept.

Suppose that the choice of tax is yours to make. Study each situation. Select the method of taxation that you prefer, and explain the reasons for your choice.

1. Shall we levy a 1 cent per package tax on chewing gum and candy bars *or* a 1 cent per loaf tax on bread?
2. Shall we levy a 2 percent tax on meat *or* a 4 percent tax on imported perfumes and whiskies?

3. Shall we levy a $5 tax on every member of a household *or* a $25 tax on every automobile *or* a $100 tax on every second or third automobile owned by the household?

4. Shall we set a 5 percent across-the-board increase in income taxes *or* a sliding-scale increase in which the lowest bracket would pay an additional 1 percent, the second lowest bracket an additional 2 percent, the third bracket an additional 3 percent, and so on? The proceeds of this tax would be returned to the community.

5. Shall we add a 5-cent-per-quart milk tax to be collected from the bottlers *or* a 10 percent sales tax on fur coats?

6. Shall we set a 10 percent fare increase on public buses *or* an additional 10 percent tax on gasoline?

Chapter 2   Inflation

In 1972 Joe DiFazio earned $13,000 a year. In 1973 the company he worked for gave him a $1,000 raise. In 1974 we asked Joe what kind of year 1973 had been for him and his family. What do you think he said?

"It was a terrible year," Joe said. "At first I thought I was better off because of my $1,000 raise. But do you know what? Vera and I couldn't buy as much with $14,000 in 1973 as we could with $13,000 in 1972. It was all because of inflation. A dollar just wasn't worth what it was worth the year before."

We checked the figures and found that Joe was right. The dollar was not worth as much in 1973 as it had been worth in 1972. Its *purchasing power* had declined. By purchasing power we mean the amount of goods and services the dollar is able to buy.

In 1973 the purchasing power of the average person's dollar went down 9.4 percent. This means that Joe DiFazio would have needed an additional 9.4 percent in salary, or $14,222 in income, just to break even in 1973. Since he received only a $1,000 raise, he really had been better off in 1972.

Rising Cost of Living

How do we account for this? Why would Joe have needed to earn $14,222 in 1973 just to have stayed even with the $13,000 he earned in 1972? The answer is that the cost of living rose in 1973. Therefore, in 1973 the dollar did not buy as much as it did in 1972.

Purchasing power declines when the cost of living rises. And what do we mean by the cost of living? The cost of living is the average price people pay for the things they need. These needs include goods, such as food and clothing, as well as services, such as medical care and haircuts. The cost of living also includes taxes, which are the payments we make to the government for the services it provides.

Increases in taxation and in the cost of living are the reasons why the purchasing power of the dollar has declined. Economists describe this situation as *inflation.* A period of inflation is one in which prices are generally rising and the purchasing power of the dollar is declining.

Inflation Affects Us All

Inflation has been with us for a long time. Since the end of World War II in 1945, there have been only two years in which the purchasing power of the dollar did *not* decline. Basically, what this means is that in order for a family (or an individual) to purchase as much in one year as in the preceding year, the family or individual had to earn more each year. The average weekly salary of workers increased from about $80 to $130 in the 10 years from 1960 to 1970. Due to increased taxes and inflation, however, the buying power of their earnings hardly increased at all.

Some groups are hit harder than others. Although inflation affects everyone, certain groups in our society suffer much more than others. The hardest hit are persons in the lower income brackets who are living on fixed incomes. The elderly, the widowed mother, the disabled—these people are usually dependent on fixed pensions. As the cost of living increases, these people have to live on money that buys less and less.

But you do not have to be poor to be hurt by inflation. Those with money in the bank will find that the money they deposited is worth less (in terms of purchasing power) when they withdraw it than it was when they deposited it.

Creditors (people who have loaned money to others) find that the money they loaned is worth less at the time it is repaid than it was when the loan was first made.

Causes of Inflation

Although economists are not totally agreed on the reasons why inflation takes place, they generally blame it on one or more of the following factors:

(1) the supply of money, (2) an excess of demand (demand-pull), or (3) increasing costs (cost-push).

THE SUPPLY OF MONEY   The supply of money in circulation at any one time is not a fixed sum. As a matter of fact, the supply is constantly changing. During wartime, for example, government spending increases to pay for the war. This increases the amount of money in circulation. On the other hand, there are times when the government reduces its spending. This could lead to a reduction in the amount of money in circulation. When the supply of money is increased, it usually winds up in the hands of potential spenders (whom we call consumers). If the amount of things that consumers can buy with their money increases by about the same amount as the money supply, not much is likely to happen to prices. On the other hand, if the money supply increases a lot more than the supply of things to buy, prices will most likely increase. The reason is that with more money to spend, people are able and willing to pay higher prices. This in turn pushes prices up and brings on inflation.

EXCESS DEMAND (DEMAND-PULL)   If for any reason consumers decide to buy more than usual, prices will be forced up. Economists describe this as *demand-pull* inflation. What they are saying is that there is more, or an *excess* of, demand than there are goods and services to satisfy that demand. Consumers therefore have to compete with one another for the things they want. This competition is what forces the prices up. During World War II, consumers were unable to buy many of the things they wanted because most factories were making war goods. When the war ended, millions of buyers eagerly purchased every thing they could get their hands on. This rush of demand, of course, "pushed" prices up sharply.

INCREASING COSTS (COST-PUSH)   Still another cause of inflation is described as *cost-push* inflation. This occurs when prices are increased because the cost of producing goods has increased. You may have read about a company that announced it was going to increase its prices because its workers had just received a wage increase. If the company produced a good (such as steel) that was used in the production of other goods, the added cost could force producers of other goods to increase their costs too. In other words, an increase in the price of steel brought on by a wage hike could lead to an increase in the price of automobiles. Thus the inflationary price increases would not have been brought on by an increase in demand (as it was in the case of demand-pull), but by an increase in *costs*.

What Can Be Done?

Ann and Ray Cambridge finally decided to buy the new home they had been looking at for the past six months. They walked into their local bank and told Mr. Jackson, who is in charge of home loans, of their decision.

"Fine," said Mr. Jackson. "Of course, you realize that your payments will now run $10 more each month than when we first discussed the loan."

"What happened?" asked Ray Cambridge. "The price of the house didn't go up."

"That's true," Mr. Jackson replied, "but the cost of *borrowing money* did go up."

"Who's responsible for that?" Ann asked Mr. Jackson. She suddenly had a feeling that everything had gone wrong.

"The rise in the cost of borrowing money is part of the government's fight against inflation," Mr. Jackson explained. "The fight is to get the public to spend less money."

"The government won, as far as I'm concerned," said Ray. "We could just barely have afforded the house at the old rate. That extra $10 is more than we can afford. Maybe we'll be able to buy a new house next year, Ann."

Ann hardly heard what Ray was saying. She was too busy fighting back the tears.

What effect did high interest rates have on the home buyers described in the text? Can you think of other groups that would be affected if people could not afford to buy new homes?

Tom Little in "The Tennessean"

The Cambridges did not buy a new home because the government had done something to make their home loan more costly. Because of this government action, there was less money in circulation than there might have been. In attempting to control inflation, the federal government directs most of its efforts toward regulating the causes we just described: the money supply, demand, and costs.

REGULATION OF THE MONEY SUPPLY The federal government can and does control the amount of money in circulation. When it does this in order to achieve a specific objective, it is carrying out *monetary policy*. This policy is carried out by the Federal Reserve System. During periods of rising prices, the Federal Reserve System can take steps to limit the amount of money in circulation. This is what happened in the case of the Cambridges. As a result, one less house was sold and less money was in circulation. When such a scene is repeated over and over again all over the country, the net result is that prices are held down.

As you might suspect, however, monetary policy alone cannot control inflation. If it could, we would not have to worry about rising prices. One reason why monetary policy alone cannot control prices is that when the Federal Reserve System reduces the amount of money in circulation, it can have an *adverse* (unfavorable) effect on business. Now if business in general should fall off, this in turn will lead to increasing unemployment. When government policy to lower prices results in a decline in business profits and increasing unemployment, many people will say that the cure is worse than the disease. Monetary policy can *help* to control inflation, but it too needs help.

CONTROL OF WAGES AND PRICES To sum up, demand-pull brings on inflation as consumers with money to spend push prices up. Cost-push, on the other hand, also brings on higher prices as businessmen pass along increasing costs in the form of higher prices to their customers. The government can limit the effect of these causes of inflation through its power to regulate prices and wages. Prior to 1971, however, the federal government had not regulated wages and prices on a national basis during peacetime. Most Americans felt that a democratic society should not be restricted to such an extent. During the world wars, the government had controlled wages and prices, and had even rationed goods that were in short supply. But this was accepted as a necessary price the nation had to pay to win the war.

By 1971, however, the country had gone through a period of nearly 25 years of steadily rising prices. And, because of the war in Vietnam, prices and wages were increasing at an alarming rate. In August 1971 President Nixon announced that the government would introduce limited wage and price controls. Under the program, wage and price increases would be limited to an amount the government deemed fair. In this way rising costs as a cause of inflation (cost-push) would be limited by fixing prices and wages. Similarly, by restricting the income received by workers and businessmen, increased demand (demand-pull) as a cause of inflation would be limited.

Wage and price controls were eased in November 1971 and again in January and August 1973. All controls were lifted in 1974. Most people are likely to agree that the wage and price control program as administered by the Nixon administration was a failure. Indeed 1973 witnessed the largest increase in prices in 23 years. Have you felt the effect of this increase? How?

Summary   In the past 25 years, inflation has been a constant problem for all Americans. Efforts to solve it have been only partly successful.

Looking Ahead   In the next chapter, we shall look at another persistent economic problem—poverty.

EXERCISES

UNDERSTANDING WHAT YOU HAVE READ   Complete the following sentences.

1. During a period of inflation, prices _____.
2. During a period of inflation, the cost of living _____.
3. During a period of inflation, the purchasing power of the dollar _____.
4. If the supply of money in circulation were suddenly increased, prices would _____.

5. When buyers decide to spend more than usual, prices are likely to
   _____.

6. One way in which the federal government tries to combat inflation is to
   _____ the supply of money in circulation.

7. Another way in which the federal government could combat inflation
   would be to _____ public spending.

8. In August 1971 the government introduced a policy of wage and price
   _____ to stop inflation.

9. When the government uses its powers to tax and spend to control
   inflation, it must use them carefully because _____ will also be
   affected.

MATCHING QUESTIONS   Match the definition in Column B with
the term in Column A.

Column A   *Column B*

1. purchasing power   (*a*) people who have loaned money
2. cost of living   (*b*) use of the government's power to regu-
3. inflation   late the money supply
4. creditors   (*c*) a period of rising prices and taxes
5. monetary policy   (*d*) amount of goods and services our
6. Federal Reserve System   money can buy
                            (*e*) average price people pay for things they
                                 need
                            (*f*) agency that regulates the money supply

HOW DOES INFLATION AFFECT THESE PEOPLE?

1. Ralph Garcia is a clothing salesman. Ralph works on a commission
   basis. That is, he earns a fixed percentage of the selling price on each
   garment he sells. The country has recently been going through a period
   of inflation. How is this inflation likely to affect Ralph?

2. Eileen Barnes, an elderly widow, is living on the fixed monthly pension
   her husband provided for her. In addition Mrs. Barnes receives a
   monthly social security payment. For the past five years the country has

been going through a period of inflation. How do you suppose this affected her?

3. Five years ago, Frank Moneypenny, a wealthy toy manufacturer, loaned $5,000 to his friend and business associate Rubin Malon. During that time the country went through a period of inflation and the cost of living increased by 20 percent. Malon repaid the $5,000 with his check for that amount this week. At the time Mr. Moneypenny said to him, "You are a lucky guy, Rubin. I loaned you $5,000 and you only had to give me back $4,000." What did Mr. Moneypenny mean by that?

4. The President of the United States has been worried about the rise in prices that has plagued the country for the past few years. He calls upon his economic advisers to draw up a program to combat this inflation. Several months later they present a three-point proposal, as follows:

    (1) Increased all taxes by 5 percent each.

    (2) Cut government spending by 5 percent.

    (3) Make it harder for people to borrow money by increasing interest charges on loans.

Explain why the President's advisers suggested each of these three remedies.

Chapter 3   Poverty

The curse of the poor is their poverty—OLD SAYING

In 1972 one out of every eight Americans was poor—over 25 million people. They were poor because their yearly incomes were lower than the amount of money they needed to live decently. This amount—called the *poverty line* by the federal government—varies with the number of people in the family and where they live. In 1972 the poverty line for an average family of four was $4,275.

Who are the 25 million poor people? Here are some typical stories that will give you some idea of who the poor are and what poverty is like.

Poverty Is . . .

Poverty is Arlo, 4½ months old, white. A bloated baby with matchstick arms and legs, he does not have enough Vitamin C in his diet, so he has had scurvy, rickets, and, now, pneumonia. He does not weigh much more now than the day he was born in a little coal-mining town in West Virginia.

Poverty is Rosalee, 15 years old, black. She was born and raised in the ghetto. Rosalee hates school. She cannot read well. She wears the same outfit to school each day and always feels that the other kids are "ranking" her (putting her down). Rosalee and her friend Patty cut classes and have fun running around and hiding when a teacher comes along the halls.

Poverty is Pablo, 11 years old, Mexican-American. Pablo works an

Rural poverty

Urban poverty

11-hour day in the potato fields. He earns $4.50 a day. During the harvest season, Pablo works seven days a week. Sometimes, Pablo goes to school.

Poverty is Linda Maria, 14 years old, Puerto Rican. Linda Maria was born in a small town in Puerto Rico. Her father was uneducated and unskilled. He moved the family up to the mainland, to a large northern city. All his life he had worked in the cane fields. In the city, all he could find to do was wash cars or dishes. One morning he left and has not been seen since, so the family is on welfare.

Poverty is Leroy, 17 years old, black. Like Rosalee, Leroy was born in a ghetto. He is one of seven children. Leroy has never seen his father. The family receives welfare payments from the government to meet its day-to-day expenses. Leroy is on drugs. He needs $40 a day to support his habit. Most of the time he gets the money by selling "bags" around the school. When he runs short of cash, he "rips off" (steals from) one of the kids, and then he's back in business.

Poverty is Tim Hutchins, 79 years old, white. Worn out by years of hard work, he is too old and sick to work. Social Security does not give him enough to make ends meet. So Tim gets a little extra money from the city's welfare department to help meet his expenses.

Poverty is Bill Creel, 39 years old, white. Bill is a farmer in Mississippi, just as his dad was, and his dad before him.

Bill's wife, Joanie, keeps asking him to give up their farm and go north to Chicago, as her brother Fred did. Joanie does not know it, but Fred can be seen almost every night in one of Chicago's North Broadway honky-tonks listening to sad songs about home—that is, the South.

The Creels have eight kids. The Creels love children, but it is hard to make ends meet. Bill often thinks that things would be easier if they had only two kids. The thought does not last long. Bill is proud that he has a large family. His neighbors, the Johnsons, are managing with 11 young ones.

The roads turn to mud when it rains. The Creels do not have indoor plumbing. There are no streetlights, and at night darkness covers the whole community. Bill's pickup truck is eight years old, and it gets tougher and tougher to keep patching it up. This year's crops were poor. Bill does not know if he can hold out much longer. With machinery coming into the area, the kind he cannot afford, he might sell out to a land developer. Maybe then he will head north.

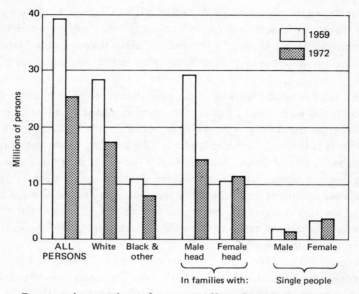

Poverty, by number of persons affected, 1959 and 1972

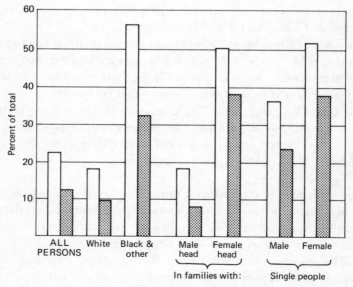

Poverty, by percent of persons affected, 1959 and 1972

What else do we know about poor people?

If you are black, Hispanic-American, or American Indian, the odds are three times greater that you will be poor than if you are white. In 1972 one out of every ten white people was poor, but three out of every ten nonwhites were poor.

A high percentage of families headed by women are poor.

Other groups with a high percentage of poverty are elderly people, handicapped persons, persons living in rural areas, single people, and families with five or more children.

Many poor people hold jobs, but they do not earn enough money to rise above the poverty line.

Causes of Poverty

Why are there so many poor people in the world's richest country? Here are some reasons—you may know a few more.

DISCRIMINATION   As we shall learn in Unit VI, Minorities, the color of our skin, our religion, and our nationality often affect the way other people treat us. Discrimination makes it harder for nonwhites, foreign-born people, and others who are considered "different" to get jobs, particularly jobs that pay well.

POOR FAMILIES   Poor people often come from poor families. This is called the *vicious cycle of poverty.* Poor people cannot live as well as other people—they cannot afford the same nourishing foods, comfortable homes, or good clothes. They often cannot afford doctors or dentists, so poverty often means poor health. This often leads to a "why-bother-trying" attitude. Children brought up in poverty see this defeated attitude all around them; sometimes it makes them work very hard in school and on the job to escape from poverty, but many times it does not. Poverty feeds upon itself—the poor remain poor and pass their poverty on to their children.

LACK OF EDUCATION   Children brought up in poverty often do badly in school or drop out, so they learn fewer skills than other children. Thus the only jobs they can qualify for are the lowest paying ones.

AGE AND DISABILITY   Some people are poor because they are too old to work or are physically handicapped (blind or crippled). Their problems are made worse by inflation, as we learned in Chapter 1. If food and almost everything else cost more this year than last year, people living on small pensions or social security can afford to buy less this year than last.

"BROKEN" HOMES   In many poor families, the father is not living at home and no other man is able to work and support the family. This leaves a woman, usually a mother, with the responsibilities of raising children and earning a living. If there are young children, she often cannot work. This explains why, in more than four out of every ten such cases, the family lives in poverty. The mother must stay at home, and she needs welfare or some other outside source of income.

REGIONAL POVERTY   There is far more poverty in some parts of the country than in others. For example, in 1972, in the states of Connecticut, Hawaii, Massachusetts, Utah, and Wisconsin, only one person in 16 was poor. In Mississippi, however, one person in three was poor; in five other states, one person in five was poor.

THE UNCOUNTED POOR   George Washington did not lose a minute's sleep worrying because he could not travel every year, did not own a car, a color television set, a stereo set, and a fancy camera, and did not have expensive tickets to theatrical and sporting events. (They did not exist, of course.) But today, when all these things are available, and are known to everyone through television, radio, and newspapers, people are very much aware when they cannot afford even some of these "good things of life." Many of these people are not poor—they earn a lot more than the poverty line figure of $4,275 a year for a family of four. But in one large American city, a survey showed that people thought $6,600 a year was the amount that families needed just to "get along." In another city, however, experts found that the family needed $10,000 a year to live "moderately well" (in a decent home, with good food and enough clothes, but with few or no extras, such as those listed above). In any case, if the poverty line were set at $6,600, instead of $4,275, millions more Americans would be classified as poor.

How Can Poverty Be Eliminated?

Most Americans now feel that the federal government must take the lead in eliminating poverty. But how? Attempts to fight poverty fall into two categories: (1) *welfare programs* and (2) *antipoverty programs*.

Welfare programs try to solve specific problems. Giving diapers and baby clothes to a family that has a new baby, food stamps to people who cannot afford to buy food, and cash to those with no money are examples of welfare.

Antipoverty programs try to get people out of the vicious cycle of poverty and into good-paying, steady jobs. An example of an antipoverty program is one that teaches people useful skills or a trade. Other antipoverty programs give people medical advice and legal aid. A different kind of antipoverty program sets up a community action program in which the people living in a neighborhood work together to improve their neighborhood.

ANTIPOVERTY PROGRAMS   Soon after the Civil War, the government gave free land to all who would settle and farm the land for a set period of time. This created jobs for thousands of people who might have been unemployed. Before World War II, the largest government effort to fight poverty came in the 1930s, during the Great Depression. Millions of people were out of work because there were no jobs. The New Deal attempted to create work for millions of people where there had been no work before.

But it was not until the 1960s that the greatest effort to fight poverty was mounted. In 1964 the government passed the Economic Opportunity Act. This act created many programs that were designed to fight poverty at many levels and in all areas of the country. Some programs, such as Head Start, were aimed at young children (under six) from poor families. Other programs, such as the Job Corps, were aimed at teenagers who needed to work and earn money while they improved their education. VISTA tried to bring young people from all parts of the country to work with poor people in their own neighborhoods. Other programs were created to combat discrimination in hiring. Discrimination had made (and continues to make) finding and keeping jobs harder for nonwhites than for whites.

WELFARE—THE BIG SYSTEM WITH FEW FRIENDS   "What I am seeking is the abolition of relief [welfare] altogether." This was President Franklin D. Roosevelt, speaking during the Great Depression. He hoped to eliminate welfare by stamping out poverty.

"What America needs now is not more welfare, but more 'workfare.'" This was President Richard M. Nixon, speaking 35 years later. Welfare programs, which were supposed to be temporary measures to fight the effects of the Great Depression, are still with us. In recent years, the number of people on welfare has expanded enormously, and so have welfare costs. The total cost of welfare assistance in 1935, during President Roosevelt's first administration, was $2 billion a year. In 1971, the cost had risen to over $18 billion a year.

Welfare programs today fall into three categories: housing, food stamps, and public assistance.

Housing programs provide living space for the poor. Sometimes these programs may provide apartments in *renovated* (repaired and updated) buildings. Most public housing programs for poor people are the familiar government-run housing projects.

The food stamp program allows poor people to buy food stamps at less than the value printed on the stamps, and then to pay for food at retail prices with the stamps. Depending on their incomes, poor families in 1973 could buy $142 worth of food for a cost of anywhere between $3 and $112. No matter how much the family actually paid for the stamps, however, they bought $142 worth of food in the markets.

Public assistance programs provide cash and other services for poor persons who are eligible for help. Money for the following programs comes from both the state and federal governments:

1. *Old-Age Assistance*—provides cash assistance for elderly poor persons.
2. *Aid to the Blind*—provides cash assistance for the blind poor.
3. *Aid to the Permanently and Totally Disabled*—provides cash assistance for poor persons who are unable to work because of physical handicaps.

     In 1970 over 2 million elderly persons, 80,000 blind people, and 900,000 disabled or blind people received assistance. But the largest program is

4. *Aid to Families With Dependent Children* (AFDC). Ten million people received benefits under the AFDC program in 1970. This program was created to help poor families with children in which there was only one parent (the mother) at home.

Many poor people do not fall into any of the four groups listed above. For example, healthy, single men and women without dependents are not eligible for help under any program, no matter how poor they are. To help these people, most states and cities have general assistance programs. These programs are paid for entirely by states and cities (the four mentioned above receive a great deal of help from the federal government). More than 500,000 people were aided by general assistance in 1970. The amounts they received varied widely, however, depending on the cities and states they lived in.

WAYS TO ELIMINATE WELFARE   Several proposals have been made to improve or wipe out the present welfare system. Here are the most important:

Family Assistance   The *family assistance program* would substitute a federal welfare program for the many different state and city programs. Under family assistance, everyone, working or not, would be guaranteed a minimum income. In order to receive benefits, unemployed people would have to register for work or for job training. In addition, all poor people would be entitled to benefits, not just those who qualify under the present system. Also, families would be allowed to earn additional income and not lose all their welfare benefits.

Under a system of guaranteed work, the federal government would guarantee that everyone who is capable of working and willing to work would have a job. This proposal calls for federal planning to provide jobs for those who cannot find them in private industry.

Negative Income Tax   Under the *negative income tax* proposal, everyone earning less than a certain amount would receive regular payments from the government to make up the difference. (This is the opposite of the regular income tax, which we pay after we earn a certain amount.) With a negative income tax in effect, no one would have an income below a set minimum. There are two advantages to this proposal. First, it would cost less than the present system because only one agency, the Internal Revenue Service, would run it.

Second, since people would automatically receive payments, the negative income tax would be less damaging to the pride of poor people than the present system. Welfare now requires hours of waiting and filling out forms and answering personal questions.

Summary   Poverty directly affects the lives of some 25 million Americans. The poor may be young, old, white, or nonwhite: they may live in city slums or on farms. Millions of poor people receive welfare assistance or are helped by anti-poverty programs. The costs of welfare programs have skyrocketed in recent years. Several new solutions to the problem of poverty have been suggested, but none has been enacted into law.

EXERCISES

MATCHING QUESTIONS   Match each term in Column A with its definition in Column B.

Column A

1. vicious cycle of poverty
2. welfare
3. antipoverty program
4. poverty line
5. AFDC
6. Family Assistance Plan
7. negative income tax

Column B

(*a*) amount of money a family needs to stay out of poverty

(*b*) aims to bring people out of poverty

(*c*) Aid to Families With Dependent Children

(*d*) poverty passes from one generation to the next

(*e*) would provide a minimum income for everyone, working or not

(*f*) aims to solve a specific problem of poor people

(*g*) people earning less than a certain amount would receive payments from the government

ESSAY QUESTIONS

1. Each of these factors seems to affect a person's chances of being poor: race, sex, and age. Give several reasons for each factor.
2. If you could solve the problem of poverty, which of the solutions proposed in the text would you favor? Give reasons. Can you think of any other ways to eliminate poverty?

PROBLEMS OF THE WELFARE MOTHER   The following is a statement made by a congresswoman before a committee of the House of Representatives:

> Ladies and gentlemen, you have heard some speakers demand that welfare mothers be given the choice to work or not to work. This demand is ridiculous. It is ridiculous because these women have never had a free choice. They have never been free to work. They have had little education. They have very few skills. Who would give them a job?
>
> Think of how these welfare mothers live. Imagine having to spend all day, every day, in a single room. The room is cold in the winter and hot in the summer. The plaster is peeling. You do not have enough beds for the family. There are no sheets. The furniture is falling apart. A bare bulb hanging in the center of the room is the only light. The plumbing does not work some of the time. There is no hot water most of the time. Your only companions are small children who are often hungry and do not have enough clothing to wear. They are your only companions, that is, except for the rats.
>
> It is a major accomplishment just to stay sane in such a situation. To give children the love and discipline they need would require a superhuman person. If we had deliberately set out to design a welfare system that would produce crime, drunkenness, and illegitimacy, we could not have improved on the system we now have.

1. What is a "welfare mother"?
2. What did the speaker mean when she said, "They [welfare mothers] have never been free to work"?
3. Explain the meaning of the last sentence in the selection.

4. The selection says that the typical welfare mother is a young, able-bodied woman. But she has had little education, so she has very few skills. And she has to care for young children. Suppose that you were in charge of the government's welfare programs. What would you do to help the welfare mother?

Unit V   Health

Chapter 1   Why Can't the Wealthiest Be the Healthiest?

Something was bothering Beth—everyone could see that. She was almost talking to herself and looked very angry. She took her usual seat in the cafeteria along with her friends, Emily, Janet, and Ann. Emily looked at Beth and decided to ask what was the matter.

"What's wrong, Beth?" asked Emily. "You look like you either failed a test or had a fight with Don."

"No, that's not it," replied Beth. "I just learned something in class that's absolutely shocking."

"You mean to say you got upset over something you learned in class?" asked Janet. She seemed surprised to learn that Beth took her classes that seriously.

"Listen," said Beth. "The United States is the wealthiest country in the world—right?"

"Right," her friends agreed.

"So, if we're the wealthiest, how come we're not the healthiest?" asked Beth.

The girls looked at one another. "Now, what is that supposed to mean?" asked Ann.

"Do you know what I learned in class today?" Beth asked. "The United States is not the healthiest country in the world. I found out that the people in many other countries live longer than Americans. More American babies die in their first year than the babies in many other countries. Poor people here get sick more often and die younger than those who aren't poor. It's just terrible!

"If we're the wealthiest, how come we're not the healthiest?"

Beth had learned her lessons well that day. The state of America's health is a real problem today. She is only one of many who have asked, "If we're the wealthiest, how come we're not the healthiest?"

Our Nation's Health

Children Who Die in Their First Year of Life
(per thousand born)

Year	Deaths
1940	47.0
1955	26.4
1965	24.7
1967	22.4
1970	19.8

Life Expectancy at Birth

Year of Birth	Years of Life
1930	59.7
1940	62.9
1950	68.2
1960	69.7
1970	70.8

Doctors for Every 100,000 People

Year	Doctors
1950	149
1955	150
1960	148
1965	153
1970	171

Look at the tables for a moment or two. What do they tell you about the state of health in America? Do you see that Americans are living longer and are less likely to die at birth than in the past? And do you notice, too, that there are more doctors for every 100,000 persons now than there ever were? Yet, despite these achievements, there are those who say that Americans get very poor health care for such a wealthy nation. Consider these facts:

1. The United States spends more per person for medical care than any other nation. But:

2. The United States ranks 17th in the world in *infant mortality*. Infant mortality means the number of children who die before they are one year old. In 16 other nations, fewer children die in their first year than in the United States.

3. The United States ranks 20th in *life expectancy*. This is the number of years the average person will live. In 19 other nations, the average person lives longer than the average American.

4. For many Americans, a serious illness can mean financial disaster.

5. The kind of medical care many Americans get frequently depends on who they are and how much money they have.

Let us look for the reasons why we lag behind other nations in several major aspects of health and medical care.

The nations that rank ahead of the United States are small countries. Almost all their people have high personal incomes and high living standards. There are no serious problems of discrimination against minority groups because most of the citizens are of the same race or national origin. The countries that rank ahead of the United States do have social problems, but they are not as numerous or as severe as the problems of the United States.

Some people think that because we spend so much on our armed forces, our space program, and foreign aid, the nation is unable to spend much for medical care. Actually, the $83 billion that we spent on health care in 1972 represented 8 cents out of every dollar spent in the country. No other nation could match this. But Americans as a nation are not the healthiest people in the world.

POVERTY AND HEALTH   In the United States, the quality of health care that a person receives frequently depends on who that person is, how much money he has, and where he lives. For example, 50 percent of the children of poor families have not had their "shots" to protect them against the common childhood diseases. The death rate for nonwhite babies is twice that of white babies, and the death rate for nonwhite mothers is six times that of white mothers. There is twice as much illness among the poor as among people with good incomes. Poor people have three times as much heart disease, seven times as many eye defects, and five times as much mental retardation and nervous disorder as the rest of the population. In 1970 there were 211 doctors for every 100,000 people in Massachusetts and 238 per 100,000 in New York. These states have high-income urban populations. But the story was different in states with low-income rural populations. Mississippi, for example, had only 83 doctors per 100,000 population, and Alabama had only 89 per 100,000.

COST OF HEALTH CARE   For all Americans the cost of health care has risen faster than the cost of any other item in their budgets. Since 1960 medical costs have risen almost twice as fast as the cost of living. Hospital costs have gone up five times as fast. In 1972 the average cost for a one-day stay in a local hospital was over $100. In certain large medical centers it was over $200 a day. The average bill for hospitalization after a heart attack was over $4,000. The cost for open-heart surgery was $10,000. Of course, many Americans do carry some form of health insurance that pays some or most of the cost of a hospital stay. But 20 percent of all Americans (over 40 million people) have no insurance coverage at all. Many of those who have insurance find that it does not cover much of the cost of a serious illness.

Case Study: How Health Insurance Fails   Bill Wing's wife Martha has just returned home from the hospital after an operation. The doctors told Bill that Martha would not be able to bathe or feed herself or do any household chores for a long time. The Wing's six-year-old son Ralph is too young to be of any help. So Bill has to hire a housekeeper to take care of Martha, Ralph, and the house. This will cost him $150 a week. Although Bill's insurance pays for the doctor's visits and the medicines that Martha needs, it does not pay for home care. So Bill Wing will have to dip into his savings to pay for this service. Bill is wondering if his savings will hold out until Martha is well. If they do not, he will have to borrow the money.

SHORTAGE OF DOCTORS   The shortage of doctors is another major health care problem. Government estimates say that the shortage of doctors necessary to maintain minimum decent health standards for Americans will run to 80,000 in 1975. Some say that the shortage of doctors is the fault of the American Medical Association (AMA), the group that represents many of America's doctors. Critics claim that during the depression of the 1930s, the AMA used its power to limit the number of graduates from medical schools. They did this, say the critics, in order to keep down the competition among doctors, so that they all could earn more money. Not until 1967, when it was too late, did the AMA admit that there was a shortage of doctors.

On the other hand, some people say it is good that the medical schools have limited the number of graduates. In this way, the schools were able to make sure that only the most qualified persons became doctors. They also point out that there are more doctors per person now than there ever were. One reason for the shortage of doctors is that people are going to doctors more now than ever before.

These children are receiving inoculations (shots) to protect them from disease

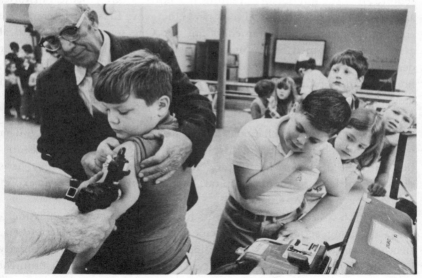

WHAT CAN BE DONE?   One proposal to solve the nation's health problem calls for a National Health Insurance program (NHI) for all Americans. NHI would operate as social security does. Today, social security funds pay for many social programs, such as old-age pensions and aid to needy children. Both employers and employees contribute a portion of their payroll and income to the social security funds, and the government also makes a contribution. Under NHI, individuals would contribute to a fund that would pay the expenses for all the medical care anyone would ever need. People could still use private doctors if they wished, just as parents can send their children to private schools if they wish. But, whether they used NHI or not, everyone would have to contribute.

Another suggestion to solve the health care problem calls for group practice. Under group practice, several doctors, including specialists, share office space, instruments, and medical know-how. Patients are free to select among the doctors in the group. Patients are assured of full-time care, even in the evening and on weekends, because the group doctors share the coverage of these off-hours.

Still another proposal to improve health care is to use *paramedics.* Paramedics are persons trained to deliver the kinds of care that do not require all of the full doctor's training and skills. Taking medical histories and giving injections, medical tests, and emergency first-aid treatment are the kinds of jobs that paramedics can do. One source of paramedical assistants is the armed forces. Many servicemen and women received a great deal of training and experience in the medical corps. To employ them in hospitals and group-practice offices would make sense, particularly in view of their special qualifications.

Summary   In this chapter we have seen that Americans live longer today than ever before. Despite this, however, many Americans are dissatisfied with the quality of health care. In many parts of the country, it is difficult to reach a doctor or a hospital. People in other countries can expect to live longer than Americans.

The high cost of medical care puts it out of the reach of many Americans, and a long, serious illness can wipe out the savings of countless others. In other countries, however, serious illness does not also mean that a family will lose its life savings. All medical care costs are paid by the government or insurance programs in these countries.

As in many chapters of this book, our study of problems has raised many questions we have not attempted to answer. For example:

Why don't more doctors want to live in small towns?

What can the small towns do to attract more doctors?

Can something be done to provide transportation for those unable to reach doctors in their own communities?

How can hospital costs be reduced when some of the lowest paid workers in the country are those employed by hospitals?

What can be done to improve the health care available to the poor and minority groups?

Looking Ahead   The chapters that follow deal with certain special problems affecting our nation's well-being: drug abuse and consumer protection. Here again, you will meet problems that remain to be solved.

EXERCISES

WRITE A LETTER   The government may be able to help improve the state of American health care. Write a letter to someone in government. It may be your mayor, or governor, your representative in the state legislature, or your congressman or congresswoman. Use one of the following as the theme for your letter:

1. What I think should be done to increase the number of doctors.
2. What I think should be done to keep down the cost of medical care.
3. What I think of the quality of medical services in my home town. (Can I find good medical care quickly if I or someone in my family have a medical emergency?)

FURTHER READING   Read the selection below and answer the questions that follow:

NATIONAL HEALTH INSURANCE IN ACTION

One day last winter, both Jim and Dolores Vasquez caught the flu. Soon their two children also had the flu. By that time Mr. Vasquez had bronchitis. The Vasquez family decided to solve its problems by going to a doctor all at one time. The visit to the doctor cost them $40, and prescriptions came to $25—a total of $65 for one illness. Meanwhile, the Aldens, a family of four living in Great Britain, also caught the flu, as did the Lindstroms, who live in Sweden. Both families also visited doctors, who gave them the same kind of examination and medicine as the American doctor gave the Vasquez family. But the Aldens did not have to pay the doctor anything for his services, and the drugs cost only $2.75. The Lindstroms had to pay about $1.75 for each family member, or a total of $7 for the doctor, and the drugs cost about $9. Had the two families lived in Denmark or Israel, the story would have been much the same.

The reason that the costs to the Israeli, Danish, English, and Swedish families are so low is that their medical bills are paid by the government. These governments have established national health insurance that protects every citizen. Under this program all or most of the expenses resulting from an illness would be covered. In the United States, on the other hand, a family's lifetime savings can be wiped out by one serious illness. The average bill for a hospitalization after a heart attack runs into thousands —around $4,000. Some families can afford to pay this amount. Others may have insurance that will pay some or most of their expenses. Still others may have to use up their savings or go into debt to pay medical expenses.

1. How much did their illness cost the Vasquez family?
2. How much did their illness cost the Aldens? The Lindstroms?
3. Why did their illness cost the Vasquez family more than the other families?
4. What is national health insurance?
5. Do you think that the United States government ought to establish a system of national health insurance? Why or why not?

Chapter 2   Drug Abuse

A hush fell as the committee members walked into the hearing room. It was the United States Senate's crime committee. The committee was investigating drug use in the nation's schools. In one corner of the room was a television crew. Reporters opened their notebooks. The first witness was called. She was a young policewoman. She was sworn in, and the committee lawyer began to question her.

LAWYER: We understand that you are going to tell the committee about the use of illegal drugs in our high schools.

POLICEWOMAN: Yes.

LAWYER: How did you get this information?

POLICEWOMAN: I posed as a student in the school.

LAWYER: What did you discover when you went to this school?

POLICEWOMAN: I spent three days in the high school. In that time I discovered much evidence of drug abuse. I saw empty glassine envelopes in the bathrooms and locker rooms. I saw students "nodding out" in the cafeteria and in classrooms. I saw girls "shooting" heroin in the locker rooms. I saw kids who had taken overdoses.

Another witness before the committee was a high school student. This was part of his testimony:

STUDENT: Nobody has to "push" drugs in our school. It is really a seller's market. I mean if a guy is holding, if he has some drugs and the word gets out, all he has to do is sit in one place and people will come to him. He is not out trying to *induce* (get) people to buy drugs. That does not occur. People will seek him out . . . he will select whom he sells to . . . he knows if he doesn't sell to you, there are four other people that want to buy from him.

Meanwhile, as the committee met, a boy walked into a dingy apartment house in another part of town. In his T-shirt and jeans, Walter looked like a great many city kids. Smaller than most kids his age, he stood only 4 feet 11 inches tall and weighed just 80 pounds. He had celebrated his 12th birthday two weeks before. Several hours after he entered the building, he was found lying on the stairs. Walter was dead of an overdose of heroin.

Next to his body, a neighbor found two glassine envelopes, a syringe, a needle, and a bottle cap—all the things Walter needed for that last shot. Of all the 500 teenagers in that city who died of an overdose of drugs from 1971 to 1972, Walter was the youngest.

Stories of death and addiction resulting from the use of drugs among America's teenagers and young people have shocked the nation. Almost everyone agrees that America has a drug problem, and that something ought to be done about it. But there is not much agreement on what that "something" ought to be. This chapter will try to give you some understanding of the problem by describing some of the more dangerous drugs that some young people have experimented with. We shall also consider some of the programs that have been developed to deal with the drug problem.

What Are Drugs?

If we were to look in a dictionary, we would find the word *drug* defined as a substance other than food taken into the body that causes physical or mental changes, or both, in the user's body. This sounds simple enough. If you ask the average person if heroin, cocaine, barbiturates, and marijuana are drugs, the chances are that you would be told yes. But what about alcohol and tobacco? Are these drugs? In one public opinion survey a sizable majority of people felt that alcohol and tobacco are not drugs. Their view was that "drugs" are dangerous substances that are taken only by criminals and sick people. After all, Presidents of the United States have been seen on television drinking toasts on state occasions. Similarly, some of the most respected persons in our society have smoked in public at one time or another.

If we accept our definition of a drug as a substance other than food taken into the body that causes physical or mental changes, however, then alcohol, tobacco (which contains nicotine, a stimulant drug), and even coffee (which contains caffeine, another stimulant) must be considered drugs. All drugs are harmful or fatal when taken in excess. Just how much of any drug is dangerous varies from person to person, but, as the frequency (number of times) with which it is used increases, so, too, does the danger. Here are some of the drugs that have been the focus of America's drug problem.

Alcohol

Alcohol has probably caused more deaths, accidents, sicknesses, and crimes than any other drug. There are from 6 to 10 million alcoholics in the United States today. These people are unable to control their drinking. As a result, they are a threat to themselves and to others.

Alcohol is a *depressant* (it lowers the rate of our bodies' activity; thus, it relaxes us). It has the same kind of effect on the body as "sleeping pills." It affects the behavior of the drinker as well as his body. It is a major cause of liver disease as well as brain and muscle damage. Alcoholics have a shorter *life expectancy* (10 to 12 years less) than people who do not drink.

Most people who consume alcohol do so in moderate quantities without any ill effects. For the 6 to 10 million alcoholics in the United States, however, alcohol is even more dangerous than heroin. If taken in large enough quantities over a long enough period of time, it is addictive. (*Addictive* means that the user will not be able to give up the drug without suffering some physical discomfort.) In attempting to give it up, the alcoholic must go through *withdrawal symptoms* known as delirium tremens (or "DT's"). These bring on, among other things, vomiting, delirium, and convulsions.

Perhaps the most dangerous thing about alcohol is that most people do not look upon it as they do heroin and marijuana, that is, as a drug. As a result they are much more willing to accept its use. One consequence of this is that more and more teenagers have been experimenting with alcohol. School authorities have been worried by the attitude of some parents who, when informed that their children had been found to be drunk in class, said, "Well, at least it wasn't drugs!"

But, of course, alcohol *is* a drug. It can be addictive. It can even be fatal. For these reasons alone it is a dangerous drug. (Perhaps its greatest source of danger, however, is that so many people look upon it not as a drug but as a beverage.)

Heroin

One group of drugs is classified as *narcotics*. Narcotics are used by doctors to relieve pain. Opium and morphine are two of the narcotics made from a poppy plant that grows in many parts of the world outside the United States. Heroin is also made from this poppy plant. Because of its ability to kill pain, heroin has medical value. It also gives the user a pleasant sensation. It is this sensation that attracts users. But it is against the law to buy, sell, or possess heroin. It can also be fatal to use heroin.

Taking heroin can be fatal because, in order to get the pleasant sensation, the user has to take a certain minimum amount of the drug. If the user misjudges the quantity, however, an overdose can cause death. The difference between the dose needed to make the user "high" and the amount that could kill is so small that many have died of an overdose of heroin.

Heroin is also addictive. If heroin is taken for a long enough period, the user is "hooked"—needs it all the time. The addict will not be able to give it up without going through nausea, cramps, twitching, gooseflesh, stomach pains, diarrhea, and other painful symptoms.

Amphetamines—The "Uppers"

"When I'm driving all night, I take one of these little green jobs. Man, it keeps me going 40 hours straight."

"My doctor gave me these yellow pills. I ate what I wanted to and managed to lose five pounds over the last ten days."

One group of drugs is classified as *stimulants* because they excite or *stimulate* the nervous system of the body. *Amphetamines* are the most commonly used stimulants. Amphetamines are produced by drug companies. Physicians may prescribe small doses of amphetamines to help overweight persons reduce. The drugs may also be used to help people with mental problems.

Some people take amphetamines because of their stimulating effects.

These "pep pills" keep the users awake or make their bodies function in high gear. Other users take even larger doses because of the tremendous sensation of well-being that these stimulants seem to give.

The use of amphetamines without the approval of a physician can be very dangerous. After the first lift, the user frequently feels worse than before taking the drug. In addition, people who have taken amphetamines to "keep themselves going" over long stretches of driving have been involved in very serious accidents.

Even more dangerous is the use of a kind of amphetamine known as "speed" (methadrine). The user of this substance, who injects large quantities directly into his bloodstream, is seeking a "super-high" feeling which can be extremely dangerous to his health. Although few people die from taking "speed," it will bring on severe nervous disorders and depression when the effects wear off. This in turn can cause violent behavior that could get the user into a great deal of trouble and harm innocent persons.

Barbiturates and Tranquilizers— The "Downers"

Barbiturates and tranquilizers have an effect opposite to that of the stimulants. They have a calming effect on the nervous system. Doctors prescribe them for relaxation and sleep. Just as small doses have a calming effect and large doses of barbiturates bring on sleep, too large a dose will paralyze the breathing center and cause death. Moreover, using barbiturates and alcohol together makes both drugs more dangerous than if they are used separately. Many accidental deaths have been caused by this combination.

Doctors give tranquilizers to calm anxious or nervous patients or to relax muscles. These drugs, too, must be used with great care. Like barbiturates, when used in combination with alcohol, tranquilizers are very dangerous, and may even be fatal.

Barbiturates and tranquilizers are found in many household medicine cabinets. Unfortunately, these drugs have also been used by young people for "thrills" in the form of a fast, pleasant, whisky-like drunk. Thus drugs, originally produced to be used in limited amounts by adults, have been misused in large quantities by young people. The results, all too frequently, have been deadly.

Hallucinogens

Hallucinogens are a group of drugs that cause the user to "see things as they aren't." (Marijuana is also a hallucinogen, but its effects are far milder than the drugs we shall describe here.) Solid objects seem to move in a wavy fashion or to melt. The senses—taste, smell, sight, hearing, and touch —become confused. Colors are "heard," sound is "seen." Mescaline and peyote are the names of two hallucinogens made from the Mexican cactus. But the best known and most dangerous hallucinogen is LSD. LSD is a chemical compound that is made in laboratories. It does not occur (grow) in nature. LSD is far more powerful than mescaline and peyote. The period of confusion is described as a "trip" by users. At first, many users of LSD talked others into taking the drug by describing the wonders of their "trips." But it was soon learned that many users had had "bad trips." During a bad trip the user becomes frightened and panic-stricken. Some have committed suicide as a result. Others, thinking they could fly or defy flames, have jumped off tall buildings or leapt into fires to their deaths.

Some artists have claimed that LSD has made them more creative. This claim has not stood up. While under the influence of the drug, the user may *think* he or she is a more interesting and creative person. But to the undrugged observer, this is not the case. This much is certain: LSD can be deadly.

Marijuana

It is against the law to produce, possess, sell, or use marijuana or hashish. Both marijuana and hashish (which is a stronger form of marijuana) come from the *cannabis* plant. Cannabis can be grown nearly anywhere in the world, which is one reason why it is so difficult to enforce the laws prohibiting its use. Marijuana affects people in a manner similar to alcohol. The user may feel happy, friendly, and relaxed. Too much use affects judgment, memory, and coordination. It may make the user so dependent on the drug that he feels that he cannot get along without it. It is important to remember that like any illegal substance, it can lead to an arrest, a fine, and jail.

One unusual aspect of marijuana use is that people who use it regularly are affected by it more than those who have just started using it. This is the opposite from alcohol, which seems to affect most those who use it the least. Marijuana is also unusual as drugs go because it does not kill, nor does it cause *physical addiction.* That is, it is possible for one to give up his marijuana habit without going through what alcoholics and heroin addicts must suffer.

Marijuana is probably the most controversial of all drugs because of the many Americans who feel that its use should be made legal. They argue that it offers the same kind of pleasures as alcohol and is far less dangerous.

Dealing With Drug Abuse

There is much disagreement in this country over what ought to be done about the use and misuse of drugs. At present we rely upon three methods to deal with the problem: punishment, rehabilitation, and education.

PUNISHMENT   The unauthorized sale and use of many drugs is illegal. Persons who violate the drug laws may be imprisoned. Sometimes the drug user will be placed in a hospital or other institution instead of a jail. But, be it jail or hospital, the addict will have to serve out his time in a drug-free atmosphere in the hope that some day his habit will disappear.

REHABILITATION   At one time the alcoholic was regarded as a sinner who could best be cured by "sleeping it off " in jail. Now, of course, alcoholism is treated more as a disease. In recent years the same change has taken place in the way society views those who misuse drugs. As a result, both government and private agencies have introduced a number of programs to help drug abusers to return to society. To achieve this most programs use one or more of the following techniques:

Therapeutic Communities   One of the reasons that many people misuse drugs is called *peer pressure.* That is, one's *peers* (one's friends) are taking drugs and thus one does too. In a *therapeutic community* drug users get away from peer pressure. They meet with other addicts, reformed addicts, and counselors. Through contact, discussion, and other activities the individual has an opportunity to "grow out" of his drug habit.

In a rehabilitation center, former addicts learn to face their problems in a drug-free environment. What do you think is the role of the woman in the center?

Psychotherapy Psychotherapy involves individual or group treatment by psychiatrists or psychiatric personnel. This is a very costly form of treatment.

Methadone Maintenance Methadone is a legal narcotic that blocks the effect of heroin. What it does is take away the heroin addict's desire for heroin. In this way it is possible for an addict to give up heroin without having to go through the withdrawal symptoms he would otherwise have to face. On the other hand, methadone is itself an addictive drug, capable of causing death. But it is not nearly as dangerous as heroin.

Antagonist Drugs Non-narcotic drugs that prevent a narcotic drug from working are called antagonists. If an addict were to take a dose of heroin while he had one of these antagonists in his system, he would feel nothing from the heroin. The idea here is that if the addict feels no pleasure from taking a drug, he will give it up. Unfortunately, antagonist drugs work only for a very short period of time (usually half a day). Thus it is up to the addict to take the antagonist before he is exposed to heroin.

EDUCATION   Many believe that the best way to fight drug abuse is through education. That is, it is far more expensive to treat drug abuse with punishment or rehabilitation than it is to talk people out of misusing drugs in the first place. After all, because of what they learned at home, in school, and from their own experience, most Americans do not misuse drugs. They know better.

Summary and Looking Ahead   In this chapter we studied the problem of drug abuse. This is a serious problem for millions of Americans. In the next chapter we shall deal with the problem of consumer protection. This is a problem faced by *all* Americans, for we are all consumers. You will learn how, as the result of the efforts of only a few people, a whole new force in American life began. You will also learn how *consumerism,* as the movement came to be called, led to the passage of new federal and state laws to protect all consumers.

EXERCISES

WHY THEY STARTED   Many doctors have asked drug addicts why they started using drugs in the first place. The following answers are the ones most frequently received:

1. I didn't want to be left out—everybody was doing it.
2. I was just curious.
3. I did it for kicks—because I knew it was wrong.
4. A friend talked me into it.

Pretend that you are the parent of a teenager who has been experimenting with drugs. When you asked why, you got one of the four reasons listed above.

1. What would you say or do?
2. What effect do you suppose your words would have on the teenager?

MATCHING QUESTIONS   Match each term in Column A with its
definition in Column B.

Column A

1. drug
2. alcohol
3. delirium tremens
4. cannabis
5. narcotics
6. amphetamines
7. methadone
8. hallucinogens
9. therapeutic community
10. tranquilizers and
    barbiturates

Column B

(a) drugs taken to relax and to sleep
(b) anything, other than food, taken into
    the body, that causes physical or mental
    changes in the body
(c) places where ex-addicts get together to
    help each other stay off drugs
(d) drugs that stimulate the nervous sys-
    tem
(e) the source of marijuana and hashish
(f) depressant drugs that relieve pain
(g) withdrawal symptoms suffered by al-
    coholics
(h) drugs that cause people to "see things
    as they aren't"
(i) a drug that has caused more illness,
    crime, accidents, and death than any
    other
(j) an antagonist drug, used to fight heroin
    addiction

Chapter 3   Consumer
Protection

Does the average consumer need protection? Consider these facts:

Over 20 million American and foreign-made cars have been called back to dealers by the car makers because the cars had or might have had safety defects.

A popular "chocolate" pudding dessert has very little chocolate but lots of strange-sounding ingredients.

Another favorite American food, the hot dog, contains about 83 percent water and fat.

Millions of Americans have been injured severely enough to require medical treatment because of accidents that resulted from using unsafe consumer products.

In this chapter we shall take a look at consumer health and safety problems. We shall see how private citizens and the government are trying to overcome these problems.

One of the most influential persons of our time is Ralph Nader. He first became known to the American public in 1965 when his book *Unsafe at Any Speed* was published. This book strongly criticized the automobile industry for turning out unsafe cars. In 1966 Mr. Nader testified before a Senate committee investigating automobile design. But both his book and his testimony might have gone unnoticed had it not been for the announcement of a dramatic piece of news.

General Motors executives were forced to admit that they had hired private detectives to investigate Ralph Nader's private life. This was an obvious effort to "get something on him" and use it to keep him quiet. There was public outrage that one of the world's most powerful corporations was using its power to attempt to stifle free speech because an individual had criticized the corporation.

The result of the Senate hearings, Nader's book, and the General Motors spy attempt was the passage of the National Traffic and Motor Vehicle Safety Act of 1966. This law gave the government the power to set safety standards in the manufacture of automobiles. The law also required that autos with defects caused in the plant must be recalled by the manufacturer. This was desperately needed, it seems, because since the law was passed, millions of cars have been recalled. In one year over 20 million American-made and foreign-made cars were recalled. In 1973 General Motors alone recalled 3 million cars that had faulty steering mechanisms.

The Rise of Consumerism

Ralph Nader's success in raising auto safety standards was only the beginning of a larger movement. In less than a decade, largely as a result of the efforts of Mr. Nader and his assistants (popularly called "Nader's Raiders") the consumer has now become a major force on the American scene. From 1967 to 1973 Congress passed or strengthened the following consumer-protection laws: the Natural Gas Pipe Line Safety Act, the Radiation Control for Health and Safety Act, the Wholesome Meat Act, the Wholesome Poultry Products Act, the Occupational Safety and Health Act, the Federal Coal Mine Health and Safety Act, and the Consumer Product Safety Act.

Ralph Nader and his followers are not the only ones interested in protecting the consumer. Thousands of consumers all over the United States, inspired by Nader's example, have formed groups to protect their interests. This movement is called *consumerism.* It seeks to protect the consumer from such hazards as dangerous food additives, harmful products, poor service, and unfair prices.

THE FOOD INDUSTRY   One of the industries that has been a key target of consumer groups is the food industry. Nutritionists say that, all too often, the foods that Americans eat have little or no *nutritional value.* The snacks and sodas and breads and cereals that we eat are often made with ingredients that have been processed so much that nearly all the vitamins and minerals (if any) in the original are gone.

Furthermore, the *additives* (artificial ingredients, or chemicals) in many foods are a source of great concern. A few years ago, artificial sweeteners called cyclamates were taken out of sodas because researchers found that cyclamates caused cancer in laboratory animals.

Additives are often used to preserve foods that would otherwise spoil quickly. Additives are also used to give color or flavor to products so that they appear to be what they are not. For example, something called an "orange drink" is not made of orange juice—it has orange coloring, and orange flavoring, but no orange juice. A "bacon-flavored" cracker contains an additive that gives it the taste of bacon, but it does not contain any bacon. A popular "chocolate" pudding dessert contains 16 or 18 ingredients, but while there is a lot of water, sugar, and chemicals, chocolate is a very small percentage of the product.

The hot dog is another food that consumer groups have criticized. Over 15 billion hot dogs are sold in America every year, but all too often they contain very little food value for their size and weight. The average hot dog is 57 percent water, 26 percent fat, only 13 percent protein, and 4 percent "other." One of the "other" ingredients in the hot dog—the one that preserves it and gives it its rosy color—is sodium nitrite. Some recent experiments indicate that sodium nitrite may cause cancer in laboratory animals.

The food manufacturers argue that additives are necessary as preservatives. Without them, Americans would have to go back to the idea of "bakery freshness"—that is, good today, stale tomorrow. Half a century ago, foods did not stay fresh very long. Cottage cheese separated. Cookies dried up in a few days. Foods made with fats and oils turned *rancid* (spoiled). Canned fruits and vegetables were soft or mushy. Without additives, the foods we eat would be like those of "the good old days." Also, just because additives are chemicals, this does not necessarily make them all bad. After all, salt, the most common additive used to preserve foods, is a combination of chemicals—sodium and chlorine. In addition, the vitamins that are added to many foods are themselves chemicals.

Another point made by those who favor additives is that the amounts used are quite small. For example, two additives used to preserve baked goods, cereals, and other foods made with fats are called BHA and BHT for short. BHA and BHT make up only four parts of every million parts of the typical American's diet. Four parts per million equals about one-eighth of an ounce of every ton of food consumed.

PRODUCT SAFETY   Another area of concern to consumer groups is that of product safety—perhaps product hazard would be a better term. According to the National Commission on Product Safety, 20 million Americans are injured badly enough to have to go to the hospital every year. Many of these injuries are a result of defective consumer products.

GOVERNMENT AGENCIES UNDER FIRE   It was not a complete shock to most Americans when consumer groups criticized the automobile and food industries. Most people were surprised, however, to learn that two agencies of the federal government had also come under attack. The agencies attacked, the Federal Trade Commission and the Food and Drug Administration, were the very ones that had been created by the federal government to protect the consumer.

A report prepared by a group of "Nader's Raiders" charged that the Federal Trade Commission favored big business at the expense of the consumer. This charge was particularly shocking because the FTC was the principal consumer protection agency of the federal government. Another report described the Food and Drug Administration as a "tool" of the food industry. The FDA is supposed to protect the nation against impure and unsafe foods, drugs, and cosmetics.

WHAT DO CONSUMER GROUPS WANT?   What are the goals of consumer groups? For one thing they want the federal agencies to do a better job of protecting the consumer. Most groups would agree that one way to get the federal agencies to perform better is by "keeping an eye on them." It is up to consumers themselves to organize for the purpose of applying pressure on the federal agencies.

Corporate Responsibility   Merely keeping after the federal agencies is not enough, however, consumer groups say. Some leaders (including Ralph Nader) feel that the big corporations are the major source of the consumer problems in this country. The lack of a truly safe automobile has caused the death or injury of hundreds of thousands of people. Wastes from industry pollute the air and waters of our country. Drug company advertising lures people into taking medicines—to sleep, to calm down, for colds, headaches, to pep up—that have little or no value. These drugs may cover up the symptoms of serious illnesses, or they may be dangerous in themselves. Recently, a nasal spray was taken off the market when it was learned that 18 children had died after using it.

Consumer advocates want federal laws changed so that the people who run the major corporations are held personally responsible for obeying health and safety laws. At present, only the company is held responsible, and if it receives a fine, that fine is so low as to be meaningless. Ralph Nader and others feel that if the people who run the big corporations knew that they may be fined or sent to jail, then they would see to it that their companies produced safe products and did not pollute the environment.

In the cartoonist's view, who is the worse offender: the car thief or the manufacturer who built unsafe cars? Copyright © 1972 The Chicago *Sun-Times*. Reproduced by courtesy of Will-Jo Associates, Inc. and Bill Mauldin.

Consumer Protection Agency   Ralph Nader and other consumer leaders are in favor of a federal agency devoted solely to consumer protection. This agency would coordinate the efforts of all the existing agencies that are concerned with protecting the consumer. This agency would testify for consumers before congressional committees. In other words, it would be there to benefit consumers, just as the Departments of Army, Navy, and Air Force work for their people.

People who oppose the consumer movement and the pressure for new laws say that there are enough such laws on the books now. They feel that if consumers spent the time to examine the information available before they buy, they would get the most for their money.

Summary   The consumer movement is on the march and it seems to be growing. As it does, it tries to arouse the support of all consumers to demands upon the government and upon industry. These demands are that consumers be treated more fairly than they have been in the past and that their health and safety be looked after more carefully. Just how much the consumer movement will actually influence government and business remains to be seen. One thing seems certain, however: Consumers are a force to be reckoned with.

EXERCISES

READING FOR FURTHER UNDERSTANDING   Read the following selection and answer the questions that follow:

MORE CONSUMER PROTECTION NEEDED:
THE NATIONAL COMMISSION ON PRODUCT SAFETY

The National Commission on Product Safety was set up by the government to examine products that consumers use in the home and during leisure activities. The purpose of these tests is to learn how safe the products are. The need for this work is clear: Accidents involving consumer products injure 20 million people a year. Of these, 30,000 people are killed and 110,000 are permanently disabled.

The commission has wide powers. It can do the following:

1. Establish standards of safety for consumer products.
2. Take to court companies that fail to live up to these standards. If

convicted, these firms could be fined as much as $500,000. The penalties against individuals could run as high as $50,000 and a year in jail.

3. Require that a product judged unsafe be recalled by the manufacturer. The product would have to be repaired, replaced, or the price refunded to the buyer.

4. Ban outright the sale of products that are judged dangerous.

In 1973 the commission drew up a list of the consumer products and places in the home that cause the greatest number of injuries each year. This information was obtained from 119 hospital emergency rooms all over the country. Some of the results of this survey are shown in the table.

Study the table. Tell how you would go about making three places or products safer for the consumer.

Activities or Places That Are Most Hazardous

Cause of Injury		Number of Injuries Reported
Sports:		
Football	230,000	
Baseball	191,000	
Basketball	188,000	609,000
Bicycles		372,000
Stairs, ramps, and landings		356,000
Nails, tacks, screws		275,000
Glass doors, windows, bathtub and shower enclosures		178,000
Cutlery (knives and other)		172,000

Read the following sentences. If they are true, write T. If they are false, rewrite them so as to make them true.

1. The major function of the National Commission on Product Safety is to find out whether consumer products are reasonably safe.
2. Only a few Americans are injured each year in accidents involving consumer products.
3. The commission can establish standards of safety for consumer products.
4. The commission itself has the power to fine and imprison those who sell dangerous products.
5. The commission was set up by the mayors of New York and Boston.

6. The most the commission can do to prevent dangerous products from being sold is to *ask* firms to withdraw unsafe products from the stores.
7. According to the commission's survey, the most dangerous product or activity was football.
8. There were approximately 188,000 injuries from basketball in the year the commission made its survey.

WHAT IS IN THE FOODS WE EAT?

1. Go to your pantry or refrigerator and take out three packaged foods. Jot down the ingredients on the labels of each. Underline the ingredients that are *additives*.
2. Why were these additives placed in foods?
3. Why are Americans worried about additives in their food?

WRITE A LETTER TO YOUR CONGRESSMAN   One of the things many consumer groups have called upon Congress to do is to create a consumer protection agency. Not everyone thinks this is a good idea, of course, and the agency has not been created.

Write a letter to your local representative or senator on this issue. In your letter you will want to say (*a*) whether you are for or against the bill creating a consumer protection agency and (*b*) why you are for or against it.

Unit VI   Minorities

Chapter 1   Prejudice and Discrimination

"You know, Kwai-ling, the Hakka are all alike. Their men folk just sit around all day and do nothing. They're lucky that their women are responsible and hard-working. Otherwise, they'd all starve to death."

"You are so right, Mei-lan. Not only that, they dress differently, they smell strange, and they speak rotten Chinese. It's a shame that there are so many of them here in Hong Kong."

Kwai-ling and Mei-lan spent another few minutes bemoaning the shortcomings of the Hakka. Finally, the two women said good night and went home.

Who are the Hakka? Hundreds of years ago a group of people migrated to southeastern China from a northern province. The people of the south called the people of the north the *Hakka*. This means "guest race," or "outsiders" in Chinese. As such, the Hakka were treated as inferiors by the Chinese people of the south. But the conversation you read did not take place hundreds of years ago. It might have taken place yesterday, for to many southern Chinese the Hakka are still "outsiders" and, therefore, are inferior to themselves. The Chinese prefer that their children do not play with the Hakka children. They see to it that the Hakka live in their own part of town. It is difficult for the Hakka to get certain kinds of jobs simply because they are Hakka. In other words, the Hakka are the victims of *prejudice* and *discrimination*.

What Are Prejudice and Discrimination?

Prejudice means that a person has made up his mind about something without knowing all or most of the facts. Sometimes prejudice is harmless or *innocuous;* sometimes it may even be a good thing. A sports fan who is convinced that his team is the greatest ball club in history may be said to be "prejudiced." After all, he has made up his mind on the subject without knowing the facts about every team in history. But this kind of prejudice harms no one. The child who stands by his mother and father in all things is *prejudiced* in their favor. Most people would agree that this is a good thing.

But prejudice can be quite harmful, particularly when it leads people to act in hostile or inhuman ways. (The Chinese in our example above showed *prejudice.*) When prejudice leads some people to compel others to live in special parts of town and makes it difficult for them to get a good education and good-paying jobs, that is *discrimination.* In other words, discrimination takes place whenever a prejudiced person does something out of prejudice that hurts someone else.

STEREOTYPES   One fairly common form of prejudice is the *stereotype.* In printing, a stereotype plate is used to print the exact same pattern over and over again. Each impression is the same as the other. In the same way some people *stereotype* others. They look upon all members of a group as being exactly the same. Here is an example of stereotyping:

"Oh, yes, those Mexicans are all alike. You see them sitting under trees sound asleep, with their *sombreros* over their faces."

The speaker is clearly prejudiced. He or she has *stereotyped* Mexicans as lazy people. Unfortunately there are a great many prejudiced people in this world. Try this one on yourself or your friends:

A father and son were driving along the highway when they had a terrible accident and the father was killed. The son was rushed to the hospital. As he was wheeled into the operating room, the surgeon looked at him and said, "Oh my God, that's my son—I can't do the operation!"

Who was the surgeon?

Did you have trouble with this riddle? The boy's father was killed, yet the surgeon said "That's my son." Well, of course, the surgeon was the boy's mother.

Why should anyone have difficulty explaining who a person calling someone his or her "son" is? Who else could it be but the mother or the father? The reason we may have trouble with this riddle is that in this case the speaker is a surgeon. A surgeon is one of the most highly trained and skilled of doctors. But most people have a stereotype of the surgeon: They automatically assume that a surgeon is a man. They also have stereotypes of women: Women are supposed to like to cook and clean; women who work are secretaries; women do not understand scientific things. Women are not surgeons. These are the stereotypes. Stereotyping is a form of prejudice.

Do you stereotype women? Are you prejudiced?

In America there are those who are prejudiced against certain people. The discrimination that has emerged from this prejudice has hurt many Americans. They have found it more difficult than others to find decent jobs and homes, to get a good education, or just to be accepted as human beings.

Minority Groups

Minority groups are usually identified by their race, nationality, religion, or language. Blacks and Orientals (Chinese and Japanese) are two minority groups whose race sets them apart from everyone else. At different periods in United States history, the Irish, Poles, Scandinavians, Italians, and others have been discriminated against on the basis of their nationality. The Amish, Mormons, and Jews have been victims of prejudice and discrimination—their religions set them apart from other groups. Americans of Mexican and Puerto Rican descent, along with other Hispanic people, have found that the Spanish language marks them as being "different." They too have been victims of prejudice and discrimination. Some people say that sex discrimination has created a minority group of women. They argue that some Americans, because they are women, are unable to obtain certain jobs or enjoy the rights and responsibilities they might have had if they had been men.

Summary   Among minority groups today, those suffering most from prejudice and discrimination are blacks, Hispanic-Americans, American Indians, and Orientals. The typical member of each of these groups earns less, has poorer housing, poorer health care, and a shorter life expectancy than other Americans. *Prejudice* and *discrimination* may not be the only reason why members of these minority groups do not live as well as other Americans, but they are certainly a major factor.

Looking Ahead   In the pages that follow, we shall meet some of the people who belong to these minorities and learn something of their problems.

EXERCISES

WHAT DID THEY MEAN?   Read the following quotations on the subject of prejudice. In your own words, explain what the writers meant.

1. "The chief cause of human error is to be found in the prejudices learned in childhood." (René Descartes, 17th-century French philosopher)

2. "He finds his fellowman guilty of a skin not colored like his own." (William Cowper, 18th-century English poet)

3. "I have a dream that my four little children will one day live in a nation where they will not be judged by the color of their skin but by the content of their character." (Martin Luther King, Jr., 1963)

4. Little Children, Sioux or Crow,
   Little frosty Eskimo
   Little Turk or Japanee,[1]
   Oh! don't you wish that you were me?

   You have curious things to eat,
   I am fed on proper meat;[2]
   You must dwell beyond the foam,[3]
   But I am safe and live at home.
                        (Robert Louis Stevenson, 19th-century English writer)

[1] *Japanee*—Japanese
[2] *proper meat*—the kind of meat people ought to eat
[3] *foam*—ocean

TABLES TELL A STORY   Tables may tell us many things, but they cannot tell us all we want to know. Some of the statements that follow the tables are true, some are false, and some cannot be answered because the tables do not give sufficient information. Write T if a statement is true, F if a statement is false, and NS if the information given is not sufficient. If the statement is false, correct it by substituting the correct words for the ones in italics.

Families Living in New York City That Had Incomes Under $5,000 in 1968

Blacks and Puerto Ricans	58 percent
Others	19

Families Living in New York City That Had Incomes Over $10,000 in 1968

Blacks and Puerto Ricans	7 percent
Others	32

Average Weekly Earnings of Families Living in Low-Income Areas of New York City in 1972

Puerto Ricans	$105
Blacks	121
Others	128

1. More than half of the black families and Puerto Rican families living in New York City in 1968 earned *more than $5,000*.
2. Among families other than blacks and Puerto Ricans living in New York City in 1968, about *one in five earned less than $5,000*.
3. Blacks and Puerto Ricans earned less than other groups in New York City *because they found it harder to find jobs*.
4. *About the same percentage* of black families and Puerto Rican families earned more than $10,000 in 1968 as other groups living in New York City.
5. Blacks, Puerto Ricans, and others living in the poor neighborhoods of New York City in 1972 all *earned about the same average income*.
6. Most of the families with low incomes received *welfare assistance*.

PREJUDICE OR FACT?   Look at the statements that follow. Some are true, so label them T. But the other statements are prejudiced in some way. Some of the prejudiced statements are *innocuous*—that is, they harm no one. Label these PI. Others, however, could lead to harmful discrimination. Label these PH.

1. Orientals have brown eyes.
2. Blue is the best color for a carpet.
3. These people are all born with rhythm.
4. Cats are better pets than dogs.
5. Italian food is better than Chinese food.
6. Foreigners are very clannish—they always stick together.
7. Teenagers don't know how to spend their money.
8. Teenage drivers have a higher auto accident rate than older drivers.
9. He doesn't have a Chinaman's chance.
10. A simple people, they are unable to deal with the problems of the modern world.

ESSAY QUESTIONS
1. Study the information contained in the tables on page 145. What reasons would you give for the differences in incomes?
2. Should the same percentage of blacks, Puerto Ricans, and others have the same incomes? Why?

Chapter 2   Hispanic-Americans

Alfredo's fingers skimmed effortlessly over the skins of the *bongos,* two bucket-like tom-toms joined together, which he held between his knees. Charlie Martinez rubbed a stick along the notched side of his *guiro,* a hollowed-out gourd, to produce a soft scraping sound. The beat was Afro-Cuban and the scene was an apartment in Spanish Harlem, New York City.

Alfredo Hernandez's father came to New York from the Dominican Republic. His mother is from Puerto Rico. Both of Charlie's parents are Puerto Rican, but his grandparents on his mother's side were born in Cuba. Charlie and Alfredo were born in New York City, and both speak Spanish as well as English. All the students at their high school are either Hispanic-American or black.

One day last summer Alfredo and Charlie went to a swimming pool in another neighborhood. Most of the people there were not like them. One fellow called Charlie a bad name. Charlie wanted to fight him, but Alfredo knew that they were outnumbered so they left the pool.

Charlie did not like being called a name. Charlie is proud of his background, his race, and his parents' language.

What really got Charlie mad was that the kid said to him, "Go back where you came from."

"Can you beat that!" Charlie said. "That kid's parents probably came from somewhere in Europe. America isn't just the United States. My ancestors lived in Latin America hundreds of years before most Europeans

even thought of coming over here. And my Indian ancestors were here to
show Columbus around."

Who Are Hispanic-Americans?

Mejicano! Hispano! Español! Puerto Ricano! Latino! Chicano! These are
some of the names that describe the more than 280 million people of
Spanish origin living in the Americas.

Many years ago, part of the Roman Empire was called *Hispania.*
Modern Spain was once part of Hispania. If you look closely at the word,
you will see that it is similar to the word *Spain.* (The Spanish language is a
form of Latin. Latin was the language of the ancient Romans.)

When Columbus "discovered" the New World, he was working for the
king and queen of Spain. Later Spanish explorers discovered more lands in
the New World. Over the years, the culture of Spain was adopted by the
people living in the Americas.

Spain had lost most of her empire in the New World by 1820.
However, from 1492 to 1820 is a long time! Spanish soldiers had long since
married Indian women, and their children were neither pure Spanish nor
pure Indian. They were a new group, who now call themselves *la Raza* ("the
race"). When Africans were brought as slaves to the New World, they too
in time became part of *la Raza.* In some areas, the Hispanic-American is
mostly a mixture of Spanish and Indian. Mexico is an example of one such
area. In Cuba, however, the mixture is more black than Indian. In Puerto
Rico, blacks worked in the cane fields along the coast. In the mountain
areas, the racial mixture is more Indian and Spanish than Spanish and black.

The Hispanic-American, then, developed through the mixing of peoples and cultures from three continents. Spaniards, from Europe; blacks,
from Africa; and "Indians," the native people of the New World. This
culture—Spanish-African-Indian—has persisted even though conquerors
have come and gone.

The United States and Hispanic-America

The United States went to war with Mexico and defeated her in 1848.
As a result of that war, vast stretches of Mexican territory were added to the
United States. All or part of the states of California, Nevada, Utah,

Colorado, Arizona, New Mexico, and Texas once belonged to Mexico. The people in this territory became United States citizens.

Fifty years later, in 1898, the United States went to war with Spain. The United States won that war too, and one of the spoils of war was the island of Puerto Rico. In 1917 Puerto Ricans were granted American citizenship.

As the United States gained new territories in Hispanic-America, the people living in these territories became citizens of the United States. (However, in much of this Hispanic territory the people held on to their languages, culture, and traditions.) Most Hispanic-Americans, then, are *born* American citizens.

Summary   Hundreds of years before the Declaration of Independence was signed, Hispanic-Americans lived in parts of what are now the United States. Hispanic-Americans built homes and churches, raised livestock, farmed the land, and mined gold and silver. Their roots are deeply planted in the soil of the New World (America).

Looking Ahead   In the next chapter, we shall take a look at the largest group of Hispanic-Americans, the Mexican-Americans. Most Mexican-Americans live in the Southwestern United States. You will see why they share many of the problems of all Hispanic-Americans. You will also learn about some of the special problems of Mexican-Americans.

EXERCISES

ESSAY QUESTIONS   Write a paragraph answering each of the following questions:

1. Alfredo and Charlie are *Hispanic-Americans*. Explain.
2. Why did Charlie think of himself as more an American than most people?
3. Where did the term *Hispanic* come from?
4. What does *la Raza* mean and why is the term used today?
5. How did many Americans of Mexican ancestry come to live in the United States?
6. How did Puerto Rico become part of the United States?

Chapter 3 Mexican-Americans

There is a movement today among Mexican-Americans. It is called *la Causa* (the "Cause"). *La Causa* means many things to the Mexican-American. It means pride in being part of what he calls *la Raza* ("the race" or "my people").

La Raza

La Raza would include all the Spanish-speaking Mexican-Americans living in the United States. To some *la Raza* also means pride in being called a *Chicano*. The Spanish word for Mexican is *Mejicano*. English-speaking Americans dropped the *Me*, sounded the *j* as *ch*, and thus pronounced the name "Chicano." At the time Mexican-Americans thought "Chicano" was an insult. Today, however, they are proud to be called Chicanos. *La Causa* also represents a giant effort to make a better life for Mexican-Americans.

Some 7 million Mexican-Americans live in the United States. This makes them the largest of the country's Hispanic-American groups. Most Mexican-Americans live in the Southwest, in states that once belonged to Mexico—California, Texas, Colorado, New Mexico, and Arizona.

The pride in being a part of *la Raza*, in being called a *Chicano*, comes from many things. It comes from pride of ancestry. The Chicano was "born" when the Spanish conquerors married the Indian women of the New World. Thus the Chicano's ancestors were living in the Americas long

150

before any other group arrived, as we learned in Chapter 2. The Mexican-Americans had a highly developed society.

Mexican-Americans are proud of the fact that their ancestors taught the pioneers how to be cowboys. The *vaquero* (Mexican cowboy) rode the plains of the Southwest in much the same way as the American cowboy did in the 19th century. Many of the special words the American cowboy used came from Mexican cowboy's words, such as *bronco, rodeo,* and *corral.*

Mexican-Americans are also proud of the Spanish language, which they still speak, and their customs and traditions, which they still maintain.

Problems of Mexican-Americans

But Mexican-Americans face a number of very great problems. These problems must be resolved if they are to share fully in the *American Dream.* The most serious of these are the problems of (1) poverty, (2) discrimination, and (3) lack of education.

POVERTY   Think about this for a moment: How well could you live if all you had to spend for food, rent, and clothing was $39 a week? Or suppose you had a husband or wife and three children and your income was $100 a week—how well could you live? Nearly one out of every four Mexican-Americans has to make do on that little. Many Mexican-Americans are poor. In fact, their poverty is greatest in certain parts of the country, where they live in large numbers. In New Mexico, for example, one out of every two Mexican-American families is poor. Doctors learned that the children in one village ate only one meal a day—the free lunch they received at school. When doctors examined the children in another village, they found 50 needed eyeglasses. None could afford them.

Another poor area with much poverty is the delta of the Rio Grande Valley in Texas. Some 400,000 Texans live there. Of this number 75 percent are Chicanos who earn less than $2,400 a year.

But most Mexican-Americans now live in cities. For some, urban living has brought a better life. For many, however, it has meant living in some of the worst slums in America.

DISCRIMINATION   Mexican-Americans face many of the same kinds of problems experienced by blacks and other minority groups. Mexican-

Americans are also a *visible* minority. As a result they have suffered from similar kinds of discrimination. One can see this discrimination at work in the neighborhoods and homes they live in. One can see it in the jobs they do and the wages they receive. In some parts of the country Mexican-American children still attend segregated schools.

LACK OF EDUCATION   Mexican-Americans as a group are among the most poorly educated people in the United States. As recently as 1971, one out of every four Chicanos had not gone beyond the fourth grade. In that same year only one out of every twenty-five white Americans had so little schooling.

Many young Chicanos leave the high schools of the Southwest before graduating—about four times more than any other group. Why do these young people drop out of school in such large numbers? One reason has to do with language. It is often difficult to adjust to situations in which only English is spoken. Another reason is family poverty. Parents may want their children to leave school to get a job and help support the family. But by dropping out of school, the Chicano youngster does not get the education required for good-paying jobs. The Mexican-American is often not qualified for anything but the lowest paying jobs. Thus we have a vicious cycle: Because they are poor, young people drop out of school to support their families. Because they drop out, they stay poor when they are adults.

Another reason for the high dropout rate is that the things taught in school often do not have much meaning for boys and girls from Mexican-American homes.

What Is Being Done?

Like all minorities suffering from prejudice and discrimination, Mexican-Americans have tried many ways to improve their lives. Here are some of the ways:

LA CAUSA—**TO BE BROWN AND PROUD**   In the past, few Americans were aware of the terrible problems and suffering of Mexican-Americans. In recent years, however, the activities of certain groups have made the entire nation aware of Mexican-Americans' plight. Some groups have tried to combat poverty and discrimination by making the people

Political action is a way to fight poverty and discrimination

proud of their heritage. Those who favor this approach refer to it as *la Causa*. This movement has led to demands that the schools accept the fact that Mexican-American children are *bilingual* (speak two languages). Therefore, it is argued, some lessons should be taught in Spanish. Also, it is urged that Mexican-American history and culture be taught in the schools.

THE LAND QUESTION Before 1848 the American Southwest and California were part of Mexico. After the Mexican-American War of that year, these territories were acquired by the United States. According to the treaty that ended the war, Mexicans living in the conquered lands could become American citizens and still hold on to their lands. Over the years, however, most Mexicans lost their lands to the *Anglos* (white Americans). Recently, there have been demands for payment to Mexican-Americans for the lands that were lost.

CÉSAR CHAVEZ AND THE UNITED FARM WORKERS Some of the worst-paid workers in America are migratory farm workers. These workers move from state to state and from farm to farm picking the crops as they are ready for harvest. Most of the farm workers live in poverty or near

César Chavez

poverty. In California and the Southwest, most of them are Mexican-Americans. In the past, wages were kept down because of the almost unlimited supply of workers living just across the border, in Mexico. Hundreds of thousands of Mexicans entered this country legally as immigrants. Hundreds of thousands more entered illegally. (These were the "wetbacks," so called because most of them "slipped" across the Rio Grande.) Upon arrival in the United States, they were met by American employers who put them to work at very low wages. Since these immigrants were willing to work for very little money, all wages were kept down.

The Chicanos of California and the Southwest have recently become active supporters of labor unions. The best known of these unions is the United Farm Workers (UFW). Headed by César Chavez, the UFW in 1970 won a five-year-long strike against the California grape growers. Since then, the UFW has continued its active campaign to improve the wages of migratory farm workers.

Will *la Causa* help the Mexican-Americans? Will the discrimination against them finally disappear? Will their jobs and education improve? Is there some other approach that should be tried to solve their problems? These are some of the questions that all Americans will have to deal with in the coming years.

Summary Mexican-Americans suffer from poverty and discrimination. Recent efforts have made them aware of their heritage and proud of their culture and language. Union activity has improved the lives of many poorly paid migrant workers.

Looking Ahead   In the next chapter, we shall look at the problems faced by another Hispanic-American minority group—the Puerto Ricans.

EXERCISES

MATCHING QUESTIONS   Match the term in Column A with its definition in Column B.

Column A

1. *la Causa*
2. Chicano
3. *la Raza*
4. Anglo
5. *vaquero*
6. César Chavez

Column B

(*a*) the community of Hispanic-Americans living in the United States
(*b*) the movement to improve the life of the Mexican-American
(*c*) a Mexican cowboy
(*d*) term meaning a Mexican-American
(*e*) leads union of migratory farm workers
(*f*) term meaning a white American

ESSAY QUESTIONS

1. Explain what Mexican-Americans mean when they say that their ancestors lived in America before any other group arrived.
2. What proof can you offer to show that Mexican-Americans suffer from poverty?
3. Why do many Mexican-American children drop out of school sooner than children from other groups?
4. Mexican-Americans are a *visible minority*. Explain this statement.
5. How has illegal immigration affected the lives of some Mexican-Americans?

WRITING LETTERS

1. Suppose that you are the son or daughter of a Mexican family. Your home is in Mexico City. Your family has a good income, a nice home,

and you have just about everything you want. As part of your summer vacation, your parents have decided to send you on a bus tour through Texas, Arizona, New Mexico, and California. As you travel through these states, you meet many Mexican-Americans. Today you have decided to write a letter to your parents to tell them what you have seen. You want to describe how Mexican-Americans live as compared to the people you know in Mexico City. You also want to tell your parents some of the reasons why the people live the way they do. Finally, tell what you think should be done to improve the lives of Mexican-Americans.

2. A proposal that has received a lot of attention has been to hold classes for Mexican-American children in both English and Spanish. Some people think this is a wonderful idea. Others are very much opposed to it. Pretend that you live in a Southwestern town where such a proposal is under consideration. Write a letter to the editor of your local newspaper. In the letter, tell what you think of the idea.

FURTHER READING   Read the following selection. Basing your answers on this reading, tell whether the statements that follow are true or false. If the selection does not give you sufficient information to answer true or false, write NS.

PABLO'S STORY: THE MEXICAN-AMERICAN
MIGRANT FARMWORKER

Pablo is an 11-year-old Mexican-American boy. He was born in Crystal City, a town in southwest Texas. Most of the 9,000 people in Crystal City are Mexican-Americans, or *Chicanos,* as they want to be called. About 15

percent of the people in town are white, or *Anglos,* as they are often called in the Southwest.

Pablo is the second son of Juan and Maria Hernandez. Pablo has an older brother and three younger sisters. No one in Pablo's family has ever gone as far as high school. In fact, only Jose, the older boy, ever got as far as the eighth grade.

Maria Hernandez works in the local food-canning plant during the winter. Juan and the children pick spinach and onions in the fields that stretch for miles beyond the town. Crystal City is proud to call itself the "Spinach Capital of the World." It is one of the few places in the United States where a winter crop of vegetables can be grown.

From spring (long before the school term has ended) to fall, the entire Hernandez family *migrates* (travels) from state to state to harvest one crop after another. There are 300,000 children just like Pablo and his sisters and brother. They travel with their parents from state to state to harvest the crops. When school closes, 500,000 more children will join this small army of migratory farmworkers.

This season the Hernandez family signed up with a labor contractor to pick strawberries in Louisiana. Pablo has to get up at 5 A.M. each day to get on the truck taking the workers out to the fields. They arrive at the strawberry fields before dawn. Pablo sometimes has to stoop and crawl on his hands and knees to pick the berries and fill the basket he carries with him. He works about six hours a day in hot, unshaded fields. The labor contractor says that Pablo earns 75 cents an hour, or $4.50 a day, for his work. But Pablo gets no money at all. His father gets coupons worth $4.50. These coupons can be used to buy groceries and other things at the general store.

At about 11:30 A.M., school buses come to pick up Pablo and the other children. From 12:30 to 5:00 P.M., Pablo and the other Chicano children go to school. Pablo is usually too tired to study. Besides, he will go to this school for only a short time. The crop in this area will soon be picked, and the family will be heading north to Oregon.

Pablo rejoins his family at 6 P.M. Work in the fields has ended. The family has been at work for more than 12 hours. When you add up the earnings of seven people, it may seem that they have made a lot of money. But somehow, after paying the labor contractor, the grocer, and the rent for the shack in which they live, there is not much money left over.

Pablo's home is one of many like it built by farmers for the migrants. They have one room and a kitchen. There is no electricity. The shower, which does not always work, is outside the house. The toilet, or outhouse, is shared with a dozen other families.

Pablo eats meat once a week. Most of the time, his dinner is beans fried in bacon fat. Because of his poor diet and all the hard work that he does, Pablo is small for his age.

Pablo dreams of becoming a labor contractor when he grows up. Then he won't have to work in the fields. He will hire the workers and take them by bus on the long, dusty trip from state to state.

1. Pablo attends a high school in Texas.
2. The Hernandez family owns a farm just outside Crystal City, Texas, which they work all year round.
3. Children of Pablo's age are not allowed to work in the fields while school is still in session.
4. The Hernandez family would be better off if they quit farm work and moved to a big city.
5. Pablo hates everything that has to do with farm work.
6. A migrant farmworker has a very hard life.
7. The United States government should do something to help migrant workers.

WHAT DO YOU THINK?

1. When England ruled the American colonies, *Yankee* was a term of contempt for people from New England. In fact, coming from some people, it was an insult to be called a "Yankee." With the coming of the Revolution, however, Americans were proud to be called Yankees. In what way is the history of the word "Chicano" similar to this? Identify and explain one other word that had a similar history.
2. When they first came to America, most European immigrants had to face difficult problems. Most of them were poor and knew little or no English. Compare the problems these immigrants had to those that Mexican-Americans had. In your answer include the problems of finding a job, earning a living, and getting an education.

Chapter 4 Puerto Ricans

Every year a million or so Americans happily vacation in Puerto Rico. They enjoy its lovely white beaches. They relax in the warm Caribbean sun. They explore its green hills and quiet towns. As their planes leave the lovely island, many of the tourists wonder, "Why would anyone move from such a tropical paradise? Why do so many Puerto Ricans leave their homeland to live in the slums of the mainland? Why do they give up the warm Caribbean winter for the cold, gray winter up north?"

There are two answers to this question. The first is that Puerto Ricans have left their island home for the same reason that many immigrants left Europe for the United States: to escape the poverty in which they were living. The second answer has to do with the special relationship that exists between the United States and Puerto Rico.

A Special Association

The Puerto Rican is as American as anyone born in Massachusetts, Illinois, Arizona, or Oregon. The Puerto Rican's traditions go back to November 19, 1493. On that day Columbus landed on an island the Indians called *Borinquén*. We now call this place Puerto Rico. Over the years of Spanish rule, the Indians intermixed with the Spanish settlers. Slavery, which was not abolished until 1873, brought many black Africans to Puerto Rico. They too intermixed, and the Puerto Ricans today reflect this blend of Spanish, Indian, and African cultures.

In 1898 the United States defeated Spain in the Spanish-American

War, and Puerto Rico passed into American hands. At first the United States ruled Puerto Rico as a colony. This meant that the people of the island had virtually no voice in their government. As time went on, however, the situation improved dramatically. Here are some of the highlights of Puerto Rico's march toward democracy:

1917   The United States Congress passed the Jones Act. Puerto Ricans were made citizens of the United States.

1941–45   The United States fought in World War II. Many Puerto Ricans served in the armed forces of the United States, and Puerto Rico was an important military and naval base.

1948   Jones Act amended to allow Puerto Ricans to elect their own governor. They elected Luis Muñoz Marín.

1952   Puerto Rico became a *commonwealth,* or *associated free state,* and Puerto Rico drew up its own constitution. It now elects its own officials and makes its own laws. Foreign affairs, however, are still controlled by the United States government.

1967   A *referendum* (national vote) was conducted to see if the majority wanted Puerto Rico to become a full state in the Union. The results of the referendum were overwhelmingly in favor of remaining a commonwealth, and plans for statehood were dropped.

Puerto Rico remains a commonwealth. It governs itself but leaves such things as foreign affairs and the coining of money to the United States. Although Puerto Ricans are citizens of the United States, they may not vote for the President or Vice President of the United States while living in Puerto Rico. If they move to any of the 50 states, however, they are permitted to vote in presidential elections. Puerto Ricans do not pay federal income tax as long as they live in Puerto Rico.

The census of 1970 showed that there were 1,450,000 Puerto Ricans living in the United States. Why have so many come to live on the mainland? One reason is that as citizens Puerto Ricans can come to the mainland whenever they want. This, plus regular, inexpensive flights between San Juan, the capital of Puerto Rico, and New York City, has made the move very easy. Anyone with the plane fare who wished to go to New York City could get there in a few hours.

Problems in Puerto Rico

As compared to the mainland, Puerto Rico is a very poor place. Puerto Ricans have left Puerto Rico in the hope of finding jobs and a better way of life. One cause of their poverty is that the island is very crowded. How crowded? Consider this:

In Canada there are 5 people for every square mile.
In the United States there are 57 people for every square mile.
In France there are 242 people for every square mile.
In Puerto Rico there are 796 *people for every square mile.*

One result of this overcrowding has been a shortage of housing. People had to live in the poorest of shanties. There were shortages of doctors, medical facilities, and schools. Parents had to worry about providing their children with adequate food and clothing. By the end of World War II and on into the 1950s, jobs were fairly plentiful in New York City and other parts of the Northeast. With the encouragement of a congressman, who represented the East Harlem district of New York City, and others, thousands upon thousands of Puerto Ricans left the island. Unfortunately, many have found that, in moving to the mainland, they exchanged one set of problems for another.

Problems on the Mainland

Like many other immigrants, most Puerto Ricans coming to live on the mainland are from a rural background. They were brought up in the country rather than in the city. This has created a problem because the two ways of life are quite different. City life in the United States is not like country life in Puerto Rico.

DISCRIMINATION   Like the Mexican-Americans, Puerto Ricans have also had to face the problem of discrimination. As a result of prejudice and discrimination, Puerto Ricans as a group have found it more difficult to find jobs and housing than most other American groups. Also like the Mexican-Americans, Puerto Ricans have faced a language problem, since

This Puerto Rican family has an apartment in a middle-income housing development in a large mainland city

Spanish is the language most frequently spoken at home and in daily life in Puerto Rico.

LOW-PAYING JOBS   Puerto Ricans as a group have filled the lowest-paying jobs in America's cities. This is in part a result of discrimination. It is also a result of the language problem. Many employers would prefer to hire persons who speak English well. In this respect, the Puerto Ricans' experience is much like that of the European immigrants who also were forced to take the lowest-paying jobs when they first arrived in the country.

Like the European immigrants, Puerto Ricans have also had to live in the worst housing, attend the most overcrowded schools, and find themselves exploited by greedy landlords and "easy-credit" merchants.

Puerto Ricans Try to Solve Problems

In their attempt to find better jobs, many Puerto Ricans have opened their own businesses. The *bodega* (grocery store) is one example of this. Visit any of the Puerto Rican neighborhoods and you will see many other small businesses. Another route to financial success is a high school or college diploma. More and more Puerto Ricans are finishing high school and going on to college and the professions.

They are also joining labor unions and forming civic and cultural organizations. Within the Puerto Rican community these organizations have concentrated on the following:

1. Protecting tenants. Tenants have been organized to put pressure on landlords to provide better housing.

2. Improving schools. Puerto Rican community groups have brought

Former Bronx borough president Herman Badillo addresses a New York City citizens' group. Badillo is one of the growing number of American civic leaders who are of Hispanic-American origin

Baseball player Orlando Cepeda. Less than 30 years ago, discrimination kept members of minority groups out of most professional sports

pressure to bear on local school districts to provide for the needs of Puerto Rican children.

3. Other services. Some agencies have helped teenagers find jobs, while others have helped merchants to improve their businesses.

Other Hispanic-Americans

Mexican-Americans and Puerto Ricans are American citizens from the day of their birth. But there also are a large number of Spanish-speaking people living in the United States who are not American citizens. For example, a person born in Cuba is a citizen of Cuba, not of the United States, unless he or she applies for and receives citizenship. Many Cubans came to the United States, particularly to Florida, when Fidel Castro took over Cuba in 1959. Many of these Cubans were business and professional people who emigrated for political reasons. Another group of Spanish-speaking people living in the United States are from the Dominican Republic. Job opportunities and political reasons explain why Dominicans come to the United States. New York City is the main place of settlement for Dominicans and some other Spanish-speaking people from the Caribbean islands.

Cubans, Dominicans, and other Spanish-speaking persons face the same problems faced by Mexican-Americans and the Puerto Rican-Americans. In addition some of these Spanish-speaking people came to the United States as tourists and stayed beyond the legal time they were supposed to stay. Thus they are not American citizens and are here illegally. Fearing that they will be sent back to their country, they are forced to accept the lowest-paying jobs. They cannot complain about job and living conditions because they do not want their presence known. They cannot ask for public assistance for the same reason. If caught, they will most likely be *deported* (sent back to their native country).

Summary Many of the problems faced by Puerto Ricans, Mexican-Americans, and other Spanish-speaking peoples in the United States are similar. Poverty, discrimination, and poor schooling are their major problems. To these we could add the difficulty of getting along in an English-speaking world when one's first language is Spanish. Like all other Americans, Hispanic-Americans want to feel that they are a part of society. They want to share, to learn, and to grow as individuals and as a group. It remains to be seen whether they will obtain the chance.

Looking Ahead   In the next chapter, we shall explore some of the problems faced by black people. Here again, we shall see how poverty, discrimination, and poor schooling have combined to create special problems for a large group of Americans.

EXERCISES

MATCHING QUESTIONS   Match each term in Column A with its definition in Column B.

Column A

1. Borinquén
2. Jones Act
3. Luis Muñoz Marín
4. referendum
5. commonwealth
6. the mainland
7. San Juan
8. East Harlem
9. bodega

Column B

(*a*) To a person living in Puerto Rico, this is where the cities of New York, Chicago, and Los Angeles are located.

(*b*) Indian name for Puerto Rico

(*c*) a self-governing territory

(*d*) a national vote on an issue

(*e*) first Puerto Rican to be elected governor of the island

(*f*) a grocery store

(*g*) made Puerto Ricans citizens of the United States

(*h*) neighborhood in New York City in which many Puerto Ricans settled

(*i*) capital city of Puerto Rico

ESSAY QUESTIONS

1. Using the information contained in the tables on page 166, compare the living standard of Puerto Ricans in New York to that of other groups in the city. (Helpful note: *Living standard* refers to the way that people live—the kinds of homes they live in, the foods they eat, the clothes they wear.)

2. From what you have read in this chapter, and what you knew even before you read the chapter, what would you say were the reasons for the situation you described in the answer to question 1?
3. Tell whether the statements that follow the tables are true or false.

Racial Groups Living in New York City in 1970

Group	Total Number Living in City	Number Living in Low-Income Areas
White	7,896,000	2,443,000
Black	1,467,000	1,165,000
Puerto Rican	812,000	692,000

Average Weekly Earnings of Workers Living in Low-Income Areas in 1970

Group	Average of All Workers	Male Head of Family	Female Head of Family
White	$128	$144	$106
Black	121	135	112
Puerto Rican	105	113	95

Among those living in low-income areas of New York City:

1. The combined total population of blacks and Puerto Ricans was larger than the number of whites.
2. Of all Puerto Ricans living in New York City, more than three-quarters lived in low-income neighborhoods.
3. Of all whites living in New York City, more than one-third lived in low-income neighborhoods.
4. Of all blacks living in New York City, four-fifths lived in low-income neighborhoods.
5. On the average, Puerto Ricans earned more than blacks but less than whites.
6. On the average, white workers earned more than either black or Puerto Rican workers.
7. Women who are heads of families have higher incomes than men who are heads of families.
8. Puerto Rican women who are heads of families earned an average of $105 a week.

Chapter 5   Black Americans

Not long ago, in many American communities, black Americans were not permitted to take any seat they wanted in a bus or movie theater. The law said that they had to take seats in the rear of a bus. Laws also required that blacks sit in the balcony or in a special section of a theater. In many of the same communities, water fountains and public restrooms were labeled "Whites Only" or "Colored Only." Most hotels and restaurants in America did not serve black people. Some schools and colleges would accept only white students. Blacks in some areas had to go to "their" schools.

This situation no longer exists in America. No one today can legally refuse to accept a customer because of race. Public facilities must be made available to all people. Schools can no longer be "for white children only." Segregation has been made illegal. But has it been wiped out?

The Problems Remain

Consider the following:

In 1974 the average income for white families in the United States was $13,271. For black families it was $7,807.

In 1974 some 9 percent of all white families were poor; 30 percent of all black families were poor.

In 1974 some 5 percent of all white workers were unemployed; 9.9 percent of the black labor force was unemployed.

What do these statistics tell us about the life of blacks as compared to whites? They tell us that blacks earn less, are more likely to be living in poverty, and have a greater chance of being unemployed than whites.

Statistics also tell us something about the *quality of life* for black people. A white baby born in the 1970s can expect to live for 72 years. A black child can look forward to 66 years.

The great majority of working blacks hold menial jobs. Three-quarters of all blacks work at unskilled, low-paying jobs. One-half of the blacks in this country live in slum housing. Despite the elimination by law of separate schools for blacks and whites, more than one-half of the black children in the country still attend segregated schools. Later in the chapter, we shall see why this is still true.

"TWO SOCIETIES, SEPARATE AND UNEQUAL" In short, even though legalized separation of the races has been outlawed, segregation still exists in the United States. A commission created by President Lyndon B. Johnson stated the facts in this way: ". . . our nation is moving toward two societies, one black, one white, separate and unequal. . . ."

The federal government has tried to stop the creation of two unequal societies. One way in which it has done this has been to try to raise the income of black families. A second way is to provide more and better educational opportunities. In both efforts, however, the government has come up against the problems of racial prejudice and discrimination. It is difficult to raise the incomes of black families because discrimination in hiring keeps many blacks from higher paying jobs. Discrimination has also led to school segregation. Most white children attend schools where the enrollment is almost all white. Most black children attend schools whose enrollment is nearly 100 percent black.

Let us see how the government has dealt with these twin problems of discrimination on the job and in school.

JOB DISCRIMINATION Don Loris entered the office. He was nervous. The sign on the door had read: *Equal Employment Opportunity Commission—United States Government.*

"What does the government want with me?" he thought.

"Come in, Mr. Loris. Please have a seat. Mr. Loris," said the government agent, "you are the owner of the Bonac Seafood Company. Is that correct?"

"That's right," Don replied.

"Well, Mr. Loris, we have examined your employee records. They show that you have 150 employees. We are concerned about the number of minority group workers in the 150. You see, this agency, the EEOC, tries to prevent discrimination because of race, religion, or sex."

"Oh, in that case there's no reason for me to be here," replied Mr. Loris. "Fifty of the men and women on our payroll are blacks. I've always hired blacks."

"I understand," said the government agent. "But tell me, Mr. Loris, how many of your 50 black employees have *managerial jobs?*"

"Well," Don replied, "now that you mention it, all our black people are packers or sweepers. None of them are managers."

The government agent thought for a moment and said, "Tell me, Mr. Loris—how many managers, supervisors, and foremen do you use on the job?"

"About 12," replied Don. "Two of our foremen are going to retire soon, so we'll probably promote a couple of workers to take their place. I imagine that we will name them in the next week or two."

The government agent handed Mr. Loris a paper. "Mr. Loris," the agent said, "we think that under the circumstances your business should have at least two black supervisors. This is a copy of our decision. I would suggest that you hire the two people as soon as possible. You can use them to fill the two vacancies you now have."

"But sir, we have some people who have been waiting for a long time for a promotion. How can we put blacks into the jobs ahead of them?"

"Mr. Loris," replied the EEOC agent, "your company has been in business for many years. In that time we feel you should have had some qualified blacks come along who deserved promotions. Since, however, you don't have even *one* black supervisor, we have to assume it is a result of discrimination. Now I am sure you don't want us to take this matter to the courts, so why don't you hire the two blacks?"

The conversation you just read did not really take place. But it *might* have. The Equal Employment Opportunity Commission was established by the Civil Rights Act of 1964. In its efforts to prevent discrimination, the EEOC has compelled many businesses to hire blacks and other minority-group workers. In addition the United States Department of Labor maintains an office that does the same thing with companies that do business with the government.

Integration in blue-collar work and in white-collar work

What this policy means is that blacks and members of other minority groups are given *preference* for certain jobs. Supporters of this approach argue that certain minorities have suffered from discrimination in the past. (We have mentioned the fact that 75 percent of all black workers hold low-paying menial jobs.) The only way, they argue, that members of minorities will get better jobs is by forcing companies to hire a certain percentage of minority workers.

Critics of this plan say it is discrimination "in reverse." That is, if a company hires a person *solely because the person is black,* then the company most likely rejected someone else *because that person was white.* Thus, they say, the white worker was the victim of discrimination.

SEGREGATION IN EDUCATION   The effort to improve the educational opportunities for blacks and other minorities has also led to great controversy. Many studies have shown that minority-group students do better if they attend schools with middle-class whites. Unfortunately, however, one-half of all the black children in the country still attend schools that are all, or almost all, black. But over 20 years ago the Supreme Court declared segregated schools unconstitutional. Why are so many schools still segregated? The answer lies in the concept of the "neighborhood school." Traditionally, Americans have gone to schools in the neighborhoods in which they lived. Since blacks, Puerto Ricans, Mexican-Americans, and other minorities usually live together in certain sections of the community, they attend a segregated school because only minority-group children live in the neighborhood. In recent years many middle-class white families have left the cities and moved to the suburbs. One of the reasons was to make

Busing has been a controversial issue in America ever since the Supreme Court in 1954 held that separate (segregated) schools were unconstitutional

certain that their children went to a neighborhood school in which there were few or no minority-group children.

How then can black children and white children be brought together in integrated schools? Two solutions are most frequently suggested. Both have aroused bitter controversy.

Solution 1—Busing   School segregation exists where there are black neighborhoods and white neighborhoods, each with its own school. Suppose, however, that one-half the students in the white school were transferred to the black school and one-half of the students in the black school were transferred to the white school. Then we would have two integrated schools rather than two segregated schools. But the question was asked, How would the students living in one neighborhood get to the other? The answer is simple: by bus. For more than 25 years, American children, particularly in suburban and rural areas, have gone to school by bus. These same buses could be used to integrate the schools.

The suggestion set off many, many arguments.

"My daughter's school is only two blocks from here. Why should I send her all the way across town on a bus?" said one white parent.

"We have a voice in the educational program of our school. If they start busing in white kids to our school, their parents will get control of the whole program," objected a black parent.

"Those black and Puerto Rican kids will pick on my boy. He won't be safe in that neighborhood."

"Those white kids are just waiting to get their hands on my child. He won't be safe in that neighborhood." Thus spoke two other parents.

Should buses be used to bring about school integration? What do you think?

Solution 2—Integrated Neighborhoods   Another suggestion, just as controversial as busing, is that the government create integrated neighborhoods by building low-income housing in middle-income neighborhoods. Those who favor the idea argue that it is the "natural" way to bring about the integration of schools. If neighborhoods are integrated, the neighborhood schools would be too.

Some leaders of the black and minority communities are opposed to the idea of integration. They would like to let segregated neighborhoods remain as they are. These leaders feel that their people can best solve their problems when they control their own community. They feel that with integration, the communities would be controlled by whites.

But most of the opposition to integration comes from white property owners. Some feel that, if the government builds low-cost housing in their neighborhood, the value of their homes will go down. Others feel that they bought their property in order to escape from the nonwhite minorities and their problems. The *last* thing they want to see happen is poor families moving into their neighborhoods. (See reading, page 255.)

Should the government promote integration by building low-cost housing in middle-class neighborhoods? What do you think?

Summary   It was as long ago as the 1960s when the government realized that ". . . our nation is moving toward two societies, one black, one white, separate and unequal." Much of the inequality referred to in that statement still exists. We have seen that most blacks do not hold nearly as many good jobs as other Americans do. We have seen that most blacks are not as well educated as other Americans. We have seen that blacks do not earn as much or live as long as other Americans. We have also seen that prejudice and discrimination have made these problems very difficult to solve.

Looking Ahead   In the next chapter, we shall take a look at America's first minority group—the Indians. As you read about the problems that Indians face, you may want to compare these problems to those confronting other minority groups. In what ways are they similar (alike)? In what ways are they different?

EXERCISES

MULTIPLE-CHOICE QUESTIONS   For each question, write the letter of the best answer.

1. As compared to white families, black families earn (*a*) less (*b*) a little more (*c*) about the same (*d*) far more
2. As compared to the percentage of poor white families, what percentage of black families are poor? (*a*) a far larger percentage (*b*) a far smaller percentage (*c*) a slightly higher percentage (*d*) about the same percentage
3. The average life expectancy of whites born in the 1970s is (*a*) 3 (*b*) 5 (*c*) 7 (*d*) 9   years longer than blacks.
4. (*a*) Some (*b*) Most (*c*) All (*d*) No   white children attend schools that are nearly all white.
5. (*a*) Some (*b*) No (*c*) All (*d*) Many   black children attend schools that are nearly all black.
6. Busing has been a controversial topic because buses have been used to (*a*) improve transportation (*b*) replace cars (*c*) integrate schools (*d*) create traffic problems.
7. Some members of minority groups would prefer to preserve (*a*) segregation (*b*) integration (*c*) interaction (*d*) discrimination   because they feel that it allows them to control their own communities.

TIMES CHANGE—FOR BETTER OR FOR WORSE?   Read the selection below and answer the questions that follow:

THE MARCH ON WASHINGTON

It was a bright, sunny day in August of 1963. Dr. Martin Luther King, Jr., the black Baptist preacher who would one day win a Nobel Prize, stood on the steps of the Lincoln Memorial in Washington, D.C. He addressed a huge gathering of 200,000 people who had assembled in a "March on

Washington, D.C.,
August 1963

Washington" from all over the United States. Dr. King's words, like those of Patrick Henry and Abraham Lincoln, are now a part of America's history.

> I say to you today, even though we face the difficulties of today and tomorrow, I still have a dream. It is a dream deeply rooted in the American dream. I have a dream that one day this nation will rise up and live out the true meaning of its creed, "We hold these truths to be self-evident, that all men are created equal."

As Patrick Henry and Abraham Lincoln had done before him, Dr. King expressed what was in the minds and hearts of millions of Americans of his time—the 1960s. Patrick Henry's attack on King George, which ended with the immortal words ". . . as for me, give me Liberty or give me death," aroused the patriotism of American colonists of the 1760s. At Gettysburg, Lincoln's promise that "government of the people, by the people, for the people, shall not perish from the earth" inspired Americans of the 1860s. In the same way, Dr. King's remarks were inspirational to many Americans of the 1960s. But simply because Henry, Lincoln, and King inspired the people of their time is not what made their words immortal. What made these words part of America's culture is that they have kept and will keep their meaning for all people for all time. Consider what Dr. King said at the 1963 March on Washington:

> There are those who are asking the devotees of civil rights, "When will you be satisfied?"
>
> We can never be satisfied as long as the Negro is the victim of the unspeakable horrors of police brutality.
>
> We can never be satisfied as long as our bodies, heavy with the fatigue of travel, cannot gain lodging in the motels of the highways and the hotels of the cities.
>
> We cannot be satisfied as long as the Negro's basic mobility is from a smaller ghetto to a larger one.
>
> We can never be satisfied as long as a Negro in Mississippi cannot vote and a Negro in New York believes he has nothing for which to vote.
>
> No, no, we are not satisfied, and we will not be satisfied until justice rolls down like waters and righteousness like a mighty stream. . . .

1. At the March on Washington, Dr. Martin Luther King, Jr., said: ". . . even though we face the difficulties of today and tomorrow, I still have a dream." (*a*) What did Dr. King mean by the "difficulties of today and tomorrow"? (*b*) What was his "dream" about?
2. Dr. King spoke of changes that would have to take place in America before "the devotees of civil rights" would be satisfied. List these changes.
3. Suppose Dr. King were alive today. Which of these demands would he feel were satisfied? Which are still unsatisfied?
4. If he were alive today, what new demands might Dr. King add to those he made in 1963?

TABLES TELL A STORY Study the tables on page 176 and answer the questions that follow:

Gains Made by Whites and Nonwhites, from 1960 to 1972

Percentage of Men and Women
Aged 25 to 29 Who Had Completed
4 Years of High School or More

	Nonwhite	White
1960	38.6	63.7
1972	56.1	77.8

Percentage of Professional
and Technical Workers

	Nonwhite	White
1960	4.8	12.1
1972	9.5	14.6

Percentage of Unemployment

	Nonwhite	White
1960	10.2	4.9
1972	10.0	5.0

Percentage of Families With Incomes
of $10,000 and Over

	Nonwhite	White
1960	13.3	35.9
1972	33.7	59.2

Life Expectancy at Birth

	Nonwhite	White
1960	63.6	70.6
1972	65.5	72.1

Median Family Income

	Nonwhite	White
1960	$4,564	$ 8,267
1972	$7,106	$11,549

1. Among men and women 25 to 29 years of age, the percentage of whites who were high school graduates in 1960 was _____. The percentage of nonwhites who were high school graduates was _____.

2. The percentage of nonwhites who were high school graduates in 1972 was _____.

3. The percentage of nonwhites who had jobs as professional or technical workers in 1972 was _____.

4. The percentage of whites who held jobs as professional or technical workers in 1972 was _____.

5. As compared to unemployment among whites, unemployment among nonwhites in 1972 was _____.

6. The percentage of nonwhite families earning $10,000 or more in 1960 was _____, while in 1972 it was _____.

7. Whites born in 1960 could expect to live _____ years longer than nonwhites.

8. The median (average) income for white families in 1960 was
   _____.

9. The median income for nonwhite families in 1972 had increased by
   _____ dollars since 1960.

10. From what you can see in the tables, would you say that nonwhites
    were better off in 1972 than they were in 1960? Explain your answer.

Chapter 6 American
Indians

Disaster was about to strike the wagon train. The pioneers had come West to settle the new lands. And now, there they were: wagons drawn up in a tight circle, guns blazing. Around them rode a horde of screaming, wild-eyed Indians, eager to scalp them all.

Then, just as all seemed lost, the distant sound of a bugle was heard. *It's the United States Cavalry!*

Just in time to save the day, the clean-shaven troopers swooped down upon the scene. Dozens of Indians bit the dust.

The men, women, and children of the wagon train sent up a loud cheer. The audience in the theater sent up a loud cheer. The Indians went down to defeat. Everybody was happy—except the Indians in the audience.

Times have changed. Pioneers no longer threaten Indian lands. Except in movies, the bugle that ordered another cavalry charge down on Indian heads is silent. People would no longer think of saying, as they did in the past, "The only good Indian is a dead Indian."

And yet, for many Indians today, very little has changed. Although settlers no longer threaten the Indians' lands and their way of life, other, more powerful, forces do. The United States Army and white settlers no longer kill Indians, but many Indians die young.

Problems of the American Indian

While the American public no longer imagines that the Indian is a wild-eyed savage, another stereotype has replaced the savage. This stereotype is of a person in "native" dress who sells beads, blankets, and jewelry to rodeo-goers and tourists in the Southwest. It is also the stereotype of a person whom many would prefer not to have as a next-door neighbor. Indians, who at one time roamed the continent at will, have become, in President Lyndon Johnson's words, "strangers in their own land." He might also have described them as *"poor* strangers in their own land," for Indians are America's poorest minority group.

The Indians are also America's *oldest* minority group, of course. No one knows exactly how many Indians lived in what is now the United States when Columbus arrived. Estimates range from 1 million to 10 million. What is known is that in 1800 there were 600,000 Indians, but in 1850 there were only 250,000. Until a few years ago, their number was constantly getting smaller. The population of a group would normally increase over the years. What happened to the Indians?

DISEASE AND STARVATION   As whites moved into Indian lands, they brought with them their diseases. Smallpox, tuberculosis, diphtheria, and mumps were new and deadly to the Indians. In 1837 a smallpox epidemic in the Mandan tribe left alive only 31 out of 1,600 people.

Over the years, many Indians starved to death. As white men took away most of their lands, Indians were unable to feed themselves properly on the land that remained. On the Great Plains of the Middle West, for example, many Indians had relied on the great herds of buffalo for food, clothing, and shelter. Following the Civil War, white settlers killed off the buffalo herds. Many Indians starved.

In addition to disease and starvation, Indians also had to fear murder. Many white settlers really believed that "the only good Indian is a dead Indian." Ninety percent of California's Indian population appears to have been killed by the gold miners.

The so-called "Battle" of Wounded Knee, which took place in South Dakota in 1890, was more a slaughter than a battle: 300 unarmed men, women, and children of the Sioux tribe were killed by the United States Army. There were only 220,000 Indians left by 1910.

INDIANS STILL DIE YOUNG   Today the Indian population is on the increase. Although there are still not as many as there were when Columbus "discovered" them, in 1970 there were over 800,000 American Indians, a dramatic increase over the 500,000 in 1960. Despite this rise in population, American Indians do not live as long as other Americans do. Indians born today can expect to live 64 years on the average, while the white population has a life expectancy of 72 years. Twice as many Indian children die in their first year as white children.

LOW INCOME   Indians are the poorest of the nation's minority groups. In 1972, when the average white American family earned nearly $11,000, Indian families earned only about $5,000. And the situation is even worse than it sounds. The $5,000 is an *average* figure. This means that many earned far less. Indeed, many Indians earned nothing at all. For example, in one tribe, the Arizona Apache, 65 percent of the people who could work were unemployed in 1972. In the case of the Navaho, the figure was 80 percent. Overall, two out of every five Indians living on reservations were unemployed.

What is it like to be a Navaho and poor? It may mean that you live in a house made of mud and logs. You walk on dirt floors. Since there is no electricity in your home, you use kerosene lamps for light. You draw your water from a well (only one home in five has any plumbing). Your meals are cooked on a stove made out of an old oil drum, and when you go to bed at night you sleep on sheepskin mats.

Why are the Indians so poor? The old-time Indian way of life was adapted to the land on which they lived. It was the loss of their lands that lies at the heart of the Indians' problems.

LOSS OF LANDS   Although the Indians had lost most of their lands by 1887, they still held 138 million acres (the area of Nevada and Arizona combined). This too was whittled away over the years, so that now their total holdings are down to 55 million acres.

Indians lost their land in many ways. Sometimes they sold it. Sometimes the United States government took it away. At other times the Indians signed treaties in which they agreed to give up some land in exchange for guarantees that they could hold on to what remained. But many of these agreements were broken by the federal government. One writer has estimated that about 400 treaties with the Indians were broken. Here is one treaty, which was signed in 1804 with the United Tribes of Sac and Fox:

> The United States will never interrupt the said tribes in the possession of the lands which they rightfully claim, but will, on the contrary, protect them in the quiet enjoyment of the same.

The Sac and the Fox no longer own their lands.

Indians are worried about losing the remaining lands that make up their reservations. About one-half of the Indian population lives on reservations. Although the reservation lands are not well suited to farming, they do contain many natural resources. Private businesses have put pressure on the federal government to turn the remaining Indian lands over to them. As a result the Indians have seen coal companies rip open their lands to strip mine them. They have watched as utility companies built power-generating plants that polluted the atmosphere. Power lines, highways, and railways have crisscrossed their lands. Indians wonder where it will all end.

Indians Speak Out

Until only a few years ago, most people in the United States rarely saw Indians or heard much about them. A famous book, written in the 1960s, spoke of America's poor. It was called *The Other America.* Its author, Michael Harrington, said that America seemed to have forgotten its poor people. Indeed it had, and even *The Other America,* which told of America's forgotten poor, forgot to mention the poorest of all—the Indian.

Recently, however, Indians have acted. One group seized the abandoned prison island of Alcatraz in San Francisco Bay and held it for nine months. Another group occupied the Bureau of Indian Affairs Building in Washington, D.C., and destroyed much of it in the process. In still another

Wounded Knee, South Dakota, 1973

incident, eleven hostages were seized and the town of Wounded Knee, South Dakota, was occupied. (See reading, page 254.)

"What do the Indians want?", many Americans asked.

"I don't know," was a frequent reply. "I've never met an Indian."

What do the Indians want? No one group speaks for all American Indians. Therefore, it is not possible to make one list of the things they want that all Indians would agree on. There are differences among the tribes, and there are differences within the tribes. Despite these differences, however, most Indians would probably agree to the following goals:

COMMUNITY CONTROL ON THE RESERVATIONS   Indians living on reservations are represented by tribal councils elected by members of the tribe. Many Indians resent this system because it was dictated from Washington. They would rather establish their own method for selecting leaders, one that is more in keeping with Indian tradition. The present method, it is claimed, has placed in power men who have used their positions as tribal leaders for personal gain. It is charged that these leaders have worked with private industry and the federal government to give away Indian lands and Indian rights.

What the Indians really want is the right to govern themselves on the reservations. They want the power to educate, police, and tax their communities. At present these things are done by the state and federal governments.

FULFILLMENT OF TREATY OBLIGATIONS Indians speak of the "trail of broken treaties." By this they mean that for 150 years or more the federal government has failed to live up to the treaties it has signed with the Indians. In the late 1700s and early 1800s, when most of the treaties were signed, the Indian tribes were nearly as powerful as the United States government. At that time the treaties were looked upon as legal agreements between nations. As time went on, however, the Indian nations became weaker and weaker, and the United States began to ignore the treaties. Indians today would like either to have the lands that they say were illegally taken returned to them, or to be paid for those lands that were not returned.

AN END TO RACIAL DISCRIMINATION Like other nonwhite minority groups, Indians suffer from racial prejudice and discrimination. One result of this, they say, is that Indians involved in crimes are treated harshly by the police and the courts. On the other hand, whites who commit crimes against Indians are treated *leniently* (easily). The following story vividly illustrates this:

> In Custer, S.D., . . . a Sioux [man] was killed and a white gas-station attendant was accused in the slaying. When the [man's] mother protested that the white man faced a maximum of only ten years in prison if he were convicted, she herself was arrested by the white authorities and held on a charge calling for a maximum of 30 years in prison.

It was because of incidents like these and other acts of discrimination that the federal government established the Office of Indian Rights in 1973. This agency will work to protect the civil rights of Indians.

AN END TO POVERTY We have learned that Indians are the poorest of America's minority groups. How to wipe out their poverty is another matter.

During the 1950s the federal government thought it would be best if the Indians would just blend into the general population, as many other ethnic groups had. The policy of "termination," as it was called, sought to "get the Indians off the reservation" and end government involvement with them. Most Indians feel that this policy was a failure. Thousands of acres of Indian lands went into private hands, and thousands of Indians found that they had exchanged the poverty of the reservation for the poverty of the big city.

Today it seems that most Indians would prefer to live on reservation lands. They do not want to lose their identity as Indians. They want certain changes made on the reservations—improved schools, for example, so that, by studying tribal language and history, students will learn what it means to be an Indian. Yet, while education will build pride in the Indian heritage, it will not solve the basic problem of poverty. Most reservations are just too poor to support themselves. If Indian-Americans are to live as Indians on their own lands, free of government interference, the reservations will have to be turned into "paying propositions." Whether or not this can be done without destroying the Indian character remains to be seen.

Summary   Over the centuries, Indians lost most of their lands to European settlers. Today, many Indians suffer from poverty, lack of jobs, and poor education. Recently, Indians have demanded equal rights, better education, and self-government on the reservations.

Looking Ahead   In the next chapter, we shall describe the problems faced by immigrants from China and Japan.

EXERCISES

BUMPER STICKERS—SIGNS OF THE TIMES   One form of protest that is uniquely American is the bumper sticker. Wherever you travel, you are sure to see a sticker. Some stickers advertise tourist attractions; others promote political candidates. Still others announce the driver's support of a cause. Some bumper stickers are used as a form of protest. The bumper stickers quoted below were seen recently on three cars in a parking lot out West. Read them and answer the questions that follow:

> **Indians Discovered America**
> **Indian Power**
> **Custer Had It Coming**

1.   What is the meaning of the first bumper sticker?

2. The person who placed the sticker on the first car wanted to protest something. What do you suppose it was?
3. What is the meaning of the second sticker?
4. What changes do you suppose the owner of the second car would favor in order to bring about "Indian power"?
5. What is the meaning of the third sticker?

FURTHER READING   Read the selection below and answer the questions that follow:

CHIEF JOSEPH'S LAST SPEECH—1878

In 1877 the Nez Percé, a small, peaceful Indian tribe living in Idaho, were ordered by the United States Government to abandon their lands and move to a smaller reservation. Led by Chief Joseph, the Nez Percé refused to move to the reservation. The United States army attacked the tribe, and Chief Joseph attempted to lead his people into Canada. After marching over 1,300 miles, the Nez Percé were trapped just short of the border in Montana. The battle was brief and the Indians were badly beaten. Rather than fight on to certain destruction, Chief Joseph urged his people to surrender and move to the reservation (which they did). His last speech to his people is one of the most famous in the history of the American Indian. Here is what he said:

> I am tired of fighting. Our chiefs are killed. The old men are all dead. It is cold and we have no blankets. The little children are freezing to death. My people, some of them, have run away to the hills and have no blankets, no food. No one knows where they are—perhaps freezing to death. I want to have time to look for my children and see how many of them I can find. Maybe I shall find them among the dead. Hear me. . . . I am tired. My heart is sick and sad. From where the sun now stands, I will fight no more forever.

1. Why did the army attack the Nez Percé?
2. Was Chief Joseph looking for a fight? Explain your answer.
3. Why did the Nez Percé surrender?
4. Pretend that you are a member of the Nez Percé tribe trapped by the army in Montana. What advice would you give Chief Joseph?

5. Pretend you are one of the American soldiers surrounding the Nez Percé. What advice would you give your commanding officer?

THE PLIGHT OF THE AMERICAN INDIAN   Read the following selection. Basing your answers on this reading, tell whether each of the statements that follow is true or false. If the selection does not give you enough information to answer true or false, write NS.

SALLY LONGBOW'S STORY

Sally Longbow is an American Indian girl. She is one of 70,000 American Indians living in New Mexico. Sally is 17 years old and would like to find work. Last week she went into the city of Albuquerque to try to find a job, but she had no luck. About half of the adults on Sally's reservation are out of work.

The land is dry and crops do not grow well. Water is scarce in the Southwest. The tribe does have some sheep and a few hogs. But there is nothing to do on the reservation. The Indian policeman says that drinking is the reservation's biggest problem. People drink because they have nothing to do and no hope of ever getting anything to do.

Sally lives in a hogan. It is not much more than a one-room house made of mud and logs. There is a school on the reservation, but Sally does not attend. She quit to work in the home of an Anglo family in the city. She liked working for them. They had running water and plenty to eat. Everyone slept in separate rooms, and the house was filled with many things. But the Anglo family moved away, so Sally is back on the reservation. Sally hopes that she will soon be able to get another job in the home of rich Anglos.

1. About 70,000 American Indians live in New Mexico.
2. Sally is lazy and does not want to work.
3. Marijuana use among teenagers is the biggest problem on Sally's reservation.
4. Sally lives in a three-bedroom split-level house.
5. Anglos live in better homes than most American Indians can afford.
6. Sally likes living on the reservation.
7. There are fewer American Indians in the United States today than in 1800.

Chapter 7   Chinese-Americans and Japanese-Americans

The tour bus pulled up in front of the telephone booth with the little pagoda rooftop. As the doors swung open the 24 eager tourists spilled into the street. "Chinatown!" they murmured to each other.

"Isn't it fun," said one. "I mean, it's so Chinese."

"Yes," said another, "look at all those Chinese, and all the restaurants and stores."

Two hours later, on the ride back to the hotel, the tourists could talk of nothing but their visit to Chinatown.

"I never saw so many Chinese in all my life. We have a couple back home—they run a little laundry. They're cheap and they do a nice job on shirts and sheets."

"A few work in Vinnie's restaurant, dear," his wife reminded him.

"Oh, that's right. Funny how they always seem to work in restaurants and laundries."

Several other passengers remembered that the only Chinese they had seen back home were the ones who worked in restaurants and laundries.

"And you know," said one man, "they're such law-abiding people. You never hear of them getting into trouble. But it's funny, isn't it? Why do so many of them work in restaurants and laundries? Why do they all live crowded together in Chinatown? And why do they still speak Chinese—can't they learn English?"

Like blacks, American Indians, Hispanic-Americans, and others who look different from white Americans, Chinese-Americans have suffered from prejudice and discrimination. Their reaction to this prejudice and discrimination explains why so many Chinese live in "Chinatowns," speak Chinese, and work in restaurants and laundries.

Early Chinese Immigration

The first Chinese immigrants to arrive in large numbers came to the United States between the years 1854 and 1883. Like many other people, they came to the United States for three reasons: (1) they could barely earn enough to live on in their homeland; (2) their government was unable to help solve their problems; and (3) they had heard that they could earn a good living in America. Gold had been discovered in California in 1848 and by the 1850s many thousands of Chinese were making the long journey in the hope of striking it rich. Some 70,000 Chinese immigrated to the United States between the years 1854 and 1868.

"BITTER WORK AND SUFFERING"   Beginning in the late 1860s, the need for cheap labor to build the railroads across the Western United States brought thousands more Chinese immigrants to the United States. These men were called "coolies," meaning "unskilled foreign labor," by American workers. The word *coolie* actually comes from the Chinese *ku li*, meaning "bitter work and suffering," which is what the Chinese immigrant endured during those years. In the 15 years between 1868 and 1883, an estimated 200,000 Chinese immigrants came to the United States.

When the Chinese first arrived, some sought to try their luck prospecting for gold. Others tried farming and fishing, and many went to work on the railroads. But the Chinese soon found that the Californians and other Westerners resented them bitterly. Soon the miners got together and forced the Chinese off their claims. There was no use complaining to the law, since few sheriffs or marshals would defend the Chinese against white Americans.

White workers resented the Chinese laborers because they were willing to work longer hours for lower pay than whites received. Employers took advantage of Chinese workers to keep wages down and break strikes. For example, in Massachusetts in 1870, a hundred Chinese railroad workers were brought in by a shoe company to replace the workers who had gone out on strike for higher wages. When the strike ended, all the Chinese were laid off.

Meanwhile, Chinese fishermen and farmers in the West soon found that white Americans resented their competition. Here, too, they were forced to give up their businesses or face death by shooting or lynching. Even in the cities, they feared for their lives. In one terrible incident in 1871 a mob entered the Los Angeles Chinatown and lynched 23 people.

It seemed that the only way the Chinese could make a living was to do the jobs that nobody else wanted or could qualify for. Restaurants and laundries were two areas in which white Americans seemed willing to allow the Chinese to work. Others found jobs as household workers and farm laborers.

THE CHINESE AND CHINATOWNS   With hostility and danger all around them, the Chinese drifted into the cities, where they could at least find jobs. They also found other Chinese whose language and customs they understood. As more and more gathered together, the Chinatown ghettos of San Francisco and New York were created. Similar smaller communities were established wherever numbers of Chinese settled.

The Chinese soon learned that the American government could not be

Chinatown, New York City

Chinese-American family celebrates a birthday

counted on to protect them. Some states had passed laws prohibiting the Chinese from testifying against non-Chinese or even from owning property. By the 1870s some states had passed laws prohibiting the Chinese from becoming citizens. In 1882 Congress passed a law that barred persons of Chinese origin from becoming United States citizens. Chinese immigration slowed down, but about 60,000 more Chinese emigrated here until the mid-1920s. Over 300,000 Chinese people had come to the United States between the years 1854 and 1924. It was not until 1943, during World War II, when China was an ally of the United States, that the Chinese once more were admitted to the United States and were again allowed to become United States citizens.

Here were the Chinese in America. They could work for a living only if the jobs did not offend or endanger the jobs of the rest of the population. The government had one set of laws that applied to the Chinese and another set of laws that applied to the rest of the country. How were the Chinese to survive?

The Chinese survived by creating their own society within America. Chinese tradition had always called for the oldest person to be the head of the family. Families with the same last name—such as Wong, Lee, or Eng—got together to form clans, or family associations. These family associations also got together and formed *benevolent societies*. Each society was made up of people who came from the same region of China. Later the societies combined to form consolidated Chinese benevolent associations across the country. Family associations and benevolent societies performed many of the services that a government would do. They settled problems between members and aided members in need by arranging loans, helping the sick, and providing legal aid. Schools were established to teach Chinese customs and language. The associations also conducted the first census of the Chinese people in America. Perhaps the associations' most important function was to work for the repeal of the anti-Chinese laws of both the states and the federal government.

The Chinese Achievement in America

We have seen that, as compared to the white population, the Chinese have had to work under terrible handicaps in this country. For many years they were not permitted to become citizens. In addition they were denied many other rights that Americans took for granted. As a result they had to live in crowded city slums or ghettos that got to be called "Chinatown." In spite of these many handicaps, however, the Chinese in America have many achievements of which to be proud. Chinese-Americans have won Nobel Prizes in the field of science. Others have been United States senators, architects, artists, and writers. Chinese-Americans have succeeded in the worlds of business and finance and the theater. Chinese-Americans, who number about 450,000 persons at present, have succeeded in just about every field in which Americans of other origins have been successful.

NEW IMMIGRANTS   The Chinese are again immigrating to this country. Most of the newcomers settle in one of the Chinatowns. San Francisco receives the largest number of new arrivals, New York the second largest. On arrival the immigrant will see familiar faces, hear a familiar language, and enjoy some of the foods of the "old country." But while the new immigrant will find many familiar things in the American Chinatown, there is much that is new and strange. As the wall of prejudice and discrimination against the Chinese broke down, so too did the way of life for the Chinese in America. Some moved out of the crowded Chinatown ghettos to the suburbs or to other sections of the cities. Even in the Chinatowns, Western dress and customs are more the rule than the exception. Although family ties are still very strong, more and more parents worry that their children will lose touch with their Chinese heritage.

Many of the problems the new arrivals from China will face are the same as those of past immigrants who were poor. Because most do not speak English and do not know American customs, they will take jobs in factories, stores, and restaurants at very low wages and under poor working conditions. But their children will attend public schools and learn American ways. These ways will seem strange to the parents and may cause problems. Many children will attend Chinese schools in the afternoons and will keep up with the language and history of China. Some, however, may take up with street gangs and adopt their ways.

The problems of the new immigrants are, in many ways, also the problems of the Chinese community, particularly those living in the Chinatowns. Like other people living in overcrowded ghettos of the inner city, they must learn how to deal with teenage gangs, drug traffic, street crime, alcoholism, and prostitution.

In other ways, however, the lot of newly arrived Chinese immigrants is easier than the lot of those who came before. Mobs no longer attack Chinese immigrants. American laws no longer treat Orientals differently from other citizens. Those who want to can leave the Chinatowns for other places to live. Most important, perhaps, is the fact that the prejudices felt by most Americans against Orientals in days gone by seem to be fading away. If this trend continues, we may expect to see more and more Chinese-Americans in all walks of American life.

And that is the way it should be.

Japanese-Americans

Japanese-Americans use a numbering system to describe their generations in this country. *Issei* means "first" in Japanese. So *Issei* is the name of the oldest generation. They were the first Japanese immigrants to leave their homeland for America. The children of these immigrants are the *Nisei* (second), the second generation of Japanese-Americans. And their children—the third generation—are the *Sansei*. The *Yonsei* and *Gosei* are the fourth and fifth generations.

The generation to which the Japanese-American belongs is quite important because the experiences of each generation in this country were so different. Some 20,000 *Issei* came to America in the 1890s. Most of the men took jobs for very little money, as laborers. They found themselves up against the same kind of discrimination that the Chinese had to face. Only the hardest, dirtiest, and lowest-paying jobs were open to the Japanese.

Many *Issei* worked as farmhands. In time, they were able to save enough money to buy farms of their own. The *Issei* were excellent farmers. By the outbreak of World War I, in 1914, they were looked upon as serious competition by the white farmers of the West Coast. Laws were passed in California that made it difficult for the *Issei* to own land. Other laws prevented them from becoming citizens.

How do you make a go of it in a country where you are treated differently from everyone else? One answer was to band together for assistance and protection. The *Issei* maintained many of the traditions of the Japan they remembered. Like the Chinese, they sent their children to both American public schools and to special Japanese schools where they learned about Japanese customs and traditions, and learned to speak Japanese.

The children of the *Issei,* the *Nisei* (second generation), were born in the United States. They were American citizens by birth. Few ever thought that laws could be passed that could discriminate against them. Then in 1941 came the attack by Japan on the American Navy base at Pearl Harbor. Many white Americans, particularly those living on the West Coast, thought that the Japanese-Americans had helped Japan to carry out the raid.

Demands that "something be done" about the *Issei* and *Nisei* led President Franklin D. Roosevelt to issue an order giving the military commander of the Western United States the power to remove anyone he thought a threat to the safety of the United States. The "anyone" were Japanese-Americans. Soon 110,000 men, women, and children were forced to give up their homes and businesses and move to what were called "relocation centers." Others called them concentration camps. Ten camps in seven Western states were soon in operation. (Although the United States was also at war with Italy and Germany, no one suggested that all Americans of German or Italian parentage be placed in relocation centers.)

What was the effect of camp life on the American-born *Nisei?* Perhaps the most dramatic result was their reaction. Rather than becoming bitter over the loss of their rights as citizens, many *Nisei* felt they had to prove they were at least as loyal as other Americans. Many of the young men enlisted in a special all-*Nisei* unit of the Army: the 442nd Regimental Combat Team. After several years of fighting in Italy and France, the

442nd had won more medals than any other unit. By the time the war ended, it was generally agreed that the 442nd was the best unit in the entire Army.

Camp life had another effect upon the *Nisei*. Because their families had been forced to give up their businesses and farms before moving into the camps, many of the *Nisei* were free to "do their own thing" once the war ended. Camp life also made it clear to many *Nisei* that they were judged by many white Americans by the color of their skin rather than their ability. They were victims of white racism.

The *Nisei* had been taught by their parents to take difficult times without complaining, that hard work and intelligence would solve their problems. When the war ended Japanese-Americans left their camps to return to normal life. They had lost their property and therefore had to find new ways to make a living. In this they have been very successful. The 600,000 Japanese-Americans in the United States today have completed more years of schooling on average than most other minority groups. They also earn higher salaries than the average for America.

Japanese-Americans are model citizens in many other ways too. Their crime and divorce rates are among the lowest in the nation. Many distinguished people in politics, the arts, sciences, and education are of Japanese ancestry.

Today the children of the *Nisei*, the *Sansei* (third generation), have come of age. Some have already given birth to the *Yonsei* (fourth generation). In time they too will bring forth a new generation who will be called the *Gosei* (fifth generation). Each of these generations will be different from the one before it.

EXERCISES

MULTIPLE-CHOICE QUESTIONS   For each item, write the letter of the best answer.

1. Chinese and Japanese immigrants originally came to the United States because (*a*) they wanted to escape the poverty and overcrowding of their native lands (*b*) they wanted to open restaurants (*c*) the American government invited them here (*d*) their relatives in the United States wrote about the wonderful conditions here.

2. In Chinese the word *coolie* means (*a*) someone who works in a cool

climate (*b*) a laborer (*c*) someone who works for low wages (*d*) bitter work and suffering.

3. The Chinese lived in ghettos called Chinatowns because (*a*) the government built special housing projects for the Chinese in the Chinatowns (*b*) rents there were cheap (*c*) they wanted to open gift shops and sell goods to tourists (*d*) they had to protect themselves and help each other.

4. Chinese people with the same family name or who came from the same part of China got together and formed clans or (*a*) block associations (*b*) railroad companies (*c*) family associations (*d*) food cooperatives.

5. Among the important things that clans or family associations did were all of the following *except* (*a*) provide financial and legal aid (*b*) educate young people in Chinese customs and history (*c*) fight for repeal of anti-Chinese laws (*d*) restrict the number of Chinese immigrants.

6. Approximately how many Chinese immigrants came to the United States between the years 1854 and 1924? (*a*) 20,000 (*b*) 300,000 (*c*) 5 million (*d*) 100,000

PROBLEMS OF NEW IMMIGRANTS The following article appeared recently in a leading newspaper. Read the article and answer the questions that follow:

GANG FIGHT INJURES FIVE

Five persons were injured in yesterday's gang fight that took place on the streets of Chinatown. Three of the victims, two of whom were children, were innocent bystanders. As a result many people now ask, "What has happened to that once peaceful section of town?"

In answer to the question, we learned the following facts:

1. Since 1965, the population of Chinatown has tripled—from about 20,000 to more than 60,000. Before 1965, only 102 Chinese people were allowed to immigrate to the United States each year, but today 15,000 per year are allowed to enter.

2. Many of the adults who are recent immigrants work six and seven days a week.

3. Many of the children of recent immigrants drop out of school. One community worker put it this way: "They may be good in math and science, but because they speak little or no English they are put in

grades lower than they were in at home. They feel looked down upon by the American-born Chinese, so they drop out of school."

4. The youth who does not join a gang is frequently picked on by gang members, and he may join a rival gang for revenge.

5. Adult criminals in the community use teenage gangs to operate several kinds of illegal activities, such as gambling and drug pushing.

1. In recent years, what has happened to the population of the city's Chinatown?

2. How do you account for this change?

3. The normal workweek in this country is five days. Why do you think many recent Chinese immigrants work six and seven days a week?

4. What would the long workweek have to do with the rise in teenage gang membership?

5. Why do many children of recent Chinese immigrants drop out of school?

6. List and explain three reasons why youngsters in Chinatown may have to join gangs.

7. What could be done to break the power of gangs in the Chinese-American communities?

TRUE OR FALSE?   Based on your reading of the text, tell whether the following statements are true or false:

1. Japanese immigrants in the 1890s had an easy time finding good jobs.

2. The first generation of Japanese-Americans are called the *Issei*.

3. The *Issei* and the *Nisei* were accused of aiding in the attack on Pearl Harbor.

4. When they were placed in relocation centers during World War II, the *Issei* and the *Nisei* were victims of white racism.

5. *Nisei* men fought for their country in World War II.

6. When the war was over, *Nisei* men went to work in their parents' businesses.

7. Since 1945, Japanese-Americans have achieved a higher level of education than other minority groups.

Unit VII Criminal Justice

Chapter 1 The Rising Tide of Crime

The woman lived in one of the cheap hotels in the city's downtown section. Much of her day was spent watching television in the hotel lobby. For exercise she walked the few blocks to a nearby cafeteria where she ate most of her meals. Then it happened. On the way home early one evening, she was mugged. She was knocked down from behind and her purse was snatched while she lay bleeding on the sidewalk.

From that time on, she stayed in the hotel. For a while she continued to watch television in the lobby, but she seemed to quiver with fright when a new person walked into the room. After a while she stopped coming to the lobby. When friends tried to visit her in her room, she asked them to go away. She was afraid that muggers might slip in with them if she opened the door.

Several weeks later it was noticed that no one had seen or heard of her for a long time. The manager let himself into the room and discovered her body on the sofa. She had been dead for a week. The police doctor said that the woman had died of a bleeding ulcer brought on by worry and hunger. But her friends knew that she had really died of fear.

Fear of Crime

Fear of crime stalks the streets of most American cities these days. Stores in some sections close before dark. Bus riders in many cities must carry the exact change. The bus drivers carry no money in order to prevent robbery. Some people carry second wallets with a small amount of money to offer the thief when he strikes. Some parents give their children "mugging money" before they go to school, for the same reason. Others walk near the curbs, away from dark doorways. Some keep large dogs so as to frighten away burglars. Others go to karate schools to learn self-defense, carry whistles or even weapons—all out of the fear of crime.

Schools have also been hit by the epidemic of crime. Millions of dollars

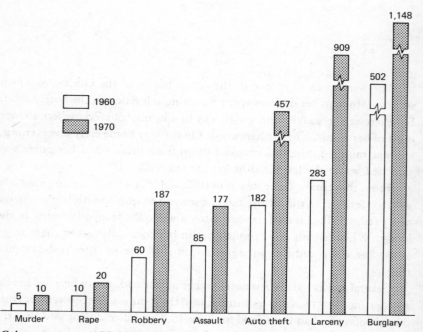

Crime rates, per 100,000 persons, 1960 and 1970. Which two serious crimes showed the largest increases?

are spent to pay for school security guards, student ID cards, and security devices.

It is not surprising that Americans seem to fear crime more these days than in the past—crime has been on the increase. According to the FBI, 1,300,000 serious crimes were committed in the United States in 1955. In 1972 this number had risen to 5,800,000, an increase of over 400 percent. (As "serious crimes" the FBI listed violent crimes, such as murder, rape, robbery, aggravated assault, and serious crimes, such as burglary, larceny over $50, and auto theft.)

You might expect the total number of crimes to increase along with the United States population. That is, if there are more people, there will be more crime. As a matter of fact, the American population has been increasing. From 1960 to 1970 it grew by 13 percent. But in that same period serious crime increased by 144 percent. In other words crime increased over 11 times as fast as the population.

CRIME RATE   When we read about crime, we often see the term *crime rate*. The crime rate tells how often a *crime* (an illegal or unlawful act) was committed. Usually, this rate is expressed by the number of crimes committed for every 100,000 people in the country. The illustration shows, for example, that in 1970 the crime rate for murder in large American cities was 10. This means that, on the average, 10 people out of every 100,000 in large cities were murdered. Using this figure, you should be able to calculate how many people were likely to have been murdered in a city of 2 million persons in 1970.

Many people take comfort in the belief that crimes are committed by a handful of professional criminals. But this belief is incorrect. A recent study found that one boy out of every six is sent to a juvenile court. And, at the present crime rate, 40 percent of all the men now living in the United States will be arrested for nontraffic offenses at some time during their lives.

Why is there so much crime in America? Why has the crime rate increased so rapidly in just a short time? Some people say the answer is in part that the average American can buy a gun almost as easily as he or she can buy a television set. The people who are tempted to commit murder or armed robbery find very little in their way when they look for the means to perform these acts.

Is Gun Control Needed?

Has America become an armed camp? Senator Edward Kennedy, a leading gun-control spokesman, estimates that Americans today own between 100 million and 120 million guns. These guns do not sit in drawers or closets either. Someone in the United States is killed or wounded by gunfire every four minutes. A person is robbed at gunpoint every three minutes. A new handgun will be sold in the time that it took you to read this sentence. Within the time span of just one minute, two used handguns will be traded.

Would strict gun-control laws stop violent crime in America? Hardly anyone thinks so. But a proposed federal gun-control law would make it more difficult to buy cheap small guns, the so-called "Saturday-night specials." This law would require dealers to register the buyer's name, height, weight, race, address, age, and place of birth. This gun registration would, it is said, help law enforcement officials to trace the owners of guns that are used in criminal acts.

The National Rifle Association (NRA) is the leading group against strict gun control. Most NRA members use guns for target shooting and hunting. The NRA's main argument against new gun laws is that most crime in America is the work of a small group of professional criminals and drug addicts. The NRA asks, "Do you believe these thugs will go away when you and I give up our guns?" Gun-control laws will not stop criminals from buying guns. The law will punish both law-abiding citizens, who need guns for protection against criminals, and sportsmen who use shotguns and rifles in target practice and hunting. The NRA insists that the way to reduce crime in America is not by strong gun-control laws but by tougher enforcement of existing laws.

Those in favor of strict gun-control laws point out that guns result in 3,000 accidental deaths each year. Over one-half of those killed in gun accidents are under 19 years of age. There are over 7,000 gun suicides and 10,000 gun murders each year. But what is even more interesting is that most of the victims knew their killers. Most murders are not committed by professional criminals. It is usually the "law-abiding citizen"—a father or mother, husband or wife, sister or brother, boy friend, or girl friend—who is the killer. If guns were not so easy to buy, would crimes of passion and rage or insanity still be committed by other means? Most authorities agree that murders of this sort would still take place, *but to a much lesser degree than is possible when guns are so easy to get.*

More people die in automobile accidents than in gun accidents. If guns are prohibited, should cars be prohibited too? No. The purpose of a gun is to shoot and perhaps to kill something or someone. The purpose of an automobile is to move people from one place to another. Even though cars are dangerous, it does not follow that we must restrict the sale of automobiles (which, by the way, *are* registered and controlled) just because the sale of guns is restricted.

Finally, the Second Amendment to the Constitution guarantees "the right of the people to keep and bear Arms." Some people say this gives them the right to own a gun. But the amendment refers only to "bearing arms" and the "militia" (National Guard). This means that citizens were allowed to keep guns in order to use them to defend the country in time of war. How many gun owners need a gun for this purpose today? Federal courts have permitted the states and the federal government to restrict and control the use of firearms by civilians.

A partial list of famous Americans who were *assassinated* (murdered) includes four Presidents—Lincoln, Garfield, McKinley, and Kennedy —and such noted figures as Robert Kennedy, Dr. Martin Luther King, Jr., and Malcolm X. Might things have been different if we had had strict gun-control laws in those days? What do you think?

Criminal Justice in America

Three *agencies* (government organizations) deal with crime: the police, the courts, and the corrections system. The police patrol the streets and engage in a number of other activities in order to prevent crime. They also arrest persons whom they suspect of having committed crimes, and take other steps to enforce the law. The law courts *try* (bring to trial) persons accused of having committed crimes. The courts pass *sentence* on those who are *convicted* (found guilty) of crimes. The corrections system receives the persons convicted by the courts. This system operates the *prisons* to which some offenders are sent. It also conducts other programs designed to return convicted persons to society.

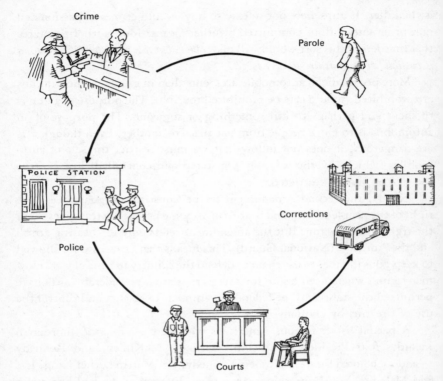

Crime

Parole

POLICE STATION

Corrections

POLICE

Police

Courts

Criminal justice system in America

The American system of criminal justice is no system at all, according to its critics. That is, the three branches—police, courts, and corrections—do not work closely with one another toward a common goal. As a result we have a poor record in dealing with crime. Consider the results:

1. Over one-half of all the crimes committed are never reported to the police.
2. Of those crimes that are reported, fewer than one-quarter lead to an arrest.
3. One-half the people who are arrested are released because the charges are dropped.
4. Almost everyone sentenced to prison is eventually released. Nearly

two-thirds of those released from prison are arrested and convicted again.

PROBLEMS OF THE SYSTEM The police declare that they work very hard to solve crimes. The work is difficult, frequently unpleasant, and sometimes very dangerous. Policemen are upset when known wrongdoers return to society on bail or because the charges against them were reduced to something less serious. On the other hand there are those who accuse the police of being corrupted by the crime they are supposed to fight. Others say that the police do not care enough to go after criminals, and that they are sometimes prejudiced against the people of the communities in which they work.

Judges complain that charges against defendants are not properly prepared, witnesses fail to show up, and cases are poorly presented. The courts, on the other hand, have been criticized for taking much too long on each case. Some people have charged judges with being so lenient that serious offenders are back on the street within hours.

Corrections officers complain about the difficulties of helping ex-convicts lead normal lives. People on parole are frequently harassed by the police. Ex-convicts find it hard to get jobs. They are forbidden by law to hold many kinds of jobs. On the other hand, jails are overcrowded. Prison guards are accused of abusing prisoners. People sometimes remain in jail for months awaiting trial. It is also charged that conditions in prisons are even worse than they have to be because of the failure of prison officials to perform their jobs properly.

There is no unified "system" of criminal justice in which police, courts, and corrections work with one another. Instead, the police blame the courts for the crime waves, and the courts blame the police. No one seems happy with the work of the corrections system.

Reducing the Crime Rate

How can the rising tide of crime be stopped? Consider these cases:

The victim lay bleeding on the sidewalk. All that the passers-by had to see was the slashed pocket that once held his wallet. They knew immediately that he had been mugged. An enraged citizen said, "Why can't the police do something about those muggers?"

"Look at this story in the paper, Diane. They caught those guys who held up Charley's liquor store last Saturday."

"That's good. I hope the police lock them up and throw away the key."

"Bless you. Wow! That's about your 94th sneeze—you have some cold."

"Yes, I know. I caught it from Nancy Baker. She sat behind me in math class yesterday and sneezed the whole time."

"What! She gave you her cold by sneezing in public? Hand me the phone. I'm going to call the police. Hello, operator? Give me the police. I want to report a person walking around in public with a cold."

This last little scene may seem ridiculous. That is, you would expect the mugging and the holdup to be criminal matters—but the common cold, or any other disease! It is a fact, however, that although sneezing caused by a common cold is not "against the law," certain behavior caused by other illnesses is. For example, the alcoholic who reels around drunk in public can be put in jail just for being drunk. Yet we know that alcoholism is a disease. The drug addict found with a supply of heroin in his pockets can be put in jail for his "crime." Yet drug addiction also is a disease.

Critics of our system of criminal justice say that it is a mistake to label as crimes those activities or actions in which there is no victim. It is true that the alcoholic and the drug addict are harming themselves—but should that be a police matter?

The bookie who handles bets and the prostitute and her customer can now be put in jail for their activities, even though no one is physically harmed by their acts. The same is true of the derelict who spends the night on a park bench or the person who uses foul and abusive language in public.

"CRIMES WITHOUT VICTIMS" What has happened, according to some critics, is that too many things are against the law. As a result the police and the courts cannot possibly handle all the so-called crimes that are committed. What is suggested, therefore, is that the so-called "crimes without victims" be taken out of the hands of the police. Rather than arresting and imprisoning drug addicts, who harm only themselves, it would be better to send these people to medical facilities for treatment. As for morals and nuisance laws, critics say that these too interfere with the most important police activity: the protection of people and their property. What is the sense, they argue, of making it legal to bet on a horserace at a track while making it a crime to bet on numbers at home? If betting at a racetrack is legal, why should betting at home be illegal?

Pornography refers to writings or pictures that are intended to arouse sexual feelings. The courts have held that it is legal to own and read pornographic books. But in many places it is against the law to sell them. What is the logic of making it illegal to sell something if it is legal to own it?

Those in favor of reducing the number of acts that are a crime say it will do the following:

1. Increase respect for law and order. Everyone applauds the police when they arrest a thief or a robber. But not everyone applauds when the police arrest a bookie or a vagrant. The feeling is that certain laws are disobeyed by so many people as to make the laws unenforceable. Such laws only create disrespect for all laws. By removing these laws from the books, it is felt, the public will have greater respect for law and order.

2. Reduce the power of organized crime. The Mafia and other organized crime syndicates make the largest part of their income by providing the public with illegal goods and services. Legalizing these services, such as numbers and bookmaking, will either put organized crime syndicates out of business or make what they are doing no longer criminal.

3. By taking away from the police the responsibility for public morals and other "crimes without victims," the police, the courts, and the corrections system will have more time to devote to protecting the public against serious crime.

Summary Crime in America is a serious problem. The number of reported crimes increased dramatically in a decade. Four out of every five crimes committed are not reported. The arrest of large numbers of people for victimless crimes—drug addiction, prostitution, and illegal gambling—prevents the corrections system from fighting serious crime as effectively as it should.

Looking Ahead In the next three chapters, we shall look at the work of the three parts of the criminal justice system and the problems faced by each. In the following chapter, we shall study the police.

EXERCISES

MATCHING QUESTIONS Match each term in Column A with its definition in Column B.

Column A

1. mugged
2. karate
3. crime
4. serious crimes
5. crime rate
6. pornography
7. agency

Column B

(a) method of self-defense
(b) any kind of written or photographed material that is intended to arouse sexual feelings
(c) attacked and robbed from behind in the streets
(d) government organization
(e) examples are murder, rape, robbery, larceny, assault
(f) number of crimes committed for every 100,000 people
(g) an illegal or unlawful act

MULTIPLE-CHOICE QUESTIONS For each question, write the letter of the best answer.

1. The main idea of this chapter is that (a) there are crimes without victims (b) the sale of guns should be forbidden (c) police work is dangerous (d) crime is a serious problem in America today.

2. An example of a *crime without a victim* is (a) robbery (b) mugging (c) gambling (d) murder.

3. Which statement is an opinion rather than a fact? (a) Most crimes are committed in the cities. (b) Policemen patrol the streets to prevent crime. (c) Conduct in which there is no victim should not be a crime. (d) Crime in America has been on the increase.

4. Alcoholism is similar to drug addiction because each is (a) immoral (b) a serious crime (c) a disease (d) harmful to others.

5. Bus riders in many cities must carry the exact change. The main reason is that (*a*) drivers refuse to make change (*b*) making change wastes time (*c*) drivers are not allowed to carry money (*d*) robbers are discouraged when the drivers carry no money.

6. The job of the police is to (*a*) arrest persons suspected of crimes (*b*) hold trials of persons accused of crimes (*c*) run the prisons to which convicted criminals are sent (*d*) sentence persons found guilty of crimes.

7. According to the chapter, the American system of criminal justice is (*a*) excellent (*b*) no system at all (*c*) approved of by most experts (*d*) the best we can do.

8. According to the chapter, reducing the number of acts that are considered crimes will (*a*) reduce respect for the law (*b*) increase the power of organized crime (*c*) increase other kinds of crime (*d*) allow more time to protect the public against serious crime.

WRITE AN EDITORIAL Imagine that you are the editor of a big-city newspaper. You want to write an editorial on crime in America. Four ideas about how to deal with crime in America are listed below. Select *one* as the opening of your editorial. Write a 100-word editorial explaining your point of view.

1. "The solution to the problem of crime is to find jobs for the poor and the unemployed."

2. "Fighting crime is the responsibility of each citizen."

3. "The idea that all criminals are sick, poor, or members of minority groups is false."

4. "Strong gun-control laws are needed to halt the thousands of senseless killings that occur in this country every year."

Chapter 2   The Police

Tom and Joe were on the 4 P.M.-to-midnight shift on a pleasant fall day. The first call they received in their squad car came at 5:05. "Woman in need of assistance, corner of Myrtle and Kirwick Streets" was all the radio said. It was rush hour and the streets were jammed, but their car was able to weave through traffic and arrive on the scene by 5:08. An elderly woman stood gazing up into a tree. When she saw Tom and Joe, she rushed over to them.

"Oh, officers, I'm so glad you're here! The big red dog that's always walking around this neighborhood scared Eloise so much she ran up a tree. And now she won't come down."

"All right, Joe," Tom said, "let's climb the tree and get the cat out of there."

The next call came at 7:15. "Holdup at candy store on Main and Woods Lane—may still be in progress." With siren screaming, the two officers arrived on the scene in short order. Guns drawn, they rushed into the shop only to find the clerk in tears and the cash register empty. They got a statement from the clerk in order to prepare the report they would have to file later that evening. As they were leaving, they heard the clerk on the phone talking to her mother. "You know the cops," they heard her say. "They're never here when you need them."

At 9:23 the call came over the radio to go to the fourth floor apartment at 12th and Ridge Streets to help settle a family argument. They could hear the screams and yells from the street when they arrived. When the apartment door was opened, the wife stood there with a knife in her hand. The husband held a hammer. Furniture lay broken and scattered all over the apartment.

"What do you want?" asked the woman.

"Who sent for you?" asked the man.

"We had a report of a loud family fight," replied Joe. "Some of your neighbors must have thought you were killing each other."

"Can't a husband and wife have a discussion without having the cops sticking their two cents in?" said the man.

"Yes," agreed his wife, "instead of wasting the taxpayers' money by interrupting family life, why don't you go lock up some of those bums who mug people and rob stores?"

"Isn't it amazing," asked Tom later, "how two people who were at each other's throats a minute ago are willing to bury the hatchet the minute we show up?"

Joe agreed. "What bothers me, though, is that they seem to want to bury the hatchet in our backs."

"Hold it, Joe, there's another call coming over. . . ."

It was 10:15. They were told to go to the aid of a man who had had a heart attack. They arrived on the scene 15 minutes before the ambulance. Tom put a blanket over the victim. Joe administered oxygen from a tank in the car. When the ambulance left, Tom and Joe took their coffee break. There was about an hour left before their shift would come to an end.

The Job of the Police

What do you think of when you hear the word "policeman"? Do you think of a big, good-natured man in uniform who helps kids cross the street and rescues kittens from treetops? Or do you think of a mean guy who is never there when you need him, who always seems to cause trouble for you and your friends? Ask ten people this question and you are likely to get ten different answers. The reason for these mixed, and often violent, emotions about the police is not hard to find. Of the agencies involved in the criminal justice system—police, courts, and corrections—the police have the most difficult job to perform.

Why is the policeman's job so difficult? For one thing the police usually arrive on the scene at a time when feelings are running high. People may be excited, frightened, embarrassed, or even violent. They are liable to say or

Two views of the job of the police: (*left*) Listening to a motorist's story (*right*) Attempting to prevent violent behavior during a demonstration against busing

do anything. The police have to size up the situation in a hurry and do something about it. There is no time for an investigation, and they cannot tell people to go away and come back after things have cooled down. The police have to act on the spot. Many times whatever they do will make somebody angry. How do you handle a situation in which a husband and wife are threatening each other's lives?

Many times the police have to help people who need help whether they know it or not. The drunk who is sleeping on a park bench in the snow and tourists wandering in search of "a good time" at night in a dangerous neighborhood often do not welcome the police help they need. Sometimes the police have to break up a lawful situation simply because it *might* lead to trouble. A man making a speech in the middle of a hostile crowd could cause a riot. A man who announces that he can "lick any man in the house," a bunch of teenagers hanging around on a corner at midnight—these are two more examples of lawful situations that could be dangerous. All these incidents call for police action to avoid a "breach of the peace" (public disturbance) or a crime. Here again, once the action is taken, it is likely that someone will be unhappy about it.

Limits on Police Powers

Another reason why the policeman's job is so difficult is that the police no longer have unlimited powers to prevent crime. Years ago most police forces in this country used the *third degree* (force or torture) to get information from suspects. Today, the third degree is illegal. (While the third degree may have helped the police to obtain some of the information they needed to solve crimes, there are very few people in the United States who would like to see it made legal.) Other laws limit the policeman's power to arrest suspects. Before he can do this, there has to be "probable cause" for such an arrest. The police power to stop, search, and question suspects about a crime has been restricted. At one time it was possible to round up everybody near where a crime had been committed, put them in a wagon, and take them to the station for questioning. Today this is no longer legal. The United States Supreme Court has limited the authority of the police to stop suspects for questioning. Indeed, in most communities, before the police question anyone, they are required to read aloud to the suspect something like this:

> You have the right to remain silent and refuse to answer questions. Do you understand?
> Anything you say may be used against you in a court of law. Do you understand?
> You have the right to consult an attorney before speaking to the police and to have an attorney present during any questioning now or in the future. Do you understand?
> If you cannot afford an attorney, one will be provided for you without cost. Do you understand?
> If you do not have an attorney available, you have the right to remain silent until you have had an opportunity to consult with one. Do you understand?
> Now that I have advised you of your rights, are you willing to answer questions without an attorney present? Do you understand?

Distrust of the Police

Still another problem that makes the job of the police very difficult is that in the ghetto or slum, where the crime rate is the highest, many people fear and distrust the police. As a result, much crime goes unreported. In addition, many people refuse to cooperate with the police in their investigations.

Nonwhites—blacks, Indians, and Hispanic-Americans—seem to trust the police least. Yet these are the same people who suffer most from crime and are most in need of police protection. These are also the same people who have suffered most from discrimination and poverty. They are the people most likely to question the "American way" and to resent government authority. It is also true that some policemen do behave badly toward members of minorities, particularly minorities living in ghettos. Even though these policemen do not represent the majority of policemen, their actions hurt the police image.

MORE POLICE NEEDED   Still another problem faced by the police is that there are simply not enough of them to handle the rising tide of crime. Although in some cities the ratio of police to citizens is more than four for every thousand citizens, in other cities it is less than one for every thousand. All the evidence seems to indicate that the higher the ratio of police to citizens, the lower the crime rate.

Improving Police Services

GUIDELINES FOR POLICE WORK   Most policemen are taught how to take a suspect into custody, deal with sick and injured persons, fill out reports, dress wounds, handle guns, and what to do about abandoned cars and lost dogs. These and many other responsibilities make up the day-to-day routine of the police officer. Training does not cover, however, some of the hardest and most common police duties.

The family dispute, the public drunk, the midnight gathering of teenagers, the public speaker in the middle of a hostile crowd—each is a special problem. Should the police officer "break it up"? Should he ignore it? Should he make an arrest? These are difficult situations that have to be handled differently at different times. The midnight gathering of teenagers may be nothing more than a conference about the next day's football game. On the other hand the gathering might be followed by stoning the school's windows or passing around dangerous drugs.

Most authorities on crime today recommend that the police departments provide their members with instruction and training in the handling of these situations. This training would instruct the police when to make an arrest and when not to, when to intervene in a family dispute and how to do it, how to protect public speakers, and when to break up public gatherings. In this way, it is hoped, policemen will not feel they are out on a limb when they make their decisions.

THE POWER TO "STOP AND FRISK"   The police have often complained that laws protecting people's Constitutional rights hinder them in their pursuit of criminals. For example, the police are not permitted to tap the telephone of a suspected criminal without a court order. They cannot stop and search every fifth person for illegal drugs. If they had these powers, the chances are that there would be less crime. The problem, however, is that we would also have much less personal freedom. After all, do you want to live in a country where the police can stop and search you whenever they choose? On the other hand, when a crime has been committed, most people would agree that the police should have the right to stop and search suspicious-looking people. In order to help the police in these situations, it has been recommended that the states pass laws to permit them to "stop persons for brief questioning" under certain circumstances, and to search them for weapons or other illegal goods, such as narcotics.

POLICE-COMMUNITY RELATIONS   Relations between the police and minorities in the ghetto have to be improved. One commission created by President Lyndon Johnson suggested there should be a citizens' advisory committee in every community. The committee should meet regularly with police officials to solve problems that arise between the police and the community. The police departments of many communities have followed this advice.

MORE POLICE PROTECTION   As we have pointed out, some communities simply do not have enough policemen to provide adequate protection. The solution is obvious: Hire more policemen. But communities also get greater protection from the police force they already have if they find ways to relieve the police force of chores that can be performed by other people. Recently, for example, San Francisco and New York City turned over to civilians the job of directing midtown traffic. Since they do not need as much training as regular policemen, and the duties they perform are much simpler, the civilians are paid less than regular policemen. Meanwhile, the police can spend more time fighting crime. Police departments throughout the country are trying to find other ways in which to free their forces from tasks that civilians can perform.

INDIVIDUAL EFFORT   But perhaps the most important ingredient in the police effort to fight crime is the quality of the individual patrolman. This is how a black police officer answered when he was asked why he had become a policeman:

> Man, when I was a little kid, I thought cops were God. I lived in the ghetto and I saw drunks, addicts, cuttings, shooting, husbands hitting wives, and kids fighting on street corners and other bad scenes every day. . . . Somebody always called the police. The police arrived in the middle of the hassle and were always cool and always got on top of the problem fast. If they could break it up by quiet mouthing, they would. If they had to bust somebody, they did it quickly and were gone. Whatever it was, they arrived on the scene, got with it fast, stopped the trouble, and split —always with a cool head. I figured that was smooth, and so I decided when I was a kid I wanted to be a policeman and do the same thing.

The speaker put his finger on two of the traits needed by all good policemen: understanding and cool-headedness. These can go a long way toward solving the problems of the police.

Summary The police have a difficult, often dangerous, job to do. Often they are distrusted by the general population, especially by members of minority groups who live in high-crime areas. There are not enough police to handle the rising tide of crime. Several solutions to these problems have been offered, but the quality of each police officer is perhaps the best answer to these problems.

Looking Ahead In the next chapter, we shall see how the courts attempt to deal with crime.

EXERCISES

MULTIPLE-CHOICE QUESTIONS For each question, write the letter of the best answer.

1. The main idea of this chapter is that the police (*a*) are corrupt (*b*) have

many difficult tasks (*c*) make too many arrests (*d*) are unfair to minority groups.

2. A suspect stopped by a policeman has all of the following rights *except* to (*a*) resist arrest (*b*) remain silent (*c*) consult an attorney (*d*) refuse to answer questions.

3. It is *not* part of a policeman's normal duties to (*a*) arrest a thief (*b*) stop a family argument (*c*) help a sick person (*d*) sentence people to jail terms.

4. In which community are fear and distrust of the police most likely to be greatest? (*a*) a middle-class suburb (*b*) a ghetto (*c*) a small rural town (*d*) a wealthy city neighborhood

5. According to the chapter, the most important ingredient in the effort to fight crime is the (*a*) number of policemen on duty (*b*) ability of each patrolman (*c*) number of weapons a policeman has (*d*) right of the police to stop and search suspects.

6. Which of the following statements would be the most difficult to prove either true or false? (*a*) The police arrive at a scene when feelings are high. (*b*) The police often have to aid people who do not want to be helped. (*c*) The police sometimes have to break up lawful situations that might lead to trouble. (*d*) Upholding the rights of suspects forces the police to allow wrongdoers to escape punishment.

FURTHER READING The following selection was taken from the book *Dark Ghetto,* by Kenneth Clark. Read the selection carefully. Basing your answers on this selection, tell whether the statements that follow are true or false. If the selection does not give you enough information to determine whether the statement is true or false, write NS.

Last night . . . the officer stopped some fellows on 125th Street. . . . The officer said, "All right, everybody get off the street or inside!" Now, it's very hot. We don't have air-conditioned apartments in most of these houses up here, so where are we going if we get off the streets? We can't go back in the house, because we almost suffocate. So we sit down on the curb or stand on the sidewalk, or on the steps, things like that . . . especially in the summer when it's too hot to go up. Now where were we going? But he came out with his nightstick and wants to beat people over the head, and wanted to—he arrested one fellow. The other fellow said, "Well, I'll move, but you don't have to talk to me like a dog."

1. The speaker lives in an area of the city called a ghetto.
2. One of the people on the street was arrested.
3. In the speaker's neighborhood, it is better to stay indoors during the hot summer months than to stay outdoors.
4. The policeman acted wisely in this situation.
5. The speaker believes that policemen treat ghetto residents fairly.
6. Better housing is one solution to the problem shown by the story.

Chapter 3　The Courts

A hush fell over the courtroom. The brilliant young defense attorney, Mason Barry, approached the prosecution's key witness. "Mr. Jones," Barry said, "you have testified that you saw my client shoot the deceased with a pearl-handled revolver. Is that correct?"

"Absolutely," said the witness. "I saw the whole thing."

"Here is the revolver," said Mr. Barry, displaying the weapon to the jury. "Please hold it as if you were going to use it." The witness took the small pistol in his hand.

"Ladies and gentlemen of the jury," said the attorney, "I ask you to observe that the handle of the gun is completely covered by the witness's hand. There is no way anyone could tell it was *pearl*-handled, as he has testified. No way at all . . . unless, of course, *it was he who fired the weapon!*"

Everyone gasped. The witness for the prosecution was the real murderer! In a few minutes he had confessed the whole thing. The accused was released. Justice triumphed again, and the commercial marked the end of another television courtroom drama.

If you watch a lot of courtroom dramas on television, you may think that this kind of scene goes on in real life. That is, that criminals are convicted only after long and exciting trials in open courtrooms. Actually, justice usually takes the following form:

The scene is a restaurant two blocks from the courthouse in a busy city. Two men waiting to pay their checks recognize each other. One is Albert

Jones, an assistant district attorney, who spends most of his time working on criminal cases. The other is George Tintner, a criminal lawyer.

> JONES: Hi, George. Funny I should bump into you today. I'm handling the case against your client Louis Green.
> TINTNER: Hey, that's a coincidence. Maybe we can settle the case right here. Al, you've got Green charged with armed robbery—you know that won't stick. There aren't any witnesses and you don't have the gun.
> JONES: I know—he probably threw it away. Look, you know we're terribly busy now. I just don't have the time to go after the evidence I need on this guy. Let him plead guilty to shoplifting and we'll call it square.
> TINTNER: O.K., Al, it's a deal. I'll see you in court in about an hour.

What Al and George worked out is far more typical of American justice than the television scene we described at the beginning of the chapter. The reason is simply that too many cases are being brought into the courts of most of our large cities. As a result most persons charged with crimes never go to trial. Indeed, in some crowded areas as many as 80 percent to 90 percent of the people arrested never get a trial. What happens is that *prosecutors* (people responsible for pressing charges against persons accused of committing crimes) and defense attorneys do what Al and George did. They work out deals. This process is known as *plea bargaining.* It allows persons accused of a serious crime to plead guilty to a less serious one. In that way sentences can be handed down without going through a costly and time-consuming trial. Plea bargaining is a result of one of the major problems facing America's courts: overcrowding. There are more cases coming before the courts than they can handle.

The courts have other problems. Before we come to these problems, let us briefly describe how courts function.

The Court System

One of the difficulties about describing America's court system is that there are really 51 court systems. Each of the 50 states has both its own laws and the courts to enforce them. In addition the federal government has its own laws and its own court system to help carry them out. Only the United States Supreme Court deals with all 51 court systems.

Each of the court systems is organized like a pyramid. At the bottom are the many *trial* courts. Above them are a handful of *appeals courts* (the number varies in each system). At the top is the highest court in the state. These high courts go by a variety of names. Many states call them *supreme courts*. In New York State, however, the supreme court is lower than the court of appeals.

Criminal cases (as well as noncriminal cases) first go to the trial courts. If either side does not like the *verdict* (decision), the case can be taken to an appeals court. In small states, all appeals are handled by the highest court in the state. In large states there is usually a court that stands between the trial courts and the highest court. This "middle" court's verdicts may be *appealed to* (brought before) the highest court. The highest state court has the last

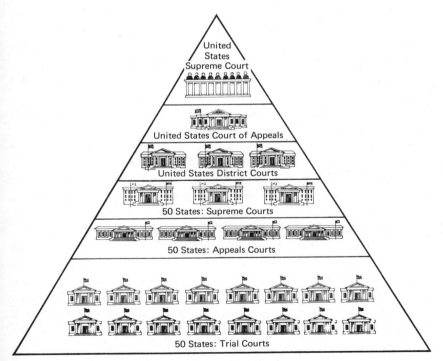

Court system in America

word on violations of the state's laws. In rare cases, when there is a question of federal law, it is possible that the state court's decision may be appealed to the United States Supreme Court.

The federal court system handles cases in which federal laws may have been broken. The lowest-level federal court is called the district court. Decisions of a district court may be appealed to the court of appeals. Verdicts of the court of appeals may be appealed to the United States Supreme Court.

Most cases are handled by state courts. That explains why there are 8,000 state court judges but only 400 federal court judges.

Court Procedures

The rights of people charged with crimes are protected by the Bill of Rights and by state laws. These rights are referred to as *due process.* This term means that a defendant must be formally notified as to the charges against him. There are still countries in the world in which this is not followed, and people have been thrown into prison without knowing why.

Due process also means that a number of other things must happen in a criminal trial. The accused has the right to hear witnesses testify against him. He has the right to question witnesses on their testimony. He can present evidence in his own defense, and he has the right to have a jury decide which side is correct. The defendant also has the right to be represented by an *attorney* (a lawyer).

The system also protects the defendant in a criminal action by setting limits on how the case against him may be presented. For example, the case must be proved "beyond a reasonable doubt." He can remain silent throughout the trial without penalty. Furthermore, no statement or confession he makes after his arrest can be used against him unless it was made voluntarily and with the knowledge that he could have remained silent if he had so chosen. He cannot be required to produce documents that might incriminate him. Another rule that protects defendants in criminal cases says that evidence must be obtained in a lawful manner. So, for example, if the police tapped a suspect's phone without first obtaining a court order, any information they got could not be used as evidence.

Problems of the Courts

All the safeguards built into our court system never really apply to most of the people arrested for crimes, however. Because many more people are arrested than the courts can handle, most cases are settled before trial through plea bargaining. But this is not the only problem facing the courts. Once a person has been convicted of a crime, a judge must hand down a sentence. Exactly what that sentence will be is largely up to the judge. All kinds of people come before the courts. Some are first offenders who, having made a mistake, are not likely to do it again. Others are first-timers on their way to a career in crime. Still others are hardened criminals who have been through the process many times.

Most of us would agree that society ought to be protected from hardened criminals and those who are setting out on a life of crime. We would probably also agree that not much is to be gained by being severe with the person who has made one mistake but is not likely to repeat it. But how is the court to know which is which? This requires the services of probation officers, social workers, and others, who can study the lives of convicted persons. These services are costly, and very few communities are willing, or able, to pay for them. As a result, most judges have to rely on their feelings when it comes to deciding whether to be harsh or lenient.

ARE COURT DECISIONS FAIR?   When judges hand down sentences based on their own estimate of the character of the criminals, the decisions appear to many to be unfair. For example, in one New York City case, a policeman convicted of selling half a pound of heroin received a suspended

A probation officer listens as a young man tells how he started using LSD

sentence. (This meant that he did not have to go to jail.) In another case, tried before a different judge in New York City, an addict convicted of selling 1/73 of an ounce of heroin got a 30-year sentence.

How do courts treat minority groups and poor people? One study showed that federal judges sentenced blacks to prison terms almost one-third longer than the sentence given to whites. Another study revealed that poor defendants who had court-appointed lawyers received prison sentences that were twice as long as those received by defendants who had their own attorneys. The record also shows that people convicted in the overcrowded courts of New York City receive shorter sentences than those convicted of crimes upstate.

Who Are Our Judges?

How does a person get to be a judge? In many cases judges are elected at the same time that we elect our mayors, representatives, senators, and presidents. Most voters do not know enough about the candidates for judgeships to make sound choices. Voters will often pick the candidate who runs the best or the most expensive campaign, or they will vote for the judge who is running on their party's ticket. Judges in some states are appointed by the governor or by the legislature. But it is too easy to give a judgeship in return for a favor or as a reward for a political job well done. One study recommends that before anyone is appointed or elected to a judgeship, his or her qualifications for the job be approved by an impartial screening panel.

Summary   In this chapter we have seen that America's courts are overcrowded, overworked, and understaffed. As a result most of those who are arrested never get a trial. We have also seen that sentences are frequently too long or too short. This may be because judges have not had enough information to go on when handing down sentences. It may also be a result of the way in which we select our judges. That is, we may have too many unqualified judges in the courts. What can be done to improve the situation? What would you suggest?

Looking Ahead   In the next chapter, we shall study the corrections or prison system in the United States.

EXERCISES

MATCHING QUESTIONS   Match each term in Column A with its definition in Column B.

Column A

1. plea bargaining
2. trial courts
3. supreme courts
4. due process
5. suspended sentence
6. appeals court

Column B

(a) convicted person does not have to go to jail

(b) a person accused of a serious crime may plead guilty to a less serious crime or offense

(c) the rights guaranteed to an accused person

(d) where a court case might go if either side does not like the verdict

(e) where criminal cases are first tried

(f) courts that make the final decisions about trial cases

TRUE OR FALSE?   Based on what you have read in this chapter, tell whether each of the following statements is true or false.

1. The main idea of this chapter is that America's courts are overcrowded, overworked, and understaffed.
2. Plea bargaining takes more of the court's time than would a regular trial.
3. Most persons charged with crimes never get to trial.
4. The courts, as they are now set up, can easily handle all of the cases that come before them.
5. There are really 51 different court systems in the United States.
6. The United States Supreme Court deals with all 51 court systems.
7. The lowest-level federal court is called the district court.
8. The highest-level federal court is called the court of appeals.
9. Most criminal cases in the United States are handled by the federal courts.

10. Due process protects the rights of persons charged with crimes.
11. No matter who you are or where a case is tried, the penalties are always the same for the same crime.
12. One of the main ideas of this chapter is that, if our criminal justice system is to work effectively, the police, the courts, and the corrections system must work together.

ARE CRIMINALS BABIED?   In the 1960s the United States Supreme Court handed down several decisions to protect the rights of an individual accused of a crime. The Court ruled that the police must immediately tell a suspect that (1) he has a right to remain silent; (2) anything he says may be used against him; (3) he has a right to have a lawyer; and (4) if he cannot afford a lawyer, one will be provided free.

1. Do you think that guaranteeing an accused person these rights is "babying criminals"? Explain your answer.
2. Do you think that any of the rights mentioned above is or is not important?
3. One opponent of the Court's recent decisions has stated that we are becoming so concerned with protecting the rights of criminals that the scales of justice are unbalanced. According to this view, it is the criminal who receives favored treatment in our society at the expense of the honest, law-abiding citizen. As a result we are losing the ability to control the crime and violence in our cities. What do you think?
4. Those who favor the Court's rulings protecting the rights of an accused person say that these decisions have not hurt district attorneys in their work. Suspects will talk, regardless of the warnings. Furthermore, they suggest, more evidence is needed than a confession. Better police work is needed to investigate and collect evidence in a case in order to win a conviction and make the charges stick. What do you think?

Chapter 4   Corrections

The prisoner stood before the judge. "Adam Caine, you have been convicted of stealing an apple from the store of Mary Julian. I hereby sentence you to have the hand with which you stole the apple chopped off. Take him away. By the way, bailiff, there is something wrong with my calendar. What is today's date?"

"It's August 28, 1694, your honor."

Chop off his hand?

That's what they did. Before the 1700s, people found guilty of serious crimes were either tortured or put to death, or both. The thief could have a hand chopped off. The person who said something he should not have said might have his tongue ripped out. Anyone convicted of a serious offense could also have received a death penalty. Many people were thrown into jail for the rest of their lives because they could not pay their debts or because they had offended an important person.

Early Prison Systems

In 1786, in what was considered a merciful act, the Quakers of Pennsylvania proposed the idea of using prisons as places of *penitence.* That is, the prisoner would have time to sit in his cell, think about his guilt, and feel *penitent* (sorry) that he had done wrong. To this day *penitentiary* describes a prison. In order to make sure that the prisoner would not be tempted to think about anything else, the Quakers saw to it that he was locked in a cell all by himself. In this *solitary confinement* the prisoner had nothing to do day in and day out but sit with his thoughts. Many solitary prisoners either died or went insane. So in 1825 New York State introduced a system in which several prisoners were allowed to share a cell and work at hard labor. Of course, it was hardly a pleasant way to spend the day. Prisoners had their heads shaved, worked and ate in silence, wore special uniforms, and marched from place to place in lockstep. Many jails in the United States still use some features of the system introduced by New York in 1825.

Why Are Jails Needed?

TAKE CRIMINALS OFF THE STREETS   Some form of jail has been in existence since people realized the need for laws. To some people jails are the one sure way to get rid of crime in the streets. "Lock up all the crooks, throw away the keys," they say, "and you won't have to worry about crime." Although this obviously cannot be done, it does explain one reason why society builds jails: *to keep off the streets people who might commit crimes.*

PUNISHMENT   A second reason why society builds jails is to *punish* wrongdoers. When government was weak, or when there was no government at all, people who were wronged took the law into their own hands. Perhaps you have seen this happen in Westerns and crime shows. The story is about a person, family, or group that seeks to "get even" with another group for a wrong they did. Often, after the first group evened the score, the other side felt that it was *their* turn for revenge. So revenge and more revenge could go on for years. But society today has taken on the responsibility for finding out who was guilty in the first place (something that private individuals usually overlooked) and for punishing that person or group. Once society has punished the guilty, there is no need for private revenge.

DISCOURAGE POTENTIAL OFFENDERS   A third reason for punishing people is to discourage others who might want to commit the same crimes. However, the *severity* of the punishment does not seem to have much effect on the *crime rate.* That is, even when thieves were tortured and hanged, robbery and burglary were still common. More recently, we can look at the murder rate to make the same point. In 1930 some 200 people were executed for murder. But in 1966 only one person was executed for murder. From 1930 to 1966, however, the murder rate went down to one-half of what it had been in 1930. In other words the death penalty did not seem to have had much to do with the number of murders committed. For this reason, people who study crime (*criminologists*) tell us that it is not the *severity* of the punishment that keeps people from committing crimes. It is the *certainty of punishment* that discourages crime. Most people will not break the law if they are almost certain they will be caught.

DETERMENT   The fourth reason for sending people to prison is to discourage them from returning to a life of crime. The idea is that if jail is unpleasant enough, the former inmate will want to "go straight" in order to avoid going back to jail some day.

TREATMENT   A fifth reason for imprisonment is to allow society to *treat* the offender. The goal of the treatment is to enable the offender to live in normal society once he is free. This may involve teaching him a trade or skill, treating a physical or mental problem, or helping him to "get off" drugs.

CRIMINAL SOCIETY   Taking an offender away from criminal society is another possible goal of imprisonment. Some people have been around crime all their lives. All their friends are in crime. It is next to impossible for such persons to avoid returning to a life of crime when they are released from prison unless something is done to help them change their ways of life.

These are the answers one is most likely to hear when the question why we still have jails is raised. After hearing these answers, you may then ask, "Have we been successful in achieving these goals?"

Most experts would probably say, "Hardly at all." Just look at the terrible record our jails have: *Two-thirds of those released from prison will return within five years!* What is wrong with the system?

Too Many People Are Behind Bars

About 200,000 Americans are "behind bars," in prisons. Many of these prisons are overcrowded. A recent study of one large city's prison showed that 900 inmates were housed in a jail with room for about 500. Because of this overcrowding, 200 to 300 people had to sleep on bare steel springs or on the floor.

Prison overcrowding often occurs because people are kept behind bars for many months while awaiting trial. They have not even been convicted of a crime! Many are teenage first offenders, who are mixed in with the most hardened criminals. Many of these first offenders will be found innocent and set free. In order to relieve overcrowding and keep young persons who can still be saved from entering a life of crime, it has been suggested that people awaiting trial be allowed to remain *at large* (free). Of course, it would be dangerous to allow all of those accused of crimes to go free until their trials. However, most accused persons can remain at large until the trial date.

In the previous chapter we discussed the problem of too many acts being considered crimes. If the people now convicted of "crimes without victims" (such as drug addicts, alcoholics, prostitutes) were taken out of the criminal justice system, much of the overcrowding in jails would end.

Substitutes for Prison

Probation offers another way to avoid a jail sentence. The person is given a suspended sentence and is set free. If more of the people who are convicted of crimes were placed on probation, jails would be less crowded. The purposes of probation are to allow those who can to remain in normal society and to help them not to repeat their crimes. The decision as to who should be placed on probation and who should go behind bars is up to the judge.

Parole, which allows people in prison to finish their terms in the outside world, is another way of reducing the number of inmates in our prisons. But again, unless something is done to help the *parolee* (the person on parole), there is a good chance that he will wind up back in prison. In the past, a parole officer used to keep in touch with the parolee and tried to help him set up a normal life. Recent studies have found, however, that parole officers themselves need help. There are just not enough parole officers to go around. They are unable to keep the kind of close contact with parolees that was kept in the past. One system that might be an effective remedy for this problem seems to be the *halfway house.*

Halfway houses offer job- and personal-counseling services for parolees.

These houses are places where parolees can avoid old friends who know only the criminal life. Society has no control over ex-convicts who are released when their jail terms are up. While a person is on parole, however, authorities at halfway houses can keep very close contact with parolees and help with problems of returning to normal life.

Jails Breed More Crime

In addition to the problem of too many prisoners for the system to handle, most critics agree that correctional institutions fail to "correct." That is, the experience of too many prisoners is so horrible as to destroy their chances for success when they return to society.

A study of jails in a large Eastern city showed that, in two years, 1,500 individual prisoners had been assaulted by others. Another study of the Midwestern jails also described a large number of assaults as well as the sale of drugs by guards to prisoners.

Other reports describe guards' mistreatment of prisoners. This ranges from beatings and torture to the assignment of "troublemakers" to the cells of dangerous prisoners. The result of such harsh treatment was summarized by the head of one state's correctional system when he said:

> It is my feeling that correctional institutions generally have contributed to violence in exactly the same way that ghettos have made their contribution. . . . The correctional institution . . . regiments, represses, and demeans the individual in countless ways.

The question here is, "How can the treatment of prisoners be improved?" In answer to this a national commission made several proposals.

Improving Prison Conditions

Educational and vocational training in prisons should be improved. The idea is to give all prisoners the opportunity to learn a trade they would like to learn. A possible way to handle this is for prisons to specialize in certain areas. For example, one prison might specialize in teaching agriculture, another in technology, and another in white-collar skills.

A second proposal is to provide inmates with the opportunity to save their earnings. A national savings and loan association for prisoners has been proposed. This would be a bank where prisoners could set aside their earnings so as to be able to meet their expenses when finally released.

Prisons should help prisoners to prepare for their return to society. When released from prison, the former inmate must be able to feel comfortable with law-abiding people. If, instead, he feels "at home" only with his old friends and way of life, he may soon be in trouble again. Some prisons have given up their large-group procedures. That is, lines of men marching in silence and long rows of men eating in silence are being replaced. Instead, where changes have been made, the men are allowed to move informally from place to place. They eat at a square table, as in restaurants.

Where prisons are truly concerned about the inmates' future, they have allowed social workers into the prisons to aid the convicts. Work-release programs have been started. These programs allow prisoners to take jobs outside the jail during the day, while spending the night back in their cells. Increasing the number of visitors permitted and the amount of mail allowed are other steps that have been taken to help prisoners maintain contact with the real world.

Can our corrections system be improved? It will have to be if society is to be protected from criminals and if we truly want to help those who have committed crimes to return to lawful society.

Summary   In this chapter we took a look at America's corrections system. We saw that attempts to "correct" or punish or reduce criminal behavior have been with us for a long time. We saw that our present system is a gigantic failure. Four out of every five serious crimes are committed by people with police records.

A number of reforms have been suggested to improve our corrections system. It remains to be seen if the reforms will be adopted. It also remains to be seen whether they will be successful in reducing the rate of crime if they are adopted.

EXERCISES

MATCHING QUESTIONS Match each term in Column A with its definition in Column B.

Column A

1. penitent
2. solitary confinement
3. criminologist
4. probation
5. on parole
6. at large
7. halfway house

Column B

(*a*) studies management of prisons
(*b*) free; not in prison
(*c*) center where a parolee can stay
(*d*) sorry for wrongdoing
(*e*) place where a prisoner is locked alone in a cell
(*f*) allowed to return to normal life, under supervision, not sent to jail
(*g*) allowed to finish a jail sentence out of jail

TRUE OR FALSE? Read each of the following statements carefully. Based on what you have read in this chapter, tell whether the statement is true or false.

1. The main idea of this chapter is that jail is an attempt by society to preserve law and order.
2. According to this chapter, nothing can be done to reform an individual who commits a crime.
3. The origin of the word *penitentiary* indicates that prison was supposed to be a place where a criminal could sit and think about what he did wrong and feel sorry about it.
4. In the 1700s the Quakers used solitary confinement to torture the inmates of prisons.
5. In the 1800s when two or more prisoners were given hard work and allowed to share the same cell, this was considered a prison reform.
6. Prison is so unpleasant that, once a prisoner is released, it is unlikely that he will ever do anything that might send him back.

7. We can reduce the number of persons in jail by making greater use of probation and parole.

8. Although jail is supposed to discourage crime, it very often breeds crime.

9. According to this chapter, there are too many people in prison.

Unit VIII   Dissent

Chapter 1   What Is Dissent?

A man sits down at his desk and writes a letter:

Dear Congressman Fink:

I think you made a big mistake when you voted for the highway bill. You should have saved your vote to help mass transportation.

Very truly yours,

Harry Wainscott

That night, the six o'clock news shows these scenes:

A line of people carrying signs marching up and down outside the governor's office. These *pickets* (marchers) are protesting the governor's call for a statewide tax increase.

Twelve people being arrested. They had formed a human chain to prevent others from entering a movie theater. The theater was showing an *"X"-rated* (adults only) film that they felt should not be shown in their town.

Women handing out leaflets in front of supermarkets throughout the state. These women were protesting rising food prices. The leaflets

233

called on the public to reduce its food spending by 10 percent that week.

Dissent in a Democracy

The letter writers, pickets, protesters, and women distributing leaflets all had something in common. They were *dissenters*. Dissenters are people who disapprove of certain policies of government or society and *let others know how they feel.* This last statement is essential to dissent. True dissent means letting others know how you feel. If you think the mayor of your town has done something foolish, but if you keep that feeling to yourself, that is not dissent. If a citizen thinks that prices are too high but does not say anything, that is not dissent. But the people we described above did let others know how they felt. They were dissenters.

Dissent Is Vital to the Life of a Democracy

A *dictatorship* (system of government in which one person rules) can allow no dissent. A successful dictator must convince the public that he "can do no wrong." If others were allowed to question his decisions, it would suggest that he might, on occasion, make a mistake. Such an idea is intolerable to a dictator.

In a democracy, on the other hand, no one person holds absolute power. It is rather the majority that rules through its elected representatives. But people in a democracy do not believe that the majority is *always* right. For this reason, the rights of the minority must be carefully protected. After all, they *might* be the ones who are correct on a particular issue. In such a case, the sooner they are able to convince the majority of the wisdom of their position, the better it will be for the rest of the country.

For this reason Americans look upon their right to dissent as necessary to the life of their democracy. Our Constitution and our laws guarantee this right.

In demonstrating their disapproval, dissenters are, of course, expected to obey the law. In other words, just as the government protects the rights of the minority, it must also protect the majority. The demonstrators who were objecting to the "X"-rated film were arrested because they tried to deprive others of their right to see it.

In this unit we shall take a look at dissent in America. We shall see that dissent may be lawful or unlawful, depending on how people carry it out. We shall also see that there is a special place for dissent in a democracy, and that dissent has a special place in American history.

Types of Dissent

Dissent can take a variety of forms. For instance, it might be:

>*violent* or *nonviolent*
>*group* or *individual*
>*organized* or *spontaneous*
>*action* or *withdrawal*
>*at the ballot box* or *in the streets*

After the assassination of Dr. Martin Luther King, Jr., in 1968, riots broke out in black neighborhoods throughout the country. This was *violent group action*. It was also *spontaneous* (because it had taken place without planning), and it took place in the *streets.*

In another case groups of people have said that they did not like the way American society was functioning. To show their dissatisfaction they let their hair grow long; the men did not shave. They dressed in old or strange clothes, refused to vote, and formed their own societies, or "communes," as they called them. This dissent was *nonviolent*. It was organized by a *group* as an act of *withdrawal* (because they removed themselves from society). The dissent took place in the streets. The public could see that the protesters looked different from everyone else. This dissent affected the *ballot box* because these dissenters refused to vote.

Listed below are a number of acts of protest that took place in the past. Which of the terms listed above best describes the kind of dissent these acts represent?

1. In protest against the high price of meat, millions of housewives throughout the country observed one "meatless week," during which they did not buy meat.
2. A government survey indicated that there was an increase in the number of home vegetable gardens. The government felt that many people had decided on their own to plant gardens as a protest against rising food costs.

3. A public opinion poll in one large city found many people who were not going to vote in the next election for mayor. This apparently was the result of the work of an independent group that called upon the public to *boycott* (not take part in) the election. The boycott was called to protest the poor quality of mayoral candidates.

4. To show their opposition to the military-training program at their college, a group of students seized and occupied the program's office and set fire to its files.

5. In protest over the small number of blacks and other minorities in a certain construction union, a civil rights group picketed the union's offices.

6. A vigorous campaign was conducted to defeat the *incumbent* (the person in office) governor of an Eastern state. The campaign was sponsored by people who favored a strict law regulating hand guns. They wanted to defeat the governor because he had come out against such a law.

Summary   Dissent occurs when people disapprove of the policies or activities of a social group or a government. Dissent is vital to the health of democracy. The right to dissent is guaranteed by the United States Constitution.

Looking Ahead   In the next chapter, we shall take a look at the role of dissent in United States history.

EXERCISES

WHAT DID THEY MEAN WHEN THEY SAID . . . ?   Here are three statements on the subject of dissent that were made by famous Americans. Read the statements slowly. Then see if you can (*a*) explain the meaning of each statement, and (*b*) tell why you agree or disagree with it.

The best test of truth is the power of a thought to get itself accepted after competing with other thoughts.

Our country . . . may she always be in the right; but our country, right or wrong.

Those who agree with their government even when the government is wrong are themselves wrong. They are wrong because they get in the way of others who want to correct the wrong.

MATCHING QUESTIONS Match each term in Column A with its definition in Column B.

Column A

1. dissent
2. violent
3. nonviolent
4. dictatorship
5. democracy
6. picket
7. boycott
8. incumbent

Column B

(*a*) system of government in which the majority rules
(*b*) person holding an office
(*c*). active protest against society or government policies
(*d*) system of government in which one person rules
(*e*) passive, inactive
(*f*) to refuse to take part in an activity
(*g*) to march in protest
(*h*) active; using physical force

ESSAY QUESTIONS Answer the following questions about dissent:

1. Why are dictatorships unable to allow dissent?
2. Why must there always be a minority in a democratic society?
3. "The rights of the majority also need protection." Tell whether you agree or disagree with this statement.

FURTHER READING Read the story and answer the question that follows:

WILL THE REAL MRS. DARVAS PLEASE STAND UP?

Just as they were about to enjoy their Sunday lunch, Mrs. Darvas and her daughters heard the sound of chanting and drums from the street below. Rachel and Maxine, the Darvas twins, rushed to the window.

"Mother," called Maxine, "it's another one of those dumb demonstrations. I wonder what they're complaining about this time."

"It's about the abortion law," said Rachel. "Do you see that first sign the man is carrying: "ABORTION IS MURDER"? I wish they'd pass a law to get these people off the street. I mean, why can't they just keep their ideas to themselves?"

"Darn right," chimed in Maxine. "There's something un-American about the way these people are always finding fault with the way things are. I mean, if you can't go along with what the majority wants, then maybe you ought to just leave."

"Now, wait a minute!" said Mrs. Darvas. "Did I understand you to say that people who demonstrate against something are un-American?"

"Absolutely," said Rachel. "This is a free country, a democracy, and the majority rules. We elected our state government and its legislature passed a law making abortions legal. It's the duty of citizens to accept the will of the majority without complaint. That's democracy."

"It sure is," said Maxine. "It's the American way."

Mrs. Darvas squirmed uncomfortably as she listened to all this. It bothered her to think that the kids believed what they were saying. She certainly did not. She felt quite strongly that the marchers had every right to do what they were doing. She thought for a moment about what she wanted to say to her daughters. Then she spoke:

On a separate sheet of paper, write what you think Mrs. Darvas told Rachel and Maxine.

Chapter 2   Dissent in United States History

Dissent is nothing new in the United States. After all, it took a revolution for the United States to win its freedom. But even before the Revolutionary War, dissent was making American history. Do you remember reading about the Boston Tea Party of 1773? The Bostonians who dressed up as Indians and threw an entire shipment of tea overboard were protesting a tea tax. Before that, in 1734, a newspaper printer named John Peter Zenger went on trial for printing articles that criticized the governor of the New York colony. The governor wanted Zenger punished because he had dared to criticize the government. Finally, after Zenger had been in jail for nine months, the case was decided. Zenger was a free man. He was *acquitted* (found not guilty) because the articles he had printed about the governor were true.

The Zenger case was a landmark in the history of free speech in this country. The right of the press to criticize the government was established.

Constitutional Guarantees

This right was further strengthened in 1791, after the American colonies had won their independence from England. The First Amendment to the Constitution said: "Congress shall make no law . . . abridging the freedom of speech, or of the press; or the right of the people peaceably to assemble, and to petition the Government for a redress of grievances."

Free speech was further strengthened after the Civil War when the

Fourteenth Amendment was *ratified* (passed) in 1868. This amendment made it illegal for the states to pass laws that limit the individual's rights. Thus the rights of Americans to dissent are guaranteed by the Constitution. Every American is guaranteed a free press, free speech, the right to hold meetings, and the right to petition.

Throughout our history, Americans have relied on these rights to protest against policies they disliked. Here are some of the more famous issues about which they have expressed dissent:

The Whisky Rebellion occurred in 1794 in Pennsylvania. Farmers were outraged by a government tax on whisky. It was not until President Washington sent troops into the state that the farmers' protest was put down.

The War of 1812 was very unpopular, especially in New England. This led to the Hartford Convention of 1814 in which representatives of the New England States met to demand an end to the war. Some of the delegates even demanded that New England *secede* (break away) from the union if their demands were not met.

Major Issues Since 1865

One of the principal areas of dissent after 1865 was the struggle for the rights of industrial workers. This eventually led to the recognition of labor unions and the passage of laws designed to provide workers with minimum wages, maximum hours, and better working conditions.

The struggle for *woman's suffrage* (the right to vote) was another major issue through most of the 19th and in the early 20th centuries. By the 1840s women had begun to organize protest groups. These groups demanded that women be given the right to vote in all elections. The struggle was not an easy one. But eventually the work of such people as Elizabeth Cady Stanton, Susan B. Anthony, Carrie Chapman Catt, and Anna Howard Shaw had results. The Nineteenth Amendment, ratified in 1920, gave all women over 21 the right to vote.

Numerous other causes attracted followers in the years that followed the Civil War. Dissent swirled around such issues as the production and sale of alcoholic beverages (for and against); money (gold vs. silver); immigration (more vs. less); and America's entry into the Spanish-American War and World War I.

In recent years the war in Vietnam and the struggle for equal rights for minority groups and women have received the greatest share of attention. Protesters in recent years have received a great deal of attention, perhaps even more than in the past. This is partly a result of radio and television, which have brought news into our homes at the instant it happens. It is also a result of the dramatic way in which protest has been conducted in recent years. Draft card burnings, the disruption of public meetings, and the occupation of public offices and buildings have all been conducted in the name of protest in recent years. Of course, this has not been the first time in American history that protesters did something dramatic to call attention to their cause. Tea drinkers living in Boston in 1773 probably had to drink hot milk that year because of the Boston Tea Party.

Summary   Dissent has existed in American life since colonial days. The right to dissent is guaranteed in the Constitution. Great social reforms have been won by dissenters.

Looking Ahead   In the next chapter, we shall study the problem of when dissent is legal and when it is illegal.

EXERCISES

PROTEST TODAY!   The people in the cartoon below are picketing in front of the United States Capitol in Washington, D.C. Using an issue that

is of public concern today, complete the cartoon by doing the following:

1. Write a slogan for each of the three signs the pickets are carrying.
2. Write a *caption* (title) for the entire cartoon.
3. Explain why the pickets are carrying signs in front of the United States Capitol.

ESSAY QUESTION   Do you think that pickets should be allowed to demonstrate for or against anything they wish?

Chapter 3   What Is Lawful Dissent?

At first no one noticed the man as he moved to the front of the crowded movie theater. Suddenly, he began to yell as loudly as he could, "Fire! Fire! Everybody run for your lives!"

As the crowd rushed to the exits, the man sat down. He burst into laughter. "April Fool!" he called out. "Now I've got a good seat."

The manager was not amused by the trick. He called the police, who placed the man under arrest. The judge was not amused either. He sentenced the man to 30 days in jail.

"I thought this was a free country," wailed the man. "I thought you could say whatever you want to say."

It is true that the First and the Fourteenth Amendments to the Constitution guarantee certain basic liberties to all Americans. But it is also true that there have to be certain limitations on these freedoms. The incident above did not take place, but it might have. If it did, the man who yelled "Fire!" in the crowded theater would certainly have been put in jail. His act might have caused terrible injuries to people who raced toward the exits.

Limits to Constitutional Guarantees

The Constitution says that Americans are guaranteed free speech, free press, and the right to assemble and petition. Does that mean that they can say or print *anything?* Can they "assemble" anywhere? Obviously not.

The man who yelled "Fire!" as a joke might have caused the injury of many people. A newspaper is not permitted to print a story saying that Joe Jones is a thief unless the story is true. To do otherwise would deprive Jones of *his* rights.

A group wishing to protest a government action has the right to meet, but not in your backyard without an invitation. Recently, for example, a group wished to protest the slow pace of civil rights legislation. They marched on a major highway at the height of the rush hour. Traffic was backed up for miles. The group was arrested and fined. The judge said that they had no right to "assemble" on a highway. Well, then, how far can people go in what they say or do in protest?

This is not an easy question to answer because there is no one statement in the Constitution that describes exactly the limits to our freedoms. For this reason, it has been left to the courts to tell the public what the First and Fourteenth Amendments mean. The courts have ruled that protesters cannot block a highway at rush hour. The man who yelled "Fire!" when there was no fire was sent to jail because freedom of speech does not mean that we can endanger others by what we say. There have been other important cases that involved people's rights to freedom of speech, the press, and assembly. Let us look at them to get some idea as to when dissent is lawful and when it is unlawful.

LAWFUL OR UNLAWFUL DISSENT?   A man delivered a speech before an audience in a crowded auditorium. His message was one of hate. America's troubles were the result of the work of Jews and other minority groups, he said.

"Kill them all," shouted people in the audience who agreed with the speaker.

A mob gathered outside. The people outside did not like what the speaker was saying. Some threatened to kill the speaker. When the meeting ended the police arrested the speaker for "disturbing the peace." The United States Supreme Court, however, said that the police were wrong. In this case, the Court said that it was to be expected that free speech would excite some people to anger. Unless, the Court ruled, what is said presents a "clear and present danger" to the public, people should be permitted to speak.

(*above*) Picketing for jobs—see Minorities unit

(*below*) Picketing against an integrated housing development—see page 255

In another famous case, a college student mounted a platform to speak. He called the President of the United States a "bum." The student said that the local government discriminated against blacks. He called on blacks to take up arms and fight for their rights. Several people in the audience were angered by the student's words. One of them told a policeman in the audience that if the policeman did not get the speaker off the platform, he (the member of the audience) would "take care of him" himself.

The policeman ordered the student off the platform. The student refused. The policeman finally had to threaten to use force. With that, the student came down from the platform and the policeman placed him under arrest.

The Supreme Court of the United States was again asked to decide the case. In this case it held that the policeman was right. The Court agreed that the student had a right to speak. However, because what he said had nearly started a riot, which would have been a "clear and present danger" to the public, he should have left the platform when the policeman ordered him to do so. Therefore, the policeman was right to arrest the student for failing to obey his order.

In a third case, a group gathered at a state capitol to protest racial discrimination. They sang songs and clapped their hands. They were arrested for a "breach of the peace." This time the Supreme Court ruled against the police. The Court said that the right to assemble and petition for *"redress of grievances"* (to correct things that are wrong) gave the demonstrators the right to meet on capitol grounds.

A group of students gathered on the lawn of a county jail. They were protesting the arrest of several fellow students a few days earlier. The protesters sang hymns and clapped their hands. They too were arrested. In this instance, the Supreme Court ruled that the demonstrators were wrong because they chose the grounds of the jail on which to protest. In other words, the public has a right to be on the state capitol grounds—therefore, the demonstrators in the previous case were acting lawfully. But the public cannot wander in and around jails at will—therefore, these demonstrators were wrong.

The right to protest in schools against government policy has also come before the Supreme Court. In a famous case, several students were suspended because they wore black armbands to school. The armbands (a sign of mourning for the dead) were their way of protesting the war in Vietnam. The Supreme Court ruled that the students had a right to wear armbands if they did not disrupt the normal school program. The Court called this "symbolic speech." In other words, the Court said that the right of the students to wear armbands was part of their rights to free speech.

Where Does Complete Freedom End?

How much freedom of protest do Americans have? How far can they go in objecting to the policies of government? As we have seen, there are no exact limits. A demonstration on the lawn of the state capitol is legal; a demonstration on the lawn of the county jail is not. A speaker who arouses anger and hostility on the part of the audience has the right to continue speaking. A speaker who arouses his audience to illegal acts does not. Wearing armbands in school without disrupting the school program is legal, but wearing armbands to disrupt the school day would not be legal.

Summary   We can see that certain broad rules apply to dissent. These are as follows:

1. People have the right to speak out against things that they oppose when their speech does not interfere with the rights of others.

2. People have the right to organize others to support their position. They can assemble, picket, and hold demonstrations for this purpose. Here again, in so doing, they may not interfere with the rights of others.

3. Where the activities of the protesters present a "clear and present danger" to others or to society in general, the activities are unlawful.

Looking Ahead   People sometimes feel that the only way an evil can be corrected is by breaking the law. In the next chapter, we shall examine this technique of protest.

EXERCISES

PICTURES HAVE A STORY TO TELL   Look at the pictures on page 245. Then see if you can answer these questions for each picture: What is the protest about? What method of protest is being used? Do you think this method of protest is an effective way of expressing dissent? (You may not be able to answer all the questions for each picture.)

SUPPOSE YOU ARE THE JUDGE   The following incidents never took place, but let us suppose they did. In each case an arrest has been made. Suppose *you* are the judge in the case. How would you rule? In each case, give reasons for your decision.

1. "Jail is too good for that guy," said Joe Smith as the mayor of the city rode by in his limousine. "I'd like to put him in a rocket and send him to the moon." Smith was immediately placed under arrest for his remarks and brought before a judge. As the judge in the case, how would you rule?

2. In protest over discrimination against women employees by the town's largest department store, a group of women handed out leaflets to the store's customers. The protesters distributed their leaflets in the toy department. The store called in the police, who arrested the group. As the judge in the case, how would you rule?

3. An investigation revealed that the state government had many corrupt officials. High officials accepted *bribes* (cash payments) in exchange for political favors. A citizens' group was formed to gather signatures on a petition. The petition was a letter to the governor of the state asking him to remove these officials from office. (When people sign a petition, this act shows that they agree with the letter.) The citizens' group was using the state capitol's town park to gather their signatures. They had set up tables in various parts of the park. As people walked by, they were asked to sign the petition. Today the police arrested the group for "loitering in the park." As the judge in the case, how would you rule?

Chapter 4   Civil Disobedience

During World War II the Nazi government in Germany adopted the policy of murdering all the Jews it could find. By the time the war ended, some 6 million Jewish people had been killed. The truth about this horrendous crime came to light in a series of trials that were held after the war. The Nuremberg trials, as they came to be called, revealed the shocking details of Nazi brutality. The trials continued for nearly a year, and the list of atrocities grew longer and longer. Throughout the trials, the same question was asked of the accused: "How could you have done such horrible things to other human beings?"

To this question the response was generally the same:

"I was only following orders." Or:

"If I didn't do as I was told, I would have been put in jail or executed."

The judges at Nuremberg did not agree with this excuse. They felt that there is a "higher law" than that of the state. In other words, if the government's laws or commands are immoral, one's duty is to disobey them.

Thirty years now have passed since the Nuremberg trials. Much of the testimony has been forgotten. However, the idea that people have a right or an obligation to disobey an illegal or immoral law has not been forgotten. Numbers of people have acted on this principle in recent years. They have deliberately disobeyed laws that they felt were unjust or immoral. The persons who deliberately broke the laws did so in order to change them.

Many of these people have been punished for breaking these laws. This form of protest is known as *civil disobedience*.

The Fight for Civil Rights

Perhaps the best-known examples of civil disobedience in America took place in the South during the 1950s and 1960s. At that time the Southern states had laws that were designed to keep whites and blacks *segregated* (apart). Blacks were not allowed to attend the same schools, eat in the same restaurants, or stay in the same hotels as whites. Sections of theaters were reserved "for whites only." The same was also true of trains and buses. Blacks had to use separate restrooms, swimming pools, water fountains, and other public facilities.

For nearly a hundred years, those who favored equal treatment for all Americans had tried to persuade the states to change their laws. For the most part, these efforts were a failure. By the 1950s some leaders of the *civil rights movement* (the effort to achieve equality for black Americans) called for civil disobedience as a means to achieve their goals.

Foremost among these leaders was Dr. Martin Luther King, Jr. In 1963 Dr. King led an effort to end segregation in Birmingham, Alabama. At the time, all groups needed permits to parade. Dr. King's group wished to march to protest discrimination, but they could not obtain the parade permits they had requested. The march went on despite the lack of "legal" authority to do so.

At the time it was illegal for blacks to sit at the same lunch counters as whites. Groups of blacks "sat in" at "white-only" lunch counters. Dr. King was arrested and sent to jail. While he was in jail, several black clergymen asked him how he could justify his behavior. After all, they pointed out, Dr. King was himself a clergyman, a man of God. How could he lead others into breaking the law?

Dr. King answered that there is a higher law, a "law of God," which is more important than that of any government. If the government's law violates the law of God, it is an unjust law. Dr. King went on to say: "I would agree with Saint Augustine that 'an unjust law is no law at all' . . . one has a moral responsibility to disobey unjust laws."

We have seen that Dr. King was not the first to argue that people should not obey unjust laws. This thought was included in the Nuremberg trials decision. As a matter of fact, the same idea was expressed in our Declaration of Independence. Think for a moment about the meaning of: "We hold these truths to be self-evident, that all Men . . . are endowed by their Creator with certain unalienable Rights. . . ."

The person who breaks the law deliberately, Dr. King went on, must be willing to accept punishment for his behavior: "An individual who breaks a law that conscience tells him is unjust, and willingly accepts the penalty by staying in jail to *arouse the conscience of the community over its injustice,* is in reality expressing the very highest respect for law."

Here we also see one of the primary goals of civil disobedience: *to arouse the conscience of the community.* By going to jail because he had broken an unjust law, Dr. King hoped to arouse the majority in support of his movement. In this case, civil disobedience was successful. The city of Birmingham came to an understanding with Dr. King and his followers in which many of their demands were met.

Dangers of Civil Disobedience

The war in Vietnam led to many acts of civil disobedience. Many Americans felt that it was an unjust and immoral war. Some people, in order to dramatize their feelings, resorted to acts of civil disobedience. Selective Service (draft board) offices were invaded and records were destroyed. The President and members of the government were interrupted when they attempted to make public speeches. Colleges and universities were shut down by demonstrations against the war.

As these illegal acts were taking place, those who committed them argued that they broke the law to protest a far greater crime: American participation in the war. Many Americans questioned this attitude. How could our government function, they asked, if people could take it on themselves to break laws? Could a bank robber claim that he took the money as an act of protest against immoral banks? What would happen to our government if Democrats decided to ignore laws passed by Republican majorities, or vice versa?

Civil disobedience, they remind us, is not possible in a dictatorship. Those who deliberately break laws to protest actions of the government would soon disappear from sight in countries such as the Soviet Union, China, Spain, or Cuba. In a democracy, on the other hand, minority

Civil disobedience at Berkeley, California, during the antiwar protests of the 1960s

points of view are allowed. They are, in fact, an absolute necessity. Remember, a democracy is a government ruled by the people. This means *all* the people. But when people take the law into their own hands, there is no longer any government. In many other parts of the world democracies have disappeared because they were unable to govern. The fear that civil disobedience will destroy our democracy has led some well-known leaders to argue that civil disobedience should never be used.

The Place for Civil Disobedience

Are citizens ever justified in breaking a law? Is it possible for a person who believes in democracy to say, "I will not obey the will of that majority"?

If you believe that it is right in some instances to disobey unjust laws, who, would you say, should be the one to decide which law is unjust? Should every individual have the right to decide which laws are just and which are unjust, and then obey only those of which he or she approved? Suppose a person decided that the government was spending citizens' tax money incorrectly. Should the private citizen be allowed to decide for himself or herself whether or not to pay taxes?

How far should civil disobedience go? Blocking traffic, as an act of protest, is an example of nonviolent civil disobedience. But protesters have also used violent means to object to certain government policies. Is violence ever justified as a means of protesting an unjust policy or law? Those who answer "yes" frequently point to gains that were achieved after violence.

"Had there been no riot, we would not have achieved the reforms we did," they argue.

Those who are opposed to violence say that it is never justified as long as there are other ways of bringing about change. Since it is always possible in a democracy to change laws through peaceful means, it is wrong to hurt others through violence.

Summary   Is there room for civil disobedience in a democracy? There is no right or wrong answer to this question—at least not one to which everyone would agree. The answer, then, is up to you.

EXERCISES

MATCHING QUESTIONS   Match each term in Column A with its definition in Column B.

Column A

1. civil disobedience
2. civil rights movement
3. "higher law"
4. segregation laws

Column B

(*a*) the effort to achieve equality for black Americans
(*b*) deliberate violation of certain laws in an effort to bring about change in the law
(*c*) designed to keep blacks and whites apart
(*d*) moral law, or the law of God

FURTHER READING   Read the selection and answer the questions that follow:

Civil disobedience as an act of conscience . . . is permissible only as a last resort to obtain justice when all other remedies . . . have been exhausted. Civil disobedience can only be justified when a civil law is . . . in conflict with a higher law—namely our Constitution, natural law, or divine law. In this extreme case, nonviolent forms of civil disobedience, accompanied by willing acceptance of any penalty the law provides, are the only means that can be justified in our democratic society.

Terence Cardinal Cooke, Archbishop of New York

Based on what you have read in this chapter and Cardinal Cooke's statement, indicate whether each of the following statements is true or false. If the statement is false, correct it by changing the words in italics.

1. According to Cardinal Cooke, civil disobedience is *sometimes justified*.
2. If a law is unjust (or in conflict with a higher law) it should be disobeyed *immediately*.
3. Civil disobedience is *always* violent.
4. Those who engage in civil disobedience should be willing to *accept the consequences* of their acts.
5. An example of nonviolent civil disobedience is the *collection of names on a petition*.

CIVIL DISOBEDIENCE IN ACTION   Read the two selections below and answer the questions that follow:

THE RETURN TO WOUNDED KNEE

In 1890, at the tiny hamlet of Wounded Knee, South Dakota, the United States Cavalry massacred 300 men, women, and children of the Sioux Indian tribe. On February 27, 1973, some 300 Sioux and other members of the militant American Indian Movement (AIM) took over the town of Wounded Knee. Seizing 11 residents as hostages, the Indians barricaded themselves in a hilltop church and vowed not to come out until their demands were met. (See photo, page 182.)

1. Why do you suppose the members of AIM chose the town of Wounded Knee for their demonstration?
2. The seizure of Wounded Knee was an act of civil disobedience. Would you say it was violent or nonviolent? Explain your answer.
3. What did the Indians expect to achieve by seizing the town and taking hostages?
4. Do you think that what the Indians did was a good idea?

URBAN INTEGRATION

Early on a cold December morning several years ago, State Assemblyman Anthony Imperiale and an associate chained themselves to the fence that surrounds the construction site of Kawaida Towers. Kawaida Towers is a middle-income apartment house that will be erected in the heart of Newark, New Jersey's predominantly Italian section. At the time that he chained himself to the fence, Assemblyman Imperiale said he would willingly be arrested "again and again if necessary."

The Assemblyman explained that he and his followers were opposed to the construction of Kawaida Towers because of its size. He pointed out that all of the other houses in the neighborhood were one- and two-story dwellings or *low-rise* (six floors or fewer) apartment houses. A 16-story building would, they argued, crowd too many people into the neighborhood. (See photo, page 245.)

Leaders of Newark's black community disagreed with this point of view. They said that the real reason for the opposition to Kawaida Towers was the fear that it would bring blacks into the all-white neighborhood.

1. When Assemblyman Imperiale and his associate chained themselves to the fence, they performed an act of civil disobedience. Was this act violent or nonviolent? Explain your answer.
2. What did Assemblyman Imperiale hope to accomplish by such an act?
3. Do you think this act was a good idea?

Unit IX   Metropolitan Areas

Chapter 1   The Decay of the Cities

It's Monday morning. Moving time!

Shirlene helped her mother wrap the last cups and saucers in newspapers, put them with the other dishes in the big wicker basket, and load the basket on the truck Uncle Ed had brought down to help them move. Shirlene is happy to leave the dusty, broken-down wooden house she has lived in all of her 16 years. Yet she is a little afraid of what she'll find in the big city of Detroit. She knows she will miss the fields, the farm, and even the hot Mississippi weather.

Tom couldn't wait to get into the family car. The moving van was just about loaded and Tom was anxious to get to the new house before the van. "It's going to be great moving out of this city!" he thought. The new house really won't be too far from everything. Tom could always borrow the family car to visit his friends. He probably would get his own car pretty soon. Mom and Dad had talked for years about moving to the suburbs. Well, they finally made the move, and Tom was glad that they had.

Maria was frightened as she waited in the hot San Juan airport. The jet would be ready to board soon. Maria was not sure that she wanted to leave Puerto Rico and live in New York City. Her father was already there and he said that they would have a better life on the mainland. Maria wasn't too sure about that, but she had to go with her family. It wasn't easy to say goodbye to her friends, especially Eduardo.

A hundred years ago, most Americans lived in *rural* (farm or country) areas. By 1910 most Americans lived in small towns, close to rural areas, but also close to larger *urban* (big city) centers. By 1920 it was clear that America was no longer a nation of farmers. By this time more Americans lived in urban areas than in rural areas.

The movement of Americans from rural areas to urban areas has continued to this day. In fact, the population of the cities has grown so large that it is spilling over into the surrounding areas. We call these surrounding areas *suburbs*. By 1970, seven out of every ten Americans lived in the cities or in the suburbs. By the year 2000, 90 percent of the population will live in the cities or in the suburbs.

What Is a City?

A city is sights and sounds and smells. It is streets filled with people walking to or coming from some place. It is schools and libraries and factories. It is tall office buildings and wooden-frame houses, and parked cars that serve as a background for children playing in vacant lots or in the streets. A city is a policeman directing traffic and three clanging fire engines racing to a burning building. A city is going to a concert and having a picnic in the park. Throbbing action and smoke, crowds and all, but most important, a city is people.

People have lived in cities since ancient times. In the United States today, a city is an important town that has been given a charter by the state. The city has the right to govern itself within a given area and under limited conditions.

METROPOLITAN AREAS   A city and its suburbs form what is called a *metropolitan area*. Many people work in the *central city* (that is, the city itself), but live in the outlying areas, or suburbs. (For example, Tom's father works in the city but lives in the suburbs.) By using their cars or

City life

public *rapid transportation,* such as trains and buses, *commuters* can cover as much as 75 miles in one day. (Commuters are people who travel from the suburbs to the city to work.) As the population grows and the means of transportation improve, the trend toward suburban living will probably continue.

MEGALOPOLIS   Many of the cities and suburbs join other cities and suburbs to form what seems like a vast network or chain. The result is one giant-sized metropolitan area. The huge metropolitan area is called a *megalopolis.* One such "supercity" stretches down the East Coast from Boston to Washington, D.C. A second supercity includes the Midwest region from Pittsburgh to Chicago, and a third megalopolis runs down the West Coast from San Francisco to Los Angeles in California.

FLIGHT FROM THE CITY   In the past 20 years, the central cities have been losing population while the suburbs have been gaining population. In the early 1960s it was estimated that white families were leaving the cities at the rate of 150,000 people each year. In the 1970s the rate is close to 500,000 people each year. About 12 percent of the United States population is nonwhite, yet about 95 percent of the people living in the suburbs are white.

A good number of the families remaining in or moving into the central cities are the poorer families. They are mainly older persons, families headed by women, large families with many young children, and "broken" families. One more fact: Although nonwhites make up about 12 percent of the entire population, they account for about 22 percent of the central city population.

Put together what we have said thus far. First, metropolitan areas are growing, but the growth is mostly in the suburbs. Second, thousands of middle-class white families are leaving the cities every year. The middle class, because of its size, is the group that can afford to pay the taxes needed to support the city. But poorer and nonwhite households are increasing in the central cities. These groups are the ones most likely to need city services, but they are least able to afford to pay the taxes needed to support a city. What happens? This is what happens: We have problems—*urban problems.*

Urban Problems

We can see four major problem areas that American cities face today. These problems are: (1) problems of the slums, or ghettos; (2) problems of city government: rising costs and loss of taxpayers and industries; (3) problems of public services: transportation and utilities; and (4) problems of pollution.

SLUMS, OR GHETTOS   Fear is a steady companion of the slum resident. Compare two areas in a large city. Each area has about the same number of residents. The 25th Police Precinct is in a low-income black area. The 114th Precinct is in a white middle-class area. Although both areas reported about the same total number of crimes, almost half of the crimes in the middle-class area were car thefts. The number of violent crimes (murders, rapes, and armed robberies) in the 25th was much higher than in the 114th.

A slum is an area in which many people live in overcrowded conditions. The people are poor. Many of the families living in the slums depend upon their welfare checks to live. Many of the buildings are rundown and infested with rats and disease-carrying vermin. Litter and garbage are everywhere. Slum buildings are often firetraps. Schools are overcrowded. Streets are often unsafe after dark. Juvenile delinquency, crime, and drug use are common.

When a slum area has a large minority group population, the slum is often called a *ghetto*. The ghetto is usually the home of the most recent minority group coming into the country or a metropolitan area. Therefore, the ghetto population is constantly changing. Ghettos that once were the homes of German, Irish, and Jewish immigrants are now the homes of blacks, Hispanic-Americans, and Appalachian whites. But poverty does not care about your skin color or where you were born. Poor whites live in slums too. If we leave out rural slums, however, most of the white people living in slums are old people whose children have moved away. Most black and Hispanic-American ghetto residents are young people.

Crime   The ghetto is a breeding place for crime. Jobless men hang around on doorsteps during the day and pack the bars at night. Hustling is the big thing—policy slips, numbers, heroin—anything goes. Drugs and drug pushing are part of the life of the ghetto. Broken homes, filth, and the hopelessness of it all turn many ghetto youngsters off. Then they turn to drugs to turn themselves on. Many ghetto youngsters do not believe that anything will ever change—at least, not for the better.

Housing   Living in the ghetto is not cheap. Since rents keep going up all over the city, few people can afford to move to better housing. Maria's father got a fairly good job in New York City, but he cannot afford the high rents in most parts of the city. So he and his family must live in the ghetto. Private builders do not put up apartment buildings in the ghetto. They put up apartment buildings for the well-to-do in urban areas. Low-income public housing is not being built fast enough to house the increasing number of people in the ghetto. What is more, landlords are abandoning sound old buildings in the ghetto. Rising real estate taxes, high interest rates, low rents, and the high costs of upkeep for old buildings make them bad investments. The landlord often takes what he can and leaves.

What happens to an abandoned building? Drug addicts rip out the plumbing and sell it to support their habit. The old boiler needs repairs and finally stops working. Tenants go without heat and hot water. Pipes freeze and burst in winter. Water drips onto electric wiring and causes short circuits. Lights go out and fires start.

Every night, in a grimy Chicago tenement Cloe Weston rolls her baby's crib away from the wall in her bedroom "to keep the rats from climbing in."

Jennie Singleton, two years old, was so hungry that she ate pieces of ceiling paint that had fallen onto the bed. She was rushed to the hospital suffering from lead poisoning.

In New York City alone, there are over 500,000 decaying apartments. This is enough to house the entire population of the state of Arizona!

"Why don't *they* build new housing?" you ask. If *they* are private builders, the answer is that private builders build where they can make a profit. New, low-rent buildings are not profitable. However, government-*subsidized* (financed) housing projects can be built. But where should housing for the poor be built? In slum areas? If this is done, black and Hispanic-American families stay in the same bad neighborhoods. The ghetto does not disappear; it just changes its shape. New slums are in the making.

If publicly aided housing is built outside the ghetto, in middle-class areas, this may bring about greater integration in society. If housing is integrated, schools will be integrated too. But many middle-class whites, who are afraid that large numbers of poor black and Hispanic-American families will move into their neighborhoods, have resisted efforts to build public housing. Efforts to build public housing in the suburbs have met the same resistance.

CITY GOVERNMENT

Rising Costs   Urban areas are caught in a *tax squeeze.* The cost of government operations keeps going up. The two major expenses of most cities are education and welfare. The poor need more services than the middle class. For example, Shirlene attends a ghetto school. Shirlene's school needs more remedial reading teachers, guidance counselors, and free lunches than Tom's middle-class suburban school. As for medical and hospital care, the middle class is usually covered by medical and hospital insurance or it can afford private care. Poor citizens often depend upon the city for free medical services.

Here is where the "squeeze" comes in. Many of the people who are able to afford to pay city taxes—the middle-class whites—are running away from the city to the suburbs. The people who cannot afford to pay more city taxes—the poor and the elderly who remain in the city—demand more and better services. They want better schools, more health services, and cleaner

In the cartoonist's view, why is big business leaving the city?

Warren King in the New York *Daily News*—1967

and safer streets. This means that cities must spend a great deal more money.

Industry Leaving City   Another thing to keep in mind is that many industries are leaving the cities and going to the suburbs. Taxes are lower, land is cheaper, and living is more pleasant in the suburbs. But not enough new industries come into the cities to replace the ones that left. With the flight of industries paying high wages from the city, fewer jobs are available. Unemployment increases, particularly for the poor who cannot afford to follow jobs into the suburbs. If the worker is black or Hispanic-American, he would have a hard time finding housing for his family in the suburbs even if he could afford it.

PUBLIC SERVICES

Transportation   A comedian once said that the way to solve a city's traffic problems is to make all streets go one way—out of town. Cities depend upon transportation in much the same way that people depend upon air and water. Food, merchandise, and raw materials must be brought into the city, and finished goods must be sent out of the city by trains and trucks. Cars and trains, buses and subways carry people into and around the city. Pipelines bring in oil and gas. Cables carry electricity to factories and homeowners and enable city people to watch television, use the telephone, and run electric appliances.

As the city grows larger, its transportation needs also grow. The daily movement of thousands of people—in cars, taxis, trucks, and buses—causes traffic tie-ups. This is particularly true during rush hours when large numbers of people are going to or coming from work.

Utilities   Telephone and electric companies have been the subject of many jokes and angry words from city people. These utilities have not been able to increase their services as fast as the demand for their services has grown. Some years ago, not many homes or offices had air conditioning. Now many—in some areas, most—do. Millions of people have electric freezers and laundry equipment. The result has been a tremendous increase in the use of electric power. The fear of power failure is now an annual summer event in many localities.

Imagine a hot summer night. You have just taken a cool drink from the refrigerator and sat down in your air-conditioned living room. Suddenly, all the lights go out. The refrigerator stops. The air conditioner dies. Dad is not home yet—and he works on the fourteenth floor downtown and then has to take a subway train run by electric power. Does this sound impossible? It has already happened once in the Northeast. It could happen again.

POLLUTION   Cities are full of factories, homes, and cars. Their smoke and exhaust fumes fill the air with poisonous gases. Soot falls everywhere. Smoke and soot pollute (make impure or unclean) the air we breathe. City people throw away cans, papers, cartons, and leftovers, and use detergents to wash clothes and dishes. Cities must dispose of human wastes. Where do all the wastes go? What happens to that milk container you threw away after lunch? What happens to the plastic bottles and the old newspapers and the tin cans you put into the garbage?

The problems that all cities face—providing pure water, disposing of wastes, and keeping the air clean—are serious. As America's urban population increased, and people became accustomed to consuming more and more goods, the pollution problem became worse. We can no longer keep dumping sewage into lakes, streams, rivers, and oceans if we want pure water to drink and fresh fish to eat. We cannot keep sending poisonous gases into the atmosphere if we want to be healthy.

Summary   Urban problems have developed as more and more of the population of the United States moved into the cities and their suburbs. Cities are often called upon to provide services that were unheard of a generation ago.

Looking Ahead   In the next chapter, we shall examine some of the problems that develop when suburbs grow.

EXERCISES

MATCHING QUESTIONS   Match each term in Column A with its definition in Column B.

Column A

1. rural
2. urban
3. city
4. suburb
5. metropolitan area
6. megalopolis
7. slum
8. ghetto
9. commuter

Column B

(*a*)   an area where poor people live in run-down, overcrowded buildings

(*b*)   an area that includes the central city and the surrounding suburbs that depend upon it

(*c*)   a slum area that is populated largely by a minority group

(*d*)   a very large area that includes cities and suburbs

(*e*)   an important town that is given the right to govern itself by the state

(*f*)   an area made up mostly of farms or small towns

(*g*)   describing a heavily populated area, or city area

(*h*)   the area that surrounds a city

(*i*)   a person who travels from the suburbs to the city to work

MULTIPLE-CHOICE QUESTIONS   For each item, write the letter of the best answer.

1. The main idea of this chapter is that (*a*) cities are bad (*b*) suburbs are nice places to live in (*c*) cities have problems (*d*) cities are nice places to visit.

2. Most Americans live (*a*) in metropolitan areas (*b*) on farms (*c*) in rural areas (*d*) in suburbs.

3. Which statement would be hardest to prove either true or false? (*a*) Middle-class whites are fleeing the central cities. (*b*) Few nonwhites live in the suburbs. (*c*) The suburbs are growing faster than the central cities. (*d*) The cities are dying.

4. Which statement is a fact and not an opinion? (*a*) Cities should receive more aid from the states. (*b*) Man has lived in cities since ancient times. (*c*) It is safer to live in the suburbs than in the ghetto. (*d*) Cities are more interesting than rural areas.

5. For people who live in the suburbs, the city is often their (*a*) workroom (*b*) bedroom (*c*) residence (*d*) shopping center.

6. A chain of several cities and suburban areas that make up one giant-sized city is called a (*a*) megalopolis (*b*) metropolitan area (*c*) central city (*d*) ghetto.

7. Which statement is true? (*a*) Only old people live in slums. (*b*) Only blacks and Hispanic-Americans live in ghettos. (*c*) Most of the people living in the central cities are nonwhite. (*d*) Cities and suburbs depend upon each other.

8. Problems of transportation, pollution, waste disposal, and finance seem to be bothering (*a*) only cities with large nonwhite populations (*b*) only cities with large elderly populations (*c*) all major cities (*d*) only the cities that are parts of a megalopolis.

FURTHER READING   Read the selection below. Basing your answers on this reading, tell whether each of the statements that follows is true or false. If the selection does not give you enough information to answer true or false, write NS.

ROSALEE'S STORY: LIFE IN THE GHETTO

Rosalee is 15 years old. She was born in a ghetto and has lived in a ghetto all her life. Rosalee is not sure if she was born in Harlem or in the

East New York section of Brooklyn in New York City. As it is, Rosalee can remember living in five different places in her life.

Rosalee is the oldest child in her family. Rosalee's mother, Doreen, is 30 years old. Rosalee was born to her when she was just about the age that Rosalee is now. Besides Rosalee, Doreen has had Tom, age 13, Billy, age 12, Sara, age 9, and baby Phoebe, who was just 2. Rosalee has never known her father, and Doreen never talks about him.

Before Phoebe was born, Doreen worked in a shoe factory. She was a piece worker and usually earned about $128 a week. She had a take-home pay of about $110. Alvin, Doreen's gentleman friend, used to help out with money. Rosalee called Alvin "Doreen's Old Man."

A few months after Phoebe was born, Alvin left and never came back. Alvin had thought that they could make a go of it without Doreen's salary, but there were a lot of expenses for food and rent and clothes, and Alvin did not earn enough to take care of all the children. He left because he figured that Doreen and the children would do better without him if they went on welfare.

Doreen has been on welfare for nearly two years. Welfare pays the rent and utilities. The welfare department has a way of figuring out how much to give each member of the family personally. For example, Doreen is allowed $36.04 for herself every two weeks, $39.45 for each of the teenagers, and $20.81 for Phoebe. With this money, Doreen has to buy food, clothing, household supplies, and everything else. She buys food stamps and exchanges them for food at the supermarket checkout. Food stamps help to cut the cost of family meals. Doreen does not know how, but welfare figures that she and the girls can get along on one lipstick and one deodorant each per year.

Rosalee has lived in her present home for only about five months. Before that, the family lived in a hotel for three months because their apartment building burned down. Rosalee says that this apartment is much better than the hotel. Her family lives in a building with 20 other families. Some of the buildings on the block have been condemned and boarded up, yet families have broken into them because they are desperate for a place to live.

Then there are the junkies. They are everywhere. They break into your apartment when you're out or mug you in the hallway or on a dark street. Sometimes they hurt or even kill people for just a few dollars.

Doreen plays the numbers. She bets only a nickel or a dime a day. She "hit" once for $50, so she keeps playing in the hope that she will be lucky again. Everyone in the neighborhood plays the numbers.

Rosalee knows many kids who are hooked on "horse" (heroin). She says that dope is not for her. But she does not mind "ripping off" some of the girls at school for a dime or quarter. The free lunch in school is not much good, and Rosalee spends the money on potato chips and soda.

Rosalee does not know what she wants to be when she grows up. She says she does not care. She just wants to live each day and, as she puts it, "later for that."

1. Rosalee has lived in Harlem all of her life.
2. When Rosalee's mother, Doreen, gave birth to her first child, she was the same age that Rosalee is now.
3. Rosalee hates her father.
4. Rosalee's family receives welfare.
5. Rosalee is no better nor any worse off than any other 15-year-old in America today.
6. Rosalee is one of the best students in her class at school.
7. Gambling, stealing, and drug taking are common activities in the neighborhood in which Rosalee lives.

FILL-IN QUESTIONS   Complete the statements by filling in the blank spaces. Select the fill-ins from the following list:

(a) crime   (d) low-income   (g) tax squeeze
(b) help   (e) high-wage   (h) cramped
(c) upper-income   (f) recreation

1. The cities are crying for _____.
2. _____ groups are moving out of the cities.
3. _____ groups are migrating to the cities.
4. _____ industries are leaving the city.
5. Cities are generally _____ for space.
6. Proof of statement 5 is the shortage of areas for _____.
7. The _____ is the result of the middle-class flight to the suburbs and low-income migration to the cities.
8. Overcrowded schools and ghettos may contribute to the rise in _____.

A POEM ABOUT CITIES, BY CARL SANDBURG   Read the poem below and answer the questions that follow:

It has happened before.
Strong men put up a city and got
    a nation together,
And paid singers to sing and women
    to warble: We are the greatest city,
        the greatest nation,
        nothing like us ever was.

And while the singers sang
and the strong men listened
and paid the singers well,
and felt good about it all
    there were rats and lizards who listened
    . . . and the only listeners left now
    . . . are . . . the rats . . . and the lizards.

1. What does Carl Sandburg mean when he says, "It has happened before"?

2. According to the poem, what can happen to even the greatest city?
3. What does Sandburg mean when he writes that the rats and lizards are the only listeners left?
4. What did you study in this chapter that either supports or does not support the main idea of this poem?
5. Why do you suppose that Carl Sandburg gives us this warning?

Chapter 2   Suburban
Sprawl

"Get off the phone!" Mr. Peters shouted to his daughter Sally. But Sally hardly listened. Her father is always telling her to get off the phone. But what does he expect her to do? Sure she lives in a lovely house in a beautiful new suburban community. Yes she has her own room, television set, and stereo hi-fi. And yes they have a half-acre of land with trees. But what is there for her to do? Her friends, who live in homes just like hers, are spread out for miles around. There is no place—no community or religious center or any other place—where they all can go and get together. "Without this phone, I'd be dead," she thought.

Sally isn't the only teenager with the same problem. More and more people are moving to suburban communities. When so many people choose to live in the suburbs rather than in the cities, there must be a lot to be said for suburban life. However, as suburban areas grow, they have growth problems.

People used to say that the suburbs were the bedrooms and the cities were the workrooms of metropolitan areas. This meant that people lived in the suburbs but went to school, worked, and shopped in the cities. But in the 1970s this description of cities and suburbs is no longer 100 percent true. Many suburbs are now centers of industry because companies have moved from the central cities to the suburbs. Huge shopping centers and industrial parks have been built in suburban areas. Today, in fact, seven out of every ten people living in the suburbs work there as well.

The suburbs have also become educational centers. New schools—from elementary through college levels—have been built in the suburbs. Plays, movies, and concerts are available everywhere.

Now let us combine the information above. Jobs, stores, schools, and entertainment are available in the suburbs. At one time these were found only in the cities. But when many people moved to the suburbs, jobs and services followed them. As a result of the change, 80 percent of the new job opportunities are in the suburbs, not in the cities.

The Suburbs Are Outer Cities

All the features of a central city now exist in the suburbs. Suburban residents are no longer dependent upon the central city—many rarely go into town for any reason. What is more, they do not have to, because they can do in the suburbs most of the things that once could be done only in the central city.

POPULATION GROWTH Up until about 1960, more people lived in the central cities than in the suburbs. But today, the population of the suburbs is now larger than the population of the central cities. In 1940, for example, two out of every ten Americans lived in the suburbs (19 million fewer than lived in the cities). In 1974 almost four out of ten Americans lived in the suburbs, and this is about 19 million more than lived in the cities.

NEW HOUSING AND INDUSTRY Cities, as you know, are crowded places. There is little or no open land on which to put up new buildings in the heart of a city. It is not surprising, therefore, that 90 percent of land available for housing is outside the city limits. In other words, if new housing were to be built on land not at present being used for housing, it would have to be built away from the central city. This means that such housing will be built in the suburbs. We have seen why builders do not tear down old houses and build new ones in the central cities—especially not low-rent housing. Two out of every three dollars being spent for housing or industrial construction are being spent in the suburbs.

NEW PATTERN OF DEVELOPMENT Suburban growth looks something like rings or circles, each one just a little larger than the other.

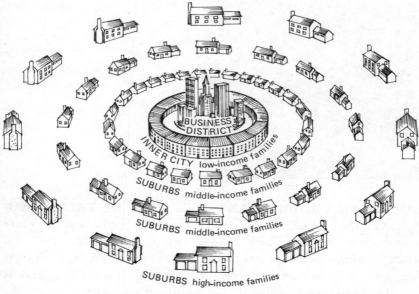

Urban-suburban pattern of American life

We can call the innermost circle the *inner city*. (This is the same area we have called the *central city*.) Located all along the circles surrounding the inner city are the suburbs, or *outer cities*.

THE SPREAD CITY   It is easy for a person who lives in one outer city to work in a second, shop in a third, and visit friends in a fourth. This means that the outer cities are in many ways connected to each other rather than to the central city. The automobile has made this spreading out easy for the people living in the outer cities. Without the automobile and the vast connecting highways, the *spread city* would not have developed.

Problems of the Suburbs

The suburbs, together with the inner city, form a metropolitan area. One suburban problem, then, is the effect that the growth of the suburbs, or outer cities, has had on the inner city. Another problem is the effect of suburban growth on the land and the people in suburban areas.

Suburban sprawl

SUBURBAN GROWTH—ANOTHER FORM OF RACIAL SEGREGATION?

Much of the middle class—in particular, the white middle class—has abandoned the inner city. As you can see in the diagram showing inner and outer cities, the poor are in the inner city. As one moves outward from the center, each suburban area or ring reached is wealthier than the one before it. The wealthiest area is farthest from the inner city.

The inner city is still the place where the rural poor must go to look for jobs. Poor blacks and Puerto Ricans have no place to go but the inner city. In 1970 the population of the city of Baltimore, for example, was nearly 50 percent black, but in the suburbs surrounding the city only 5 percent of the people were black. Throughout the nation, only about 5 percent of the people in the suburbs are nonwhite.

LACK OF PLANNING FOR GROWTH

As you drive through the suburbs, you often see an ugly mixture of shopping centers, billboard displays, drive-ins, and auto junkyards. This is because the suburbs have been allowed to develop without planning for sensible growth. To make matters worse, beautiful forests and fields have given way to miles of housing developments, where all the houses look alike. The people living in these look-alike houses are also very much alike. They probably earn nearly the same income, attend the same churches, dress the same way, and enjoy the same activities. And, most probably, they are white, since so few nonwhites live in the suburbs.

The modern highways that connect the inner and outer cities take up a lot of space. A cloverleaf intersection may take up 40 acres of land. In order to build the highways and intersections, trees had to be cleared and hillsides bulldozed or graded to meet the design of the highway engineers.

Most homes in the suburbs are built for one or two families. Therefore, a suburban community of two dozen families may occupy two to three times that many acres of land. But in the city, a single apartment building on two or three acres of land usually houses a dozen or more (often many more) families. Thus the single-family suburban home is the least economical use of land for housing.

INCREASED COSTS   The large increase in population in the suburbs has made it necessary to build new schools, hospitals, and roads, and to expand police, fire, and sanitation facilities. This costs money. Taxes on real estate, therefore, have gone up in suburban areas. These taxes are often a high price to pay just to get away from the problems of the inner city.

Some suburban communities have encouraged industries to enter their areas. The industries will pay real estate taxes and, therefore, reduce the tax burden on homeowners. This has been taking place, but not without a price. When the suburbs become outer cities, they lose some of the appeal that once was associated with suburban living (quiet, almost rural communities, made up of one-family houses; no traffic jams or overcrowded schools; fresh air and open spaces).

BOREDOM   Many people who have moved to the suburbs do not find it all that they had thought it would be. Many people—teenagers most of all—often find suburban life dull. Recent increases in drinking and drug use by suburban teenagers are alarming. Their parents, running away from the problems of the inner city, find that they are running into new problems in the suburbs.

LACK OF FACILITIES; HIGH LIVING COSTS   Suburban living is not always all it is cracked up to be. At least this is the opinion of many city people who moved to the suburbs and then moved back to the city. For one thing community facilities, such as public transportation, are often poor in the suburbs. Sally Peters complains that there is no place in her community where she and her friends can meet after school. And many services are miles from where people live. If you are used to walking to the store, school, and library, you will find it difficult to get used to the need for a car just to get around. Dad, in the meantime, also needs a car to get to work.

The costs of commuting to work in the city are often high. Suburban railroads and buses cost far more than urban subways and buses. Keeping up a home in the suburbs can be more expensive than expected. When you include local school, water, and property taxes, taxes are often higher than in city areas. Gardening may be fun, but it can be expensive, particularly if your house was built on a marshy or sandy area.

Summary   The suburban areas are growing in size and population. In many ways, the suburbs are like small outer cities surrounding an inner city.

The growth of the suburbs has been at the expense of the rest of society. Good land has been stripped to make room for suburban houses. This form of land use is economically wasteful. It is by no means certain that the quality of life in the suburbs is worth the cost.

Looking Ahead   The problems of the cities and the suburbs often cross many boundaries. The problems may start in one state, county, or locality and end in another. In the next chapter, we shall see how communities in large areas of the country can get together to work out their common problems.

EXERCISES

MULTIPLE-CHOICE QUESTIONS   For each item, write the letter of the best answer.

1. The main idea of this chapter is that (*a*) it is nice to live in the suburbs (*b*) it is best to live in the central city (*c*) the suburbs are the answer to America's problems (*d*) suburbs have and create problems.
2. Which statement would be the most difficult to prove either true or false? (*a*) The suburbs are growing faster than the central cities. (*b*) Life is more pleasant in the suburbs than in the central city. (*c*) The black

population in the suburbs is not large. (*d*) Many industries are moving to the suburbs.

3. If a person lives in the suburbs but works in the city, we say that the suburb is that person's (*a*) shopping center (*b*) playground (*c*) bedroom (*d*) workroom.

4. Which area would most likely be the largest? (*a*) a city (*b*) a suburb (*c*) a metropolitan area (*d*) a spread city

5. People who live in the suburbs and work for a living probably work (*a*) in the city (*b*) in factories (*c*) in the suburbs (*d*) on farms.

6. More Americans live in (*a*) central cities (*b*) suburban areas (*c*) farm areas (*d*) rural lands.

7. Most poor Americans live in the (*a*) inner city (*b*) outer city (*c*) suburbs (*d*) spread city.

8. Most of the people living in the suburbs are (*a*) white (*b*) black (*c*) poor (*d*) farmers.

9. Which takes up the most land space for housing and transportation? (*a*) tall apartment buildings (*b*) skyscraper office buildings (*c*) central cities (*d*) suburbs

MATCHING QUESTIONS   Match each term in Column A with its definition in Column B.

Column A

1. residential area
2. inner city
3. outer city
4. spread city

Column B

(*a*) a suburb that has all of the features of a central city

(*b*) another name for the central city; or, the main part, or core, of the city

(*c*) an area where people live, as distinguished from an area where there are businesses and factories

(*d*) suburbs connected to each other rather than to the central city

UNDERSTANDING POPULATION CHANGES   Study the tables below and answer the questions that follow. Write *T* if the statement is true, *F* if the statement is false, and *NS* if there is not sufficient information given to answer true or false.

Black and White Population of Central Cities and Suburbs in Metropolitan Areas, 1970 and 1974

	1970	1974	Percent Change
Central Cities:			
Whites	48,909,000	46,427,000	−5.1
Blacks	12,909,000	13,726,000	+6.3
Total	61,818,000	60,153,000	−2.7
Suburbs:			
Whites	70,029,000	75,313,000	+7.5
Blacks	3,433,000	3,987,000	+16.1
Total	73,462,000	79,300,000	+7.9

1. Whites outnumber blacks in the central cities of the United States.
2. The greatest percentage increase shown on the chart was the increase in blacks living in the suburbs.
3. Approximately 75 percent of all whites living in metropolitan areas live in the suburbs.
4. Approximately 75 percent of all blacks living in metropolitan areas live in the central city.
5. Blacks prefer living in the central city.
6. Outside of the great metropolitan areas, we probably would find that black and white population changes during the period were the same as those shown on the chart.
7. Almost 95 percent of the population of the suburbs is white.
8. Fewer whites lived in the central cities in 1970 than in 1974.
9. Persons of Hispanic origin follow the same population patterns as shown for blacks in the chart.
10. A conclusion that one might reasonably draw from this chart is that there has been a movement of whites out of the central cities and into the suburbs.

RESEARCH PROJECT With the information that you now have, you might enjoy doing a little more research to enable you to come up with some ideas on each of the following:

1. Do library research to find out how the area you live in has changed. Get a new road map of the metropolitan area near you.
   (*a*) Identify on the map the central city or cities, the suburbs, and routes of travel connecting city and suburbs.
   (*b*) Compare your new road map with an earlier map of the same area—one about 20 years old. Which communities are the same? Which are new? What happened to the green areas of forest and fields?
   (*c*) Locate unused land in your area. Do you think that this land should be used for homes? schools? parks? industry? a combination of some or all of these? Tell why.

2. You have learned that the suburbs are growing faster than the central cities. You have also learned that more poor people and nonwhites are living in the central cities.
   (*a*) Should all-white suburban schools be forced to accept black children bused in from the inner city?
   (*b*) Should people who live in the city be allowed to use the parks and beaches paid for by taxpayers living in the suburbs?
   (*c*) If an all-white suburb passes a law that does not permit a low-cost housing project to be built in the community, should the federal government cut off housing funds to that community?
   (*d*) Should the government help poor families purchase single-family homes in middle-class suburban areas?

3. You have learned that a metropolitan area is made up of a city and the suburbs that surround it. The white middle class seems to be fleeing the cities and going to live in the suburbs.
   (*a*) What do you think the middle class living in the suburbs owes to the city?
   (*b*) What, if anything, do you think the city owes to the suburbs that surround it?

4. Can you draw? Draw a cartoon showing one of the following:
   (*a*) the flight of the white middle class to the suburbs
   (*b*) "look-alike" suburban living
   (*c*) the boredom of suburban living

Chapter 3 Regional Planning

If you have ever had a really bad cold or the flu, you will remember that your head ached, your arms and legs were tired, your nose was running, and it was hard to breathe. Perhaps you also had a sore throat and a cough that kept you awake all night. Your entire body was affected. As far as you were concerned, the important thing was to get some relief and to get rid of the cold. From head to toe you are one person, so whatever happens to one part of you affects every other part.

A nation is like a person. Most of the time we Americans do not think of ourselves in this way, but it may be time that we did. If it is true that the United States, like a person, is one whole body, then anything that happens to any part of the United States is important to every other part of the United States. If a local problem does not begin or end in the local area, then we ought to start thinking about treating local problems beyond the local area alone.

Local Problems

In other units of this book, you have read about the problems and the goals of Jimmy Green, Pablo, Rosalee, Tim Hutchins, Alfredo, and Leroy. Maybe you liked some of these people and did not like others. But one thing is certain: each individual whom you met was just that—a person, a human being. All people want a better life.

Imagine that a poor family moves into your neighborhood. The father wants to work and is looking for a job. But suppose that he cannot find a job right away. He has no money. Who should pay the cost of keeping his family together while the man is down on his luck—your community, because the man lives there now, or the community he left in search of a better life? Or should both share the costs?

If you live in a metropolitan area, you live in the central city or in one of the surrounding suburbs. If you live in the central city, you are probably used to dodging cars or waiting at street corners to get into a crowded bus. You are probably used to the noise of the city as life *teems* (moves quickly) around you. Maybe you go home to a large apartment building where many of your neighbors are strangers to you. You know what the problems of the city are.

Perhaps your family wanted to get away from all the dirt and crowding of the city and bought a home in the suburbs. Dad still commutes to his job in the city. Even though you live in the suburbs, do you still have some responsibility to the city? Should your family help to pay the costs of running the city because your dad earns his living there?

POLLUTION   If your drinking water is sudsy or has a strange taste, or if your living room drapes are loaded with soot, who is at fault? The water you drink and the soot in your drapes may have traveled many miles before they arrived at your house. The soot may have come from a factory chimney in New Jersey. Winds carried it to your home in New York or Pennsylvania.

The water you drink in Oregon may have started as snow on Mount Rainier in the state of Washington. The snow melted and then joined one of the streams that feed the rivers emptying into the Columbia River. Somewhere along its way to you, housewives used detergents to wash their dishes and clothes. The water from their homes flowed into the river. Some of the detergents were still in the water when it reached your town's water system. Which state is responsible for keeping the water pure and clear—Washington or Oregon—or are they both?

When many cities and suburbs are tied together into one giant-sized metropolitan area, this is called a megalopolis, as we learned earlier. When New York sneezes, so they say, it can be heard in Boston to the north and Washington to the south. Therefore, it is not always possible, or even practical, to solve all local problems locally. Many problems that *seem* to be local may actually involve a much wider area. Sometimes the area involved is an entire *region*.

A region is an area in which the people have certain economic interests in common. A region may cover a few square miles or many square miles. It may be within one state or it may cover several states. The important thing is that the communities within the region have a common interest. Their problem can be handled through regional planning.

POVERTY   Poverty, as you know, exists both in urban and rural areas. In fact, as jobs become scarcer in rural and farm areas, many people migrate to the cities and become members of the urban poor. Rural poverty, therefore, becomes a city problem. As suburbs grow, they take up more and more of the space that once was farmland or green space. So, if city growth is at the expense of rural land, the problem of city expansion becomes a rural problem and not a city problem alone. It should be clear, then, that rural and urban problems are closely linked.

Case Study: Regional Planning for Education   Mary Manigo went to Decker Intermediate School. Paula Janowski went to Martin Luther King Intermediate School. Mary and Paula met in a social studies class at Central High School. Although they live in different neighborhoods and had never met before they went to high school, they became good friends. In high school, they realized that they had many things in common. Most of all, both Mary and Paula wanted Central High to be the best school in the country.

Mary and Paula were active in school affairs. They quickly realized that their school was concerned with both the community that Mary lived in and the community that Paula lived in. For one thing Central High was concerned that the schools its students came from should prepare them well. Then again, Central High realized that students spend only a part of their day in school and the rest of their day in the community. Therefore, if a high school is truly interested in its students as people, the school must also be involved in the community.

Mary and Paula are members of Central's Students' Organization. They help plan dances, school plays, sporting events, and programs to bring parents and other community residents into the school. In addition, Paula serves on a committee of students, faculty members, and parents. They meet every month with the school's principal to discuss school programs and policies. All of the activities that Mary and Paula are involved in require planning that must consider the needs and wishes of the different neighborhoods that send students to Central High School. If we were to think of each neighborhood as a region, we might say that Mary and Paula were taking part in regional-planning activities.

What Regional Planning Does

Regional planning means studying everything that goes into making an area the kind of place you would want it to be. Your own community is part of a larger region. If you were asked to draw up plans for your region, some of the topics you would want to study might include the following:

LAND USE   As the population of the region increases, you will have to plan how best to use the remaining open land. For example, should the *green belt* (forest and farm areas) be cleared for housing or for industrial development? Where should parks be located? Should new housing be located outside the central city? Should a manufacturing plant or a low-rent housing development be built on vacant land?

WATER USE   Rivers, streams, and lakes in the region can serve many purposes. They can be used for recreation—such as boating, swimming, or fishing—for transportation, for sewage and waste disposal, or for drinking water. But using a body of water for one of these purposes means that you cannot use it for any of the others. So you will have to plan how the region's water resources can serve each of these needs for all of the people and businesses.

AIR USE   Factory smoke is easily carried by winds across community and state lines. Home chimneys, jet planes, as well as factories—all make use of the airways. Clean air, for example, cannot be handled by one community working alone, particularly if the cause of pollution is in another community. Regional cooperation is needed in this case.

ECONOMIC DEVELOPMENT   You would want to study and plan for the use of your region's natural resources. Do you want to encourage agriculture, industry, or both? You would have to plan an educational system that would make a supply of trained labor available. A fair tax program is needed so that homeowners and industry do not flee your region for another.

Case Study: The Tennessee Valley Authority (TVA)   When the United States was still a young nation, the region of the Tennessee River basin was rich and fertile. When the settlers arrived, they cut down the trees and cleared the land to make room for homes and cotton plantations. But years of growing cotton robbed the soil of its fertility. Winds and rains took away the rich topsoil. Without tree roots to hold the soil, the land in the region became *eroded* over the years. (*Erosion* is when the topsoil is worn away.) The people of the Tennessee Valley became poor farmers working poor soil. *Flash* (sudden) floods or *droughts* (long periods when it does not rain) could wipe out the work of the year.

It was clear that a massive regional effort was needed to save the Tennessee Valley. In 1933 the Tennessee Valley Authority (TVA) was set up to deal with the problem of water power development and use. The TVA did that and much more as well. The TVA built dams and *hydroelectric* (water power) plants along the river basin. It was able to produce cheap electric power and sell it to many farmers, who had never had electric lights. The TVA also sold electric power to states, communities, and private industries. The area served by the TVA covers some 40,000 square miles in seven states with a population of several million people.

The important thing is that, because the area crosses state and community lines, the TVA could work for the benefit of all the people of the Tennessee Valley region. For example, the TVA was able to plant new trees on the land, control floods, and increase farm production. The TVA also promoted the use of the Tennessee River for commercial purposes, built low-cost housing for its employees, and helped local health services fight malaria and tuberculosis. The TVA pushed for the agricultural and industrial development of the entire area.

Today the Tennessee Valley region is fertile again. Industry is highly developed. Electricity is cheap. Recreational facilities—swimming, fishing, and boating—are available for everyone. The area is once more a healthy and growing part of our country.

Federal Aid for States and Cities

The problems of the cities and the problems of rural areas are very closely related to each other. In fact, we have learned that the major problems of the cities are national in origin. We saw that rural problems caused many people to leave rural areas and move to the cities.

Cities and states today do not seem to have the money to deal with the problems of poverty, education, health, crime, and ecology. People living in the suburbs, we have seen, have in many ways run away from the problems of the cities. Some people have suggested, therefore, that the best way to help the cities is for the federal government to take on much of the *financial* (monetary) burden of the cities. In this way, all Americans would share in the burden of solving a national problem, not only those living in the cities where the problems come to the forefront.

Federal aid to states and cities is not new. For example, the federal government pays about 90 percent of the cost of building interstate highways. It gives money to help improve education. Because states and cities often cannot raise the money needed to attack the problems that we have discussed, the federal government must provide the money.

Summary   City, state, and regional planning boards and the federal government will all have to work together to solve the problems at home.

EXERCISES

MULTIPLE-CHOICE QUESTIONS   For each item, write the letter of the best answer.

1. Which of the following problems do you think is handled best at the local level? (*a*) welfare (*b*) pollution control (*c*) garbage collection (*d*) regional planning
2. Which service do you think would be handled best at the regional level? (*a*) public transportation (*b*) police protection (*c*) fire protection (*d*) noise control

3. Which of the following is the best example of a national problem? (*a*) Unemployment increases in all the states. (*b*) A state cuts money for school buses. (*c*) A factory moves from the inner city to the suburbs. (*d*) People looking for work move into your neighborhood.

4. Which problem may have started outside the local community? (*a*) dim street lights (*b*) sudsy drinking water (*c*) vandalism (*d*) not enough policemen

5. Which of the following is an example of regional planning? (*a*) TVA (*b*) city government (*c*) state government (*d*) interstate highways

6. What is the main idea of this chapter? (*a*) Some problems can be handled best through regional planning. (*b*) All problems should be handled on a regional basis. (*c*) Local governments can no longer handle any problems. (*d*) The federal government should do all it can to help people in need.

7. Rivers and air currents flow across state lines. This is an argument (*a*) for regional planning (*b*) against regional planning (*c*) that does not affect regional planning (*d*) for public aid to education.

8. Which statement is a fact, not an opinion? (*a*) The United States should do away with state governments. (*b*) Many rural problems spill over into urban communities. (*c*) The people in a community should solve their own problems. (*d*) States should not accept aid from the federal government.

MATCHING QUESTIONS   Match each term in Column A with its definition in Column B.

Column A

1. local
2. region
3. nation
4. erosion
5. green belt

Column B

(*a*) forest and farm areas
(*b*) the entire country
(*c*) close to home
(*d*) wearing away of topsoil by water and wind
(*e*) a large area, which may cross state lines, whose people share common economic interests

HOW WOULD YOU SOLVE THESE PROBLEMS? Here are some real problems that have faced many communities. Imagine that you could do something about each problem. What would you do?

1. You live in a small suburban town. Septic tanks have begun to overflow. The seepage is polluting the water supply. Your town's engineer says that a sewerage system is needed to replace all the septic tanks in town. This would be very expensive.

   Four nearby towns face a similar problem. Would you advise your town to build a sewerage system on its own? Or would you try to get the five towns to join in the project? Why?

2. A new bridge was built across a river that separates two states. The roads and highways in the state on one side of the river are wide and modern. You live on that side. On the other side of the river, the roads are narrow and in need of repair. Each time you cross the heavily traveled bridge, you get stuck in a traffic jam on the other side.

   Should your state pay part of the cost for improving the roads and highways on the other side of the bridge? How might the traffic problem have been avoided?

3. Suppose that you solved problem 2. Now you find that the roads are packed with trucks, buses, and cars. When you finally get where you want to go, you cannot find a parking space. Traffic and parking are handled by the local police in each community.

   Should traffic control and parking be handled by each separate community? How might regional planning help this situation?

4. Sewage and refuse from all the towns up the river are carried downstream. The water is so dirty when it reaches your town that no one can go fishing or swimming. The river has a bad smell too. Factory chimneys in the next state pour out smoke that crosses state lines and pollutes the air of your community. Highways cross state and city lines too. Exhaust fumes from the cars and trucks traveling along these highways also add to the air pollution in your community.

   Would you ask your town council to pass laws to protect your town? Could these laws work? How might regional planning help?

Unit X   The Environment

Chapter 1   The Balance
of Nature

Henry Stevens is in the ninth grade. Today his social studies class was discussing the Middle East. The map that Henry's teacher, Mrs. Ellison, placed at the front of the room showed that much of the area is a desert. Many years ago, however, a fertile area, shaped like a crescent, stretched from the Tigris and Euphrates Rivers along the Mediterranean coast and down the Nile River. Henry was puzzled why this once-fertile area had become a desert.

That evening, Henry asked his sister Mary to explain about the Fertile Crescent. Mary, who is studying ecology at college, explained in the following way:

What Is the Balance of Nature?

"The word 'ecology' comes from a Greek word that means 'house' or 'home,' " Mary said. "So ecology is the study of the home, or the environment, of living things. Plants, fish, birds, animals—including people —are living things.

"But," Mary went on, "living things depend upon nonliving things, such as air and water, for survival. Living things and nonliving things must

289

exist together in their environment. Your fishtank, for example, is an *ecosystem* (a complete unit in nature). The base of this system is its nonliving parts—water, minerals, chemicals, and the sun's energy.

"The system is so delicately balanced that even a change in temperature can affect several parts of it and throw the entire system off balance. Isn't that why you keep a thermometer in your tank and are so careful to keep the water at the same temperature?

"Once there were great oak forests in Spain and cedar trees in Lebanon. All along the coast of the Mediterranean, there were rich lands and cool forests. But when the trees were cut down, the people did not plant new ones. During the Middle Ages, huge herds of sheep were turned loose in the forests. The sheep ate the grass that held the topsoil in place. Tree roots could not hold the topsoil. The ecosystem was upset. Winds and rains washed away the topsoil. Trees could not grow without the topsoil, so the trees disappeared. The result of the upset in the balance of nature is that desert now exists where green fields and giant forests once grew."

Henry was interested in what Mary was saying. "Could it happen again? Could it happen in the United States?" he asked. Mary told him that the question is not whether it can happen here—it is happening here. Something is upsetting the balance of nature.

IT CAN HAPPEN HERE   Two of America's Great Lakes are dying. They can no longer be used for fishing or swimming.

Oil spilled from giant tankers has ruined beaches and killed birds and fish life along the coasts of California and the Gulf of Mexico. Some of America's great rivers are giant sewers.

Air pollution is so bad in Los Angeles that *smog* (*sm*oke and f*og*) is a constant problem. Smog is becoming a problem for many other American cities as well.

Pesticides are chemicals that farmers use to kill harmful insects. But pesticides kill useful insects in addition to the unwanted ones. In many orchards, for example, the destruction of bees is creating a serious problem. Bees carry the pollen needed to fertilize plants and fruit trees.

Human beings have existed on earth for perhaps a million years. Our bodies are made in such a way as not to interfere with the balance of life. For example, just like the fish in Henry's fishtank, we live in a delicate balance with our environment. We inhale oxygen and exhale carbon dioxide. We eat solid food and drink liquids, and we *excrete* (give off) solid and liquid wastes.

Plants absorb carbon dioxide, nitrogen, and minerals from animal and human wastes. Plants need these elements to live. Animals and human beings eat the plants and other animals as well, also in order to live. When animals and humans die, their bodies *decompose* (turn back to elements and minerals) and become food for the plants. This closes the cycle. Nothing is wasted. And the balance of nature is complete.

What Has Upset the Balance of Nature?

Pogo, the comic strip character created by cartoonist Walt Kelly, says, "We have met the enemy and he is us." Pogo is talking about the enemy of the environment. Pogo is right. Most of the changes that have been made in the environment have been made by mankind. As man becomes what he thinks is more "civilized," he makes more changes in the world around him. The *technology* (methods and machinery used in production) that has helped Americans change the earth and force it to serve their needs is threatening America's very survival.

Fertilizers and pesticides in the waters that drain off farmlands have *contaminated* (made unclean or unhealthy) our rivers and lakes.

American households produce tons of waste material that add to sewage and increase the pollution of our waterways. Laundry detergents containing phosphates have upset the aquatic balance of nature by causing the growth of algae that use up the oxygen fish need to live.

Many electric power plants use the water from nearby streams or rivers to cool off the machinery used to produce electricity. This water is then dumped back into the stream or river, and, of course, raises its temperature. The higher water temperature often kills some or all of the fish. People who fished for enjoyment or for food pay the cost.

Huge dams have changed the courses of rivers, and vast swamplands and marshes have been drained, destroying the natural environment of the fish and animals that once lived there. Homes and factories, streets and highways occupy land that once was open space or fertile farmland. Some day soon, there may no longer be any open land left.

Jet planes streaking across the sky leave a trail of smoke that pollutes the atmosphere. Giant jets add to noise pollution. (Superjets may even threaten the ozone balance in the atmosphere.)

The Numbers Problem

The first recorded human civilization dates back to about the year 3000 B.C., or about 5,000 years ago. There were fewer people on the entire face of the globe *then* than now live in one of America's major cities.

The population of the United States today is over 210 million persons. Experts guess that there will be at least 300 million—perhaps 400 million—of us in the year 2025.

Americans today throw away about 8 million television sets and junk about the same number of cars each year. We also throw away 200 million tires, 50 billion cans, 30 billion bottles, 4 billion tons of plastics, and 30 million tons of paper. In addition there is the usual household waste and garbage. (In one large city, the cost of removing solid waste is about $150 million a year.) How much waste will be discarded 50 years from now?

By the time you are 70 years old, you will probably have used up 26 million gallons of water and 21,000 gallons of gasoline. You will have eaten 10,000 pounds of meat and drunk 14,000 quarts of milk.

As the population of the United States increases, more and more of us will be sharing the same amount of land, air, and water. More people mean more ecological problems. Everyone will be consuming goods and discarding waste and refuse. The growth in population and the increased use of material things therefore make the environmental problem a crisis.

The Costs of Pollution

Pollution attacks everyone, rich or poor. In a sense, then, it is "democratic." The price we have to pay for pollution, however, is not democratic. The business firm or householder who is responsible for *causing* pollution does not have to pay for it. The living creature that is damaged or destroyed by the effects of pollution pays for it.

Air pollution

Water pollution

How can cities prevent the mass
junking of used cars?

Doctors say that the noise from construction, planes, cars, trucks, and radios threatens our physical and emotional health. Air pollution is probably responsible for many cases of bronchitis, emphysema, asthma, and lung cancer. If you live near a factory that spews forth black smoke, your mother will have to pay for cleaning the drapes and curtains that have become gray with soot, and your father will have to repaint the house more often. In dollars and cents, the cost of air pollution is about $850 a year to each household in the United States.

The cost of upsetting the balance in the environment is a cost that must be paid by all of us. The environmental crisis is so great that one may ask this question: If it is birds and fish today, will it be our turn next?

WORLDWIDE PROBLEM   America is not the only nation facing an environmental crisis. The great Rhine River is now sometimes called the sewer of Western Europe. The rivers and streams of Europe are suffering the same pollution problems as those in the United States. Many beaches along the coast of Europe are unsafe for bathing as a result of oil spills from tankers and the dumping of untreated wastes. Smoke from factories is eroding the famous buildings and outdoor statues of such cities as Brussels and Venice.

The United States, the greatest industrial nation and consumer of goods in the world, is the greatest polluter of all. As other nations become more industrialized and as their people consume more goods, they too will add to the pollution problem. Thus the worldwide problem will grow worse.

Summary   Ecology studies how living things depend upon each other and upon nonliving things in the environment in which they live. Ecology, then, studies the balance of nature and of life. Modern technology has upset the balance and has endangered human beings and wildlife. The problem is worldwide.

Looking Ahead   How proud we Americans are of the beauty of our country! We take pride in our mountains, deserts, and prairies and in the plants and animals that live there. Will future Americans be able to enjoy this beauty? In the next chapter, we shall describe the problem of our vanishing wilderness.

EXERCISES

MATCHING QUESTIONS   Match each term in Column A with its definition in Column B.

Column A

1. environment
2. ecology
3. ecosystem
4. pollution
5. pesticides
6. phosphates
7. smog
8. technology

Column B

(*a*) the study of the environment of all living things

(*b*) chemicals, often used in detergents, that upset the balance between fish life and plant life (algae)

(*c*) the home of all living things—people, animals, and plants

(*d*) methods and machinery used in production

(*e*) chemicals that kill harmful insects

(*f*) dirty or impure air or water

(*g*) a complete unit in nature

(*h*) *sm*oke and f*o*g

MULTIPLE-CHOICE QUESTIONS   For each item, write the letter of the best answer.

1. The main idea of this chapter is that (*a*) the Fertile Crescent is now a desert (*b*) only man can save—or destroy—the environment (*c*) people should not drive cars to work (*d*) the fishing industry in the Great Lakes is ruined.

2. Which statement would be the most difficult to prove either true or false? (*a*) Car exhausts pollute the air. (*b*) Pesticides kill useful insects. (*c*) The environment is doomed. (*d*) Man has changed the balance in nature.

3. Which of the following means of travel causes the most pollution? (*a*) buses (*b*) bicycles (*c*) subways (*d*) cars

4. Which statement is an opinion rather than a fact? (*a*) Pollution attacks rich and poor. (*b*) Americans dispose of 50 billion cans each

year. (*c*) Industry and government should pay for the costs of cleaning up the environment. (*d*) Noise pollution threatens physical and emotional health.

INTERPRETING A CARTOON   Study the cartoon below and answer the questions that follow:

© 1970 by Walt Kelly. Courtesy Publishers-Hall Syndicate

1. According to the cartoon, what is the source of pollution?
2. If we cannot do away with the source of pollution, how can we teach people how to reduce pollution?
3. The artist knows that we must live with the source of pollution mentioned, yet he says do away with it. What do you think he is *really* trying to tell us?

FURTHER READING   Read the following song lyrics and tell whether the statements that follow are true or false. If the lyrics do not give you enough information, go back to the chapter for the answer.

POLLUTION

by Tom Lehrer

If you visit American city,
You will find it very pretty.
Just two things of which you must beware:
Don't drink the water and don't breathe the air.
Pollution, pollution,
They got smog and sewage and mud,
Turn on your tap and get hot and cold running crud.

See the halibuts and the sturgeons
Being wiped out by detergents.

Fish got to swim and birds got to fly
But they don't last long if they try.

Pollution, pollution,
You can use the latest toothpaste,
And then rinse your mouth with industrial waste.

Just go out for a breath of air,
And you'll be ready for Medicare.
The city streets are really quite a thrill,
If the hoods don't get you, the monoxide will.

Pollution, pollution,
Wear a gas mask and a veil
Then you can breathe, long as you don't inhale.

Lots of things there are that you can drink,
But stay away from the kitchen sink.
Throw out your breakfast garbage, and I've got a hunch
That the folks downstream will drink it for lunch.

So go to the city, see the crazy people there.
Like lambs to the slaughter
They're drinking the water
And breathing the air.

1. American cities are ugly.
2. The air and water in American cities are polluted.
3. Smog is a form of air pollution.
4. Detergents kill fish.
5. Wildlife is rapidly increasing because animals can easily find food in garbage cans.
6. Industrial waste finds its way into drinking water.
7. Cities are dangerous places because of crime and pollution.
8. Sewage disposal plants get rid of sewage so that it no longer creates any problem.
9. The songwriter is warning America to do something before it is too late.

Chapter 2   The Vanishing Wilderness

Charlie Goodman and Tony Burgos, like many young Americans, decided that it would be great to "get back to nature" for a week of their spring vacation. The boys decided to *backpack* (carry everything they need on their backs) in Big Bend National Park in Texas. Charlie and Tony hope to see wildlife in a natural setting. On a good day, the boys have read, you can see wild animals such as cougars and bobcats, and perhaps even rare birds.

Tony had read about backpacking in several magazines. According to the articles, the first things you need are good health and a strong desire to explore the wilderness. Tony told Charlie about backpacking, and Charlie liked the idea.

Not all of Charlie and Tony's friends would go backpacking, though. Some prefer the sights and sounds of the city. Others think that backpacking is too tough to be fun. Charlie and Tony tell them that if you can walk, you can backpack. Even more important, though, Charlie and Tony believe that, if they do not hurry and enjoy the wilderness now, they may never get another chance. The wilderness is rapidly disappearing.

We Need Natural Environments

Big Bend, just like all the national parks, is an area of unspoiled natural beauty. The national parks and seashores are open spaces that we use to satisfy some of our basic human needs. Human needs include keeping

physically fit, and open spaces allow people to play games, swim, walk, cycle, or just look at nature. Human needs are also emotional, and open spaces satisfy our impulse to explore, to learn, to enjoy natural beauty, or to be alone. Open spaces link people to nature.

In 1854 the American writer Henry David Thoreau wrote a book about the year he spent living at Walden Pond, in Massachusetts. Thoreau believed that people need to get close to wild things:

> We need the tonic of wildness—to wade sometimes in marshes where the bittern and the meadow-hen lurk, and hear the booming of the snipe [birds that live in marshes]; to smell the whispering sedge [a plant] where only some wilder and more solitary fowl builds her nest, and the mink crawls with its belly close to the ground.

The American frontier, it has been said, kept the nation youthful for about a century—until 1890, when there was no frontier left. Americans today may be turning to outdoor sports as a partial substitute for the pioneer life they can never have. We also need to get away from the crowded, noisy cities and the monotony of suburbia.

Less than a century ago, the average person worked 60 hours a week. People worked six and even seven days a week. Recreation was unknown to all but the well-to-do and the rich. Most Americans thought that hard work and keeping busy were virtues and doing nothing (what we call relaxing) or playing games was a sin. Today, of course, most people work a 40-hour, five-day week. Americans have leisure time and extra money to spend, and the demand for open space for outdoor recreation has increased enormously.

To sum it up:

1. The population of the United States is over 210 million people, or 2½ times larger than in 1890. This has meant an enormous increase in the number of potential users of outdoor recreation areas. Yet much of the space available has to be used to house and feed these people.

2. The shorter workweek and longer holiday weekends give people more time to enjoy the outdoors.

3. The incomes of many American families have risen above what they need to survive. Thus they can set aside more money for leisure and recreation.

4. Automobiles, ships and boats, and jet planes have made it possible to travel hundreds of miles in a day or two. Natural wonders that once were *inaccessible* (out of reach) to most Americans are, in a way, "just around the corner."

Charlie and Tony are looking forward to backpacking in Big Bend. They want to enjoy the natural beauty of the land. But not all people think of the national parks in just this way. Buslines and railroad companies consider the parks as places to which people travel, while local governments see parks as places that bring in visitors—visitors who spend money. To many motorists, the parks are just pretty places to drive through.

NATIONAL PARKS ARE UNDER ATTACK   Our national parks make up less than 5 percent of the 2¼ billion acres of land in the United States. Even though almost half the land area of the United States is farmland, the need for more highways, more urban or suburban developments, and more minerals and lumber makes it unlikely that additional land will be set aside for outdoor recreation. Most likely, the pressure of rival claims for land will endanger the land now set aside for recreation.

The parks are being attacked by noise, pollutants, pesticides, exhaust fumes, and overcrowding. A superjet airport and flood-control projects threaten the ecosystem of the Florida Everglades. In the heart of the West's Yellowstone National Park, motels and hotels that were built to accommo-

date the growing number of tourists attract even more people. Old-timers say that the park is overused and overcrowded. In this lovely craggy wilderness, one can see boiling springs bubbling beside an icy lake and spouts of hot water (Old Faithful) shooting from the ground. During the height of the tourist season, however, the park looks more and more like a crowded city rather than a masterpiece of nature.

WILDLIFE IN TROUBLE   Coalminers used to carry a canary in a cage when they worked down in the mines. If the air down in the mine became poisonous, the canary died. The miners knew that they had to get out of the mine into the fresh open air right away.

Wildlife is man's "miner's canary." Man shares the natural environment with wildlife. Therefore, pollution will affect both man and wildlife. But most wild creatures are lower on the *food chain* than man. This means that wildlife eats vegetation, insects, animals, and fish that man may not eat. But we do eat the plants, animals, and fish that have eaten of these things. When wildlife is endangered by a poisoned environment, so is man.

Birds such as the eagle, the peregrine falcon, and the brown pelican are fast disappearing. One reason is the use of insecticides that are harmful to certain species of birds as well as to insects. Scientists say that some insecticides cause female birds to lay fragile and often infertile eggs. Another reason for the disappearance of wildlife is the loss of living space. Highways, airports, housing, and industry are eating up over a million acres of land a year that once was the home of wildlife. Even though government at all levels is trying to set aside "green acres" and wildlife living space, the lost acres still outstrip those that are saved. As a result, the number of wildlife species on the official *endangered list* (in danger of dying out) was 89 in 1969 and 102 in 1970.

WE MUST REVERSE THE TREND Technological progress and population growth have placed Americans in a very difficult position in terms of the vanishing wilderness. As the nation's population grows even larger, we shall need more and more space for campers, hikers, and other vacationers. We will also need more and more land for highways, airports, shopping centers, and industrial parks, and homesites. "Progress" has made it easier for more and more Americans to get to and enjoy their leisure time. "Progress" has also brought pollution and endangers the ecological balance of nature.

Some people are trying to reverse the trend that is destroying the wilderness. Just 65 miles southeast of Tucson, Arizona, one couple decided to turn back the environmental clock. They are devoting their 8,000-acre farm to nothing. Working with the United States Forest Service and the Arizona Land Department, Frank and Ariel Appleton have made their ranch into an ecological preserve. Instead of raising cattle in this *arid* (dry) area, where it would take 25 acres to support one cow, the Appletons are allowing their farm to return to its natural state.

In 1872 Congress established Yellowstone as the nation's (and the world's) first national park. Since then, Congress has established 37 more national parks as well as eight national seashores and four national lakeshores. Perhaps you would not want to backpack along with Charlie and Tony, but you can enjoy some spectacular sights—glaciers, swamps, prairies, snowcapped mountains, giant caves, the mile-deep Grand Canyon, or the largest and among the oldest of all living things, the giant trees in Sequoia National Park. Perhaps you would prefer to see the prehistoric cliff dwellings in New Mexico or the swampy grasslands of Everglades National Park. If you and future generations of Americans are to enjoy the natural beauty of these precious areas, their use will have to be more carefully controlled.

In addition to placing limits on the number of people who can use recreation areas at any one time, more recreation areas will have to be set aside. Here too, America must make a choice. Land is limited. There are many ways to use this limited land, and pressures are great to use it in many ways. Real estate developers want the land for homes or shopping centers. Cities and towns want new highways. Industry wants to cut the timber, build new factories, or develop natural resources. Those who wish to preserve the land in its natural setting must exert pressure and influence, through the democratic process, to counteract the pressures exerted by those who want to use the land in some other way.

Summary   As America grows in population and wealth, the pressures to use all available lands increase. The wilderness gives way to civilization. But Americans today have more leisure time and great need for open spaces and unspoiled wilderness. Wildlife disappears with the wilderness. If future generations are to enjoy the natural beauties and the wildlife that remain for us, Americans today must act to protect the ecological balance of nature. We must set aside new areas that can never be exploited or destroyed.

Looking Ahead   Americans want to enjoy the natural beauty of the country. We also want to enjoy the comforts of life: high-powered cars, air conditioning, and plastics and other synthetics. Can we have it all? Can we keep using up our resources? In the next chapter, we shall discuss the choices facing Americans.

EXERCISES

MULTIPLE-CHOICE QUESTIONS   For each question, write the letter of the best answer.

1. The main idea of this chapter is that (*a*) backpacking is fun (*b*) backpacking is hard (*c*) America's wilderness is in danger (*d*) national parks are more important than housing developments.
2. According to this chapter, open spaces (*a*) satisfy basic human needs (*b*) are expensive to keep up (*c*) are dangerous areas (*d*) have disappeared.
3. Which of the following was *not* given as a reason why more Americans are using outdoor recreation areas? (*a*) population growth (*b*) shorter

workweek (c) better transportation (d) more areas are available for recreation.

4. As the rural population declines and the number of Americans living in cities increases (a) more land is set aside for outdoor recreation (b) farms are converted into parkland (c) the pressure of rival claims for farmland increases (d) the number of farms increases.

5. Population growth and economic progress have (a) hurt the wilderness (b) helped the wilderness (c) had no effect on the wilderness (d) brought the wilderness closer to man.

6. Wildlife in the United States is (a) in danger (b) increasing (c) serving no useful purpose (d) dangerous to man.

MATCHING QUESTIONS   Match each term in Column A with its definition in Column B.

Column A	*Column B*
1. backpacking	(a) an unspoiled area set aside by the federal government for public enjoyment
2. wilderness	
3. leisure	(b) tells of the values of living in an unspoiled environment
4. *Walden*	
5. national park	(c) dry
6. arid	(d) a form of hiking and camping
	(e) period when one does as one pleases
	(f) natural area, untouched by man

WHO OWNS THE UNITED STATES?   Using the information in the charts on page 305, tell whether the statements below are true or false.

1. More than half of the land in the United States is owned by private individuals, businesses, and industry.

2. The federal government owns less land than the American Indians.

3. The states own more land than the cities and counties.

4. Farming takes up about one-quarter of the land area in the United States.

5. There are more forest lands than national parks.

6. Indian reservations are part of the national park system.

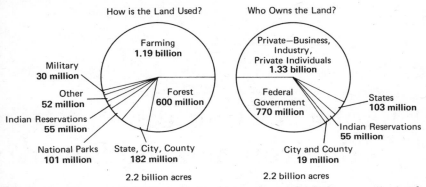

The United States   (*left*) How the land is used   (*right*) Who owns the land

PROJECTS

1. Write to or join one of these environmental protection groups: the National Wildlife Association, the Audubon Society, or the Sierra Club. These groups offer free materials about the environment and suggest possible solutions to environmental problems.

2. For several days, read your local newspapers for articles about local and national problems of the environment, wildlife, and the wilderness. Share what you learned from these articles with your class.

3. Study a map of your state. Note and list the names of national parks and seashores (if any), state parks, wilderness preserves, and bird sanctuaries. How many of each are there? How far away are they from your home?

4. Does your local library or museum have an exhibit on wilderness and wildlife in your state? What animals—if any—that live in your state are marked as endangered species? What is being done to save them? Report your findings to the class.

Chapter 3 Can the Environment Be Saved?

> The air, the water, and the ground are free gifts to men and no one
> has the power to portion them out in parcels. Man must drink and
> breathe and walk and therefore each man has a right to his fair share
> of each. —James Fenimore Cooper, *The Prairie*

No one is against fresh air and clean water. Yet much of our air and
many of our waterways are polluted. We can have a decent environment, if
we really want one, but it will be achieved only at a sacrifice. For example,
we know that present methods of generating electricity add to our pollution
problem. Therefore, we cannot constantly increase electric power output
without increasing the pollution that comes from producing that output. Is
the answer, then, to cut back output?

The Environment and Economic Growth

As a society we have devoted our energies to *economic growth* (increasing
our nation's output of goods and services) and technological progress. We
are used to, or desire to achieve, a high standard of living: color television
sets, permanent-press fabrics, and larger and faster jet planes. But as we
satisfy these demands and as our technology grows, so too does our need for
sources of energy to run these appliances and machines. And as our nation's
population grows, so does our demand for goods. What is happening, then,

is that as we grow in size and increase our demands for materials and energy resources, we may be coming close to the point where we will have used up these resources.

This constant striving for "more and better" has forced us to a point where we must now make some hard choices. These choices involve traditional American beliefs or values. For example, should private business be allowed to do whatever it chooses? Or should the government regulate business to protect the rights of all citizens to a decent environment? Should we have unlimited economic growth and abundance and leave a *plundered* (picked over, barren) and worn-out world for future generations? Or should we now restrict or regulate our consumption and our growth?

Technology vs. the Environment

The growth of technology has been mainly responsible for the problems of our environment. Economic growth too has been blamed for our environmental difficulties. On the other hand, technology may also be able to *solve* these problems. Some specialists believe that a portion of our increased output can be set aside to find the technological solutions to pollution problems. For example, it is possible to reduce air pollution from automobile exhausts to a safe level, or even to zero, with new emission systems or new types of engines using steam or battery power. *Solar* energy (from the sun's rays) may one day replace coal or nuclear energy as a major source of electric power. It *may* very well be that *some time in the future* technology will be able to bring us industry without pollution and farm production without chemicals that damage or threaten the environment.

But experts today predict that, even at present rates of *consumption* (use), supplies of basic raw materials such as copper, zinc, lead, magnesium, tin, gold, and silver will run out in 30 years. The United States, with less than 6 percent of the world's population, annually consumes 33 percent of the world's resources. Knowing this, can we force American producers to stop using these resources?

Now let us consider two of the most difficult environmental problems that, so far, defy political solution: *economic growth* and *population control.*

As the nation grows, its wealth increases. In 1972 the total value of all the goods produced in the United States was $650 billion. In 1980 it is

estimated that the total value will be over $1,000 billion! As you well
know, as more is produced, more energy is needed. This adds to pollution.
More resources will be used up. This *depletes* (exhausts or empties) our
environment.

Should growth be limited? Remember, it is only because of economic
growth that we can have the material things some of us think make life
more interesting. It is only because of economic growth that more people
have jobs (to produce the goods and services that are part of growth). A
decline in economic growth would probably mean an increase in unemployment.

Is population control needed? Because of population growth, our need
for everything will double by the year 2000. We will need to cut down
more trees for timber, build more houses, produce more food, and use more
water because we will have more people. If this is true, should population
growth be limited? If the answer is yes, who will decide how to limit this
growth? For example, should limits be based on a system of free choice, or
should some groups, such as the poor, be forced to reduce population
growth?

The Will to Do the Job

In many cases, we know what has to be done if we are to save our
environment. We know, for example, that automobiles and power plants
pollute the air we breathe. We know that air pollution is expensive in terms
of human lives lost due to lung cancer and emphysema. Pollution's dollars-
and-cents cost is seen in corroded steel and paint and decaying brick and
cement.

The world's supply of fresh (not sea) water is limited. Salt water
accounts for 97 percent of the total water on the planet, and about 98
percent of the remaining fresh water is in the polar ice caps. We know that
polluted water can result in such diseases as cholera, typhoid, and dysen-
tery. We also know that water pollution destroys fish life. It caused the
herring catch in Lake Erie to drop from 835,000 pounds in 1950 to almost
nothing in 1970.

It will cost about 12 cents per 1,000 gallons to remove up to 90 percent
of the pollutants in our water supply. The cost of pollution control devices

for automobiles runs from about $100 to $600, depending upon how high the standards are for clean air. For only about $3.50 a ton, scrap cars can be melted down, and hundreds of pounds of metal and glass can be reclaimed. Are we willing to pay the cost, and are we willing to make the hard choices needed to save our environment?

Environmental Victories

In England in 1952, 4,000 people died as a result of a dense and poisonous fog that hit London. The people of London said, "Enough." The famous gray London fog was no longer a joke. When it was found that the smoke from the soft coal burned in homes and industries combined with normal fog to cause the deadly gray fog, the government *prohibited* (banned) the use of soft coal. Today Londoners enjoy sunlight and a city that is practically free of soot and smoke.

The Dust Bowl was a vast, desert-like area of the Great Plains of the United States. Winds had blown away the topsoil. This was very much like what had happened to the Fertile Cresent. But a large area of the Dust Bowl has been reclaimed in the past 40 years.

Cities are developing sewage treatment systems. San Diego Bay, once polluted, is now dotted with sailboats, and the water, now clear of sewage, is filled with fish.

Groups all over the country have set up centers where people can bring their used aluminum cans and glass bottles. The cans and bottles are returned to the manufacturers, melted down, and *recycled* (made into new cans and bottles). In this way society does not use up as much aluminum and glass. At the same time the waste is used up and there is no problem of where or how to dispose of it.

CITIZENS FIGHT POLLUTION   Youngsters throughout the United States are cleaning up littered vacant lots and turning them into neighborhood parks. People are cleaning rivers and streams of the junk that has been thrown into them for years.

Henry Stevens joined the Ecology Club at school. He told his mother that she should not buy detergents that contain phosphates. (Partly through citizens' efforts, the use of phosphates in detergents has been banned by many states.) Henry uses only as much water as is needed and turns the lights off when he leaves a room.

Henry has convinced his mother to buy *reusables* (articles that can be used more than once) instead of *disposables* (articles that are used once and then thrown away). Mrs. Stevens buys bottles that can be returned to the store, and she uses cotton dish towels instead of paper towels.

Mrs. Stevens reads all the food labels and does not buy foods processed with additives if she can avoid them. She promised Henry that she would never buy a coat made from the fur of an animal facing extinction.

Mr. Stevens uses only plastic trash bags. He is planting more trees and bushes in his garden because they produce oxygen and help filter carbon dioxide from the air. He does not use insecticides to kill pests.

Mary Stevens belongs to a car pool. She uses only low-lead gasoline in her car. Whenever possible, Mary walks or uses buses and trains instead of her car. One day Mary saw clouds of black smoke rising from the smokestacks of a local factory. She was able to get the interest of a group in her community that was organized to defend the environment. Mary helped them to start a lawsuit against the factory.

Thus all of us can do our share to help make our world a cleaner, healthier, and more attractive place in which to live.

INDUSTRY FIGHTS POLLUTION Industry is now aware of environmental problems. Electric power producers are urging consumers to "save a watt." Producers are looking for methods of using atomic power and disposing of wastes that will not pollute rivers and kill fish.

The auto industry is experimenting with devices to control the carbon monoxide from car exhausts. New engines that operate on steam, batteries, and other fuel sources are being tested. Gasoline producers are producing or developing low-lead and lead-free gasoline for use in auto engines.

Factories burning soft coal are changing to hard coal and raising the height of their smokestacks to keep the smoke rising instead of falling. Devices are being installed on the smokestacks to wash or clean the smoke and to catch the solid wastes before they enter the atmosphere. About 10 percent of the total cost of constructing new paper mills goes for devices to control air and water pollution.

GOVERNMENT FIGHTS POLLUTION Federal, state, and local governments are passing laws to control pollution. An antismog program in Los Angeles has cut pollution a great deal. The cost to the city of Los Angeles, however, is about $4.6 million each year. New York City spends about $70 million a year on water pollution controls.

The federal government has created a Council on Environmental Quality. The council grants funds to the states for local waste disposal works and water quality control. Programs to lower the taxes of those industries that spend money for antipollution research and devices will encourage private industry to fight pollution.

Summary Rescuing our polluted environment and preserving our natural resources for future generations will not be easy. It will require the efforts of government, industry, and every individual.

EXERCISES

MATCHING QUESTIONS Match each term in Column A with its definition in Column B.

Column A

1. economic growth
2. recycling
3. disposables
4. reusables

Column B

(*a*) products such as plastic bottles that are used once and thrown away

(*b*) increasing the output of goods and services

(*c*) taking used products—cans, bottles, and paper—turning them back to their original material, and making them into new products

(*d*) products such as glass containers that can be used more than once

MULTIPLE-CHOICE QUESTIONS Select the letter that best answers the question or completes the statement.

1. The main idea of this chapter is that (*a*) industry is against plans to save

the environment (b) government is not doing enough to combat water and air pollution (c) hard choices will have to be made between more "progress" and protecting the environment (d) our nation must slow down its economic growth.

2. Which statement is not a fact but an opinion? (a) Population growth must be controlled. (b) Americans use more power per person than the rest of the world combined. (c) Americans will use more electric power in the year 2000 than they use today. (d) Pollution killed fish in Lake Erie.

3. Which of the following values is in conflict with the other three? (a) economic growth (b) protection of natural resources (c) material well-being (d) population increase

4. One problem that may result from continued economic growth is (a) unemployment (b) reduced output of material things (c) slowdown in population growth (d) increased pollution of air and water.

5. Which is *not* an example of an environmental victory? (a) rapid growth in population (b) increased use of reusable items (c) more recycling of metals and glass (d) London is practically soot- and smoke-free.

6. How can you fight pollution in your home? (a) Buy returnable bottles. (b) Use paper towels. (c) Use laundry detergents rich in phosphates. (d) Throw all cans and glass bottles into the garbage.

7. In order to win the fight against pollution, action must be taken by (a) the public (b) private industry (c) the government (d) all three.

WHAT IS BEING DONE IN YOUR COMMUNITY?   Tell how your community or neighborhood rates in each of the pollution areas listed below: Is there no problem, a minor problem, a major problem, or an extremely serious problem?

Source of Pollution

Motor vehicle exhausts	Trash dumped into vacant
Factory and home	lots, rivers, and streams
Incinerator exhausts	Industrial pollution
Traffic noise	of streams
Airplane noise	Sewage disposal
Auto junkyards	Garbage disposal
	Other forms of pollution
	not listed here

INTERPRETING A CARTOON Look at the cartoon above and answer the following questions:

1. What sources of pollution can you identify?
2. What can the citizen shown here do to combat pollution?
3. How can industry help to combat pollution?
4. What can city, state, and local governments do to combat the pollution shown here? Explain.

Unit XI   World Affairs

Chapter 1   The Balance
of Power

Earl Gibson was reading his World History homework assignment. The topic was World War II. Perhaps Earl was bored or looking for an excuse not to study. Suddenly, there flashed into his mind some words he had once read: "Blessed are the peacemakers of the world."

"If that's true," thought Earl, "then why am I always studying about the people who made wars?"

As he turned the pages of his book, Earl came upon a picture of Sir Winston Churchill, Great Britain's prime minister during World War II. Under Churchill's picture were his famous words to the British people as they faced possible defeat by the Nazis in the Battle of Britain:

Upon this battle depends the survival of [our] civilization. . . . Let us therefore brace ourselves to our duties, and so bear ourselves that, if the British Empire and its Commonwealth last for a thousand years, men will still say, "This was their finest hour."

"Funny," thought Earl. "Why does Churchill say that a battle can be a country's 'finest hour'? People talk about peace being so great, but almost any time, anywhere, some country in the world seems to be at war."

Very little in Earl's history book had to do with peace. Most of the book was about wars. Some of these wars took place thousands of years ago. Some wars seemed to stop and start again for years, even decades.

The Study of War

Earl's textbook stated that the Spanish Civil War (1936–1939) was a "minor" war. But Earl could not understand how a war in which almost a million people died could be a *small* war. Then Earl looked up *War* in his encyclopedia. He learned that between 1907 and 1945 (from the Balkan Wars that led into World War I to the end of World War II) at least 50 million people died as a result of war. What is more, World War II did not end all wars any more than World War I did. There had been and was again fighting in the Middle East between the Israelis and several Arab states. The United States had fought Communist armies in Korea and Indochina. In Africa there had been civil wars in Nigeria, the Congo, and Angola. India and Pakistan had fought over Kashmir and Bangladesh, and Protestants and Catholics in Northern Ireland had fought one another for years.

Earl wondered if the French Emperor Napoleon Bonaparte was right when he asked, "Can a few days of life equal the happiness of dying for one's country?" Or was our Civil War General William Tecumseh Sherman wiser when he said, "I am tired and sick of war. . . . War is hell"?

MUST MEN KILL ONE ANOTHER?   Was war really necessary? Earl was puzzled why men always seem to fight and kill one another. Most animals that hunt and kill have to do so to live. Earl could accept this. But man, he knew, is one of the few creatures on earth that kill their own kind. Other animals kill for food. Man kills for entirely different reasons. Is man a "natural" killer?

AGGRESSION   Some scientists say yes, man is a "natural" killer. *Aggression* (destructive or threatening behavior) is *inborn*. That is, all people are born with the tendency to act aggressively. On the other hand, Dr. Louis Leakey, a British *anthropologist* (a scientist who studies primitive people) blames civilized life for mankind's aggressive behavior toward his fellow creatures. Our remote ancestors killed animals for food. There is no evidence of murder or warfare until about 40,000 years ago. This was the time when man learned how to use fire. Dr. Leakey believes that the use of fire made man's life more secure. Dr. Leakey thinks that the human population then increased, people lived longer, and people began to fight one another for lands and possessions. As man became more civilized, the number of violent acts increased. Think about it! Doesn't it seem strange that, as we became more civilized, we also became more destructive? Today we have weapons that are capable of destroying everything on earth.

An *aggressor* is someone who threatens to harm you in some way unless you do as he says. Basically, there are only two ways of dealing with an aggressor. You can either fight or you can refuse to fight. Some people do not choose to fight because they are afraid of being hurt more by fighting than by giving in to the bully. However, there are people who refuse to fight because they consider it *immoral*. They are called *pacifists*. Jesus, for example, taught his followers to "turn the other cheek." He forgave those who crucified him. In our time Mahatma Gandhi in India and Dr. Martin Luther King, Jr., in the United States taught that love is the best way to resist an enemy. They and their followers refused to obey laws or government orders that they felt were unjust, even though this meant going to jail. For example, the followers of Dr. King went to places they were forbidden to enter—such as "whites-only" restaurants. This is known as *passive resistance*. When their enemies used violence against them, the followers of Dr. King would "turn the other cheek."

PEACE BY NOT GETTING INVOLVED   Some Americans believe that we should try to solve the problems of this country, not those of other nations. (We have examined many of our own problems in this book —poverty, pollution, discrimination, and criminal justice, to name just a few.) These people believe that we should not become involved in the problems of other nations. These people are not necessarily pacifists. Many would fight if the United States were attacked. But they do not believe that any nation would attack the United States if it would just mind its own business.

PEACE BY GETTING INVOLVED   Others believe that the United States has no choice. We must be involved, they say, even though involvement has its dangers. According to this view, involvement is like breathing. We know that there are germs in the atmosphere, but that does not stop us from breathing. To stop breathing is to die. The life of the United States, it is argued, depends upon its being involved because:

1. The United States is only one nation in a world of nations. We occupy one area of land in the world. Our neighbors are where they are. If we don't like them, we just can't pack up and move away.

2. We need more natural resources and foods than we have or can produce at home. We must buy these items (such as oil, bananas, and aluminum) from other nations. If many foreign resources were denied to us, we would not be able to exist as the nation we are today.

3. We have products to sell to other nations.

4. Americans travel abroad for business and pleasure. They expect their government to protect their lives and property while they are in foreign countries.

5. It is unlikely that the United States could survive and continue to prosper and progress if it kept itself apart from the rest of the world.

6. In the nuclear and space age, the United States is not the only powerful nation on earth. The Soviet Union, Japan, and West Germany are important industrial powers. The People's Republic of China (Communist China) is rapidly increasing in power.

7. Peace can be kept only when there is a *balance of power*. This means that if there are two opposing sides, neither will attack the other if each is about equal in strength to the other. But if one side *thinks* it is stronger, it may attack the other.

Power balances keep changing. Before World War II, Great Britain tried to keep the balance of power. After World War II, keeping the balance of power became the job of the United States. This is called *power politics*. It requires that the United States get involved in Asia, Africa, and Latin America. The purpose is not simply to spread democracy to others (as some people think), but to keep the balance of power from being upset and threatening democracy at home.

ARGUMENTS AGAINST THE BALANCE OF POWER   Some people today believe that all arguments about keeping a balance of power to preserve peace are phony. Power politics has not stopped wars. Power, they insist, corrupts, and those nations with the most power become the most corrupt. Governments may make their people afraid of enemy attack. In this way the government can use "national security" as an excuse to abolish civil rights and gain excessive power over the people.

The majority of the American people, however, believe that the best way to keep peace is to remain militarily strong. The American people support the United Nations' peace efforts. However, the UN has thus far not been able to prevent small wars from breaking out. Until all nations are willing to give up much of their independence to a world organization, such as the UN, most Americans do not think that they can rely on the UN to protect their vital interests.

Summary   The instruments of peace are not easy to develop. Some people argue that if everyone would refuse to fight, there would be no war. Others argue that this is unwise because not everyone would refuse to fight. Some suggest that the United States should mind its own business and in that way it could keep out of war. This argument is challenged by those who say that no powerful nation can keep to itself. Instead, the United States must continue to be powerful and work to keep a power balance in the world.

Looking Ahead   In the next chapter, we shall discuss how the United States has become involved with other nations. As one example of this involvement, we shall study the current situation in the Middle East.

EXERCISES

MULTIPLE-CHOICE QUESTIONS   For each question, write the letter of the best answer.

1. The main idea of this chapter is that (*a*) peace is only temporary (*b*) a greater effort should be made to study peace (*c*) power politics works (*d*) man is a natural killer.
2. According to this chapter, history books should devote more space to

(a) war studies (b) domestic problems (c) political events (d) peace studies.

3. Scientists who have investigated aggression in man (a) agree that aggression is inborn (b) agree that aggression is learned (c) think that aggression in man can be controlled (d) do not agree on this issue.

4. Someone who believes that we can have peace only by remaining strong is in favor of (a) noninvolvement (b) passive resistance (c) pacifism (d) power politics.

5. Which of the following statements would support United States involvement in world affairs? (a) We must be prepared to react to the moves of other nations. (b) Power politics has not stopped wars in the past. (c) Politicians do not want peace. (d) We should concentrate on the problems that we face at home.

6. Which of the following statements is an argument for noninvolvement on the part of the United States in world affairs? (a) No powerful nation can keep to itself. (b) Peace can be kept only when there is a balance of power. (c) We have goods which we must sell to other nations. (d) We should concern ourselves first with problems at home.

MATCHING QUESTIONS   Match each term in Column A with its definition in Column B.

Column A

1. aggression
2. inborn
3. power politics
4. pacifists
5. passive resistance
6. noninvolvement
7. balance of power

Column B

(a) people who, for moral reasons, refuse to fight

(b) when two opposing sides are of almost equal strength

(c) the idea that a nation should "mind its own business"

(d) natural for everyone to have

(e) refusal to obey laws one considers unjust

(f) destructive behavior

(g) requires that America get involved in world affairs

PUZZLING QUESTIONS IN MAN'S HISTORY See if you can answer some of the questions that people ask as they study history. Write your own thoughts on each of the questions below.

1. If war is so horrible, why do men fight?
2. If a balance of power has not prevented war in the past, why do some leading statesmen seem to think it will prevent war now?
3. What did Benjamin Franklin mean when he said, "There never was a good war or a bad peace"?
4. Why do some of our leaders tell us that we can have peace only if we mind our own business while other leaders tell us that we can only have peace if we get involved?
5. If most people seem to be against war, why can't they get together for peace?

Chapter 2 Oil, Energy, and Foreign Policy

Someday soon, as you ride with parents or friends into your local gasoline station, you may hear a conversation that runs something like this:

"Fill it up, Joe."

"Sorry, I can give you only two gallons."

"Not again! The same thing happened a few years ago. And Joe, the price is up two cents a gallon."

"Yes," Joe replies. "The shortage is back. And the prices will keep going up because the suppliers keep raising their prices."

As you drive away from the service station, you wonder why there is a shortage of gas. You understand that whenever there is a small supply of a product and a large demand for the product, its price will go up. And today's cars, with their pollution-control devices and high-powered engines, use more gas than any cars ever made. So there is a huge demand for gasoline. But why is there a shortage?

Gasoline, as you probably know, is produced from crude oil. The Middle East, and particularly the area around the Persian Gulf (see map), has perhaps two-thirds of all the crude oil reserves outside the *Communist bloc* (nations allied with the Soviet Union or Communist China). Except for Israel, the nations of the Middle East are Arab nations. Israel produces very little oil. Thus most of the world's known oil reserves are in Arab hands.

Israel and her Arab neighbors have been at war since the state of Israel was created in 1948. The Arab states believe that the United States favors Israel. They believe that American Jews, although few in number, play an

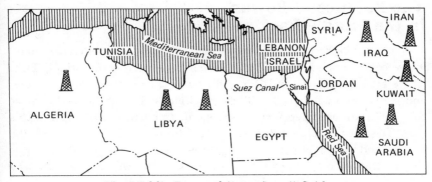

The Middle East and its major oil fields

important part in influencing American foreign policy. The Arab states therefore want to use their oil to pressure American leaders to change their policy.

Some Americans agree with the Arab leaders that it is in America's best interests to stop supporting Israel. Other Americans disagree. They believe that America is morally obligated to make sure that Israel remains an independent nation.

Containment

The United States was one of two great powers following World War II. The Soviet Union was the other. A Communist country, the Soviet Union was trying to spread Communist beliefs throughout the world. The aim of the United States since 1945 has been to stop the expansion of communism. The United States formed military alliances, gave economic and military aid to its allies, and, in some cases, used military forces to stop the expansion of communism. This policy—*to stop the spread of communism*—is called the *policy of containment*.

Containment is another form of *balance-of-power* politics. When World War II ended, the British, French, and Germans were too weak to match the power of the Soviet Union. Only the United States was able to do this. Since 1945, then, the United States and the Soviet Union have tried to keep at about equal strength—that is, to maintain a *balance of power*.

The Balance of Power
in the Middle East

The Middle East has long been called the "crossroads of civilization." Three continents—Europe, Africa, and Asia—meet at the Middle East. Three great religions—Judaism, Christianity, and Islam—began there, and Jerusalem is a holy city to all three religions. Two of the world's great early civilizations, Egypt and Mesopotamia (modern Iraq), began in this area. The Suez Canal, a direct water route from the Mediterranean to the Red Sea and the seas of Asia, was dug through Egypt. Now if we add to this the tremendous oil resources of the Arabian states, we can easily see why this region is so important to so many different nations.

The Soviet Union has long sought to gain a foothold in the Middle East. Before World War II, Britain and France kept Russia out. Since World War II, the United States has been the major power in the Middle East. American oil companies and engineering firms dominate the oil-producing, refining, and transportation (pipeline) companies in the area. The United States has given economic and military support to Israel, Saudi Arabia, and Jordan. The Soviet Union has replaced the United States as the supplier to Libya, Syria, Iraq, and Egypt. The powerful United States Sixth Fleet cruises the Mediterranean waters. The United States, then, has a strong stake in the Middle East. Many military men believe that it would be against our interests to allow the Soviet Union to gain a strong position in this area. Power politics being what it is, the Soviet Union is doing everything it can to increase its influence in the Middle East in order to create a balance of power in that area.

THE ENERGY CRISIS AND OUR ENVIRONMENT   The Middle East problem is made more complicated by another crisis facing the United States. The United States today faces an *energy crisis*. Many other sources of energy, such as coal, natural gas, electric power, and nuclear energy, are in short supply. In some areas, gas used in heating and as fuel has been *rationed* (a fixed daily allowance was given).

Ecologists (people concerned about the environment) are afraid that if we drill for oil in the oceans too near our coastlines, we will damage the oceans and shores. Ecologists are against building nuclear-powered electric plants

Balance of power

for fear that nuclear wastes (or simply the heat from these power plants) will be discharged into the streams and rivers nearby and will endanger plant and fish life. Ecologists are against the *strip mining* (surface removal) of coal reserves because this method destroys the land. So you see, new sources of energy are needed. But our interest in *ecology* limits the ways in which we can get this much-needed energy.

MIDDLE EAST OIL RESERVES   The United States expects to consume between 24 and 27 million barrels of oil daily in the 1980s. In order to meet this demand, we will have to import between 12 and 15 million barrels of oil a day. We are not alone in this rising demand for oil. The worldwide demand for oil (excluding the Communist countries) is expected to rise from about 45 million barrels daily in 1973 to some 78 million barrels daily in 1980. Most of the additional oil that we and the rest of the world need must come from the Middle East.

The Middle East produced about 20 million barrels daily in 1973. It is believed that this production might increase to between 40 and 45 million barrels daily by 1980. Will the Arab states increase their oil production to meet world demand? They might not! For one thing increasing oil production will not do the Arab states much good. They now earn so much money from oil that they are not tempted to earn more money. Furthermore, if oil reserves are kept in the ground, the oil will probably be worth much more in the future.

Money is not the Arab states' only concern. The oil-producing Arab states can see no reason to produce more oil than would best serve their own countries' interests. Why, they think, should they do the world a favor by *increasing oil production* unless the world, and the United States in particular, is ready to do them a favor? The favor the Arabs want is support against Israel.

THE SIX-DAY WAR OF 1967   In just six days of war in June 1967, the Israeli army badly beat the Arab armies. The Arabs lost land and, what is just as important, they lost "face." On November 22, 1967, the United Nations Security Council called for the withdrawal of Israeli forces from lands they had captured during the war and had occupied ever since. The Soviet Union strongly supported the Arab states and the UN resolution. The Arab states believe that the United States could influence Israel to obey the UN resolution.

THE 1973 **WAR**   Israel does not believe that the Arab states will be satisfied with the return of the territories they lost in the Six-Day War. Israel is convinced that the Arab states want to destroy Israel as a nation. Furthermore, the Israelis do not have faith that the UN will support them if the Arab states do strike out against them.

In 1973, on the highest (most solemn) Jewish holy day, Yom Kippur, when most Israelis where in synagogues, fasting and praying, Egyptian and Syrian armies attacked Israel. The Egyptians and Syrians claimed that they were being attacked by Israel. They argued that, to begin with, the Israelis did not belong in Arab territory. The Arabs felt that when they crossed the Suez Canal, or occupied the Golan Heights in Syria, they were "going home."

At this writing we do not know where events will finally lead. However, we do know several things. First, the Arab armies' victories in the early part of the 1973 war did much to raise the *morale* (self-image) of all the Arab people. The Arab armies demonstrated to themselves, as well as to the rest of the world, that, given the equipment and training, Arab troops can fight. This new spirit in the Arab world strengthened the cause of Arab unity against Israel. Second, perhaps because of their new self-confidence, Arab nations are now willing to discuss peace terms. Third, largely through American efforts, the Arabs and Israelis have agreed to exchange prisoners, pull back their troops, and allow United Nations peace-keeping forces to be placed between the two sides.

If both sides can learn to respect one another and continue to have confidence in themselves, perhaps they will continue to talk. If they talk, perhaps they will not fight. If they do not fight, a lasting peace in the Middle East may be possible.

Summary   A study of the Middle East situation today shows that the United States does get involved in world affairs. It also indicates that peaceful solutions to world problems are not easy to find. We saw that the United States has many different interests, and these interests often are in conflict with each other.

Looking Ahead   The Middle East situation is a difficult one. What do you think the United States should do? Does it matter what one person thinks? In the next chapter, we shall discuss the role of the individual in peace making.

EXERCISES

SEPARATING FACT FROM OPINION   Study the statements below. If the statement is a fact, write T. If it is an opinion, write O.

1. There is an energy crisis in the United States.
2. Increased demand and reduced supply are responsible for the energy crisis.
3. Israel produces very little oil.
4. It is in America's interest to stop supporting Israel against the Arab states.
5. The Soviet Union supports the Arab states against Israel.

6. The United States and the Soviet Union are engaging in power politics in the Middle East.
7. Israel occupied Arab territory in 1967.
8. Israel should return all territory it occupied in 1967.

MATCHING QUESTIONS   Match each term in Column A with its definition in Column B.

Column A   *Column B*

1. Communist bloc   (*a*) allies of the Soviet Union
2. balance of power   (*b*) oil still in the ground
3. containment   (*c*) a fixed daily allowance
4. energy crisis   (*d*) American foreign policy designed to stop the spread of communism
5. ecology
6. ration   (*e*) shortage of oil, coal, and natural gas
7. oil reserves   (*f*) keeping opposing sides at equal strength
                             (*g*) study of the environment

MAP STUDY   Study the map on page 323 and then tell whether the statements that follow are true or false. If the map does not give enough information to answer true or false, write NS.

1. Libya is a neighbor of Israel.
2. Egypt is a neighbor of Israel.
3. Egypt and Syria share common borders.
4. Israel is more powerful than any of her neighbors.
5. The Soviet Union is near the Middle East Arab states.
6. An Israeli soldier is better trained than an Egyptian soldier.
7. The United States is many miles away from the Middle East.
8. There are oil fields in Saudi Arabia.

WHAT WOULD YOU DO?   Imagine that you are the President of the United States. You are meeting with your Cabinet. The Secretary of the Interior tells you that fuel reserves are very low. We must build a pipeline to Alaskan oil fields and dig for offshore oil if we are to meet our energy needs. The Secretary of State warns that unless we change our policy with respect to Israel, the Arab states might cut off all oil supplies to this country. Your personal secretary has completed a count of telegrams coming to your office. They are overwhelmingly in favor of helping Israel keep its independence.

A messenger has just brought news that the Arab states, with support from the Soviet Union, have launched an all-out attack on Israel. It is believed that Soviet pilots and technicians are part of the invasion force.

What would you do?

Chapter 3 The Citizen's Role in World Affairs

A mother in Peoria, Illinois, remembers the words of a song that was popular when she was a girl, before the United States entered World War I: "I didn't raise my boy to be a soldier." Yet her son had become a soldier. He died in combat 12,000 miles from home, in a country most Americans barely knew existed—Vietnam. What could the mother have done to stop the war?

A worker in an aircraft plant in southern California wonders, "Will peace hurt me?" About 95 percent of the aircraft industry depends upon defense business. And so do three out of every ten manufacturing workers in the state of California.

A war veteran reads that the draft has been *abolished* (ended). Where will America's armies come from if they are needed to fight its enemies? What has happened to the spirit and dedication of men such as Nathan Hale, who said, "I regret that I have but one life to give for my country"?

Jim Saunders is an American who lives in Canada. Some of Jim's friends live in Sweden and Norway, and probably in other countries as well. While America was fighting in Vietnam, Jim fled to Canada. He and many young men like him want to come home. But they do not want to go to jail as *draft evaders* (young men who did not report for induction into the armed services). These men believe that they were right not to report. You will recall, from Unit VIII, on dissent, a discussion of the Nuremberg trials. The trial judges ruled that, if the laws of a government are immoral, men and women must obey a higher law (natural or divine law) and disobey the government. Jim was a dissenter. He thought that the war in Vietnam was immoral and the laws that forced young men to fight in the war had to be broken.

You may have seen, in newspapers and on television, pickets marching in front of the White House. They were carrying signs urging the President not to meet with the leader of a Communist country. These pickets were dissenters. They were letting the President know that they did not agree with his policy of establishing friendly relations with Communist nations. Yet the President met with the Communist leader, and agreed to meet again.

What can the mother in Peoria, the aircraft worker in California, the war veteran, the draft evaders, and the people who oppose making agreements with Communist countries do? The United States has a population of over 210 million people. It is a big, powerful country. Can one person, one citizen, really do anything? Before we can answer this question, we have to know more about how our country's foreign policy is made.

How Foreign Policy Is Made

In the United States the basic decisions about foreign policy are made by the *executive branch* of government: the President and his Cabinet. Congress, the *legislative branch,* becomes directly involved only when treaties must be *ratified* (approved), laws passed, nominations approved, and money *appropriated* (set aside from tax money) to carry out the President's policy.

THE WORLD SITUATION   A major purpose of foreign policy is to make it possible for the United States to cope with the world situation. Thus in the 1960s American troops were sent to fight in Vietnam. Three American Presidents thought we had to help South Vietnam defend itself against Communist aggression. So whatever is happening in the world —and this means the decisions made by over a hundred nations all over the world—is going to influence American foreign policy.

CONGRESS   Congress can and must help the President set and carry out foreign policy. In 1965 President Lyndon Johnson used a congressional resolution to defend American ships in the Gulf of Tonkin as the legal basis for American actions in Vietnam. But the war dragged on for years, with little hope of victory, and even spread to other nations in Southeast Asia. The mood in Congress turned against American military involvement in Southeast Asia. In the summer of 1973 Congress threatened to cut off funds for all military activities in Asia if President Nixon did not stop the bombing of Cambodia. The President agreed, and the bombing stopped.

THE AMERICAN PEOPLE   Congress is elected by the American people. There are two houses of Congress, the Senate and the House of Representatives. The Senate has 100 members: two senators from each of the 50 states in the union. Both senators of a state are elected by all the voters of the state. The House of Representatives has 435 members. Each member is elected by the voters in one *electoral district* of a state. (The district may be a few city blocks or several small towns.) Thus the members of Congress must consider both the local needs and the statewide interests of the people who elect them to office.

Special-Interest Groups   There are many special-interest groups in the United States. Labor unions, associations of businessmen, veterans, farmers, and bankers—all these and many more groups have special interests that they try to push forward in Congress. Of course, some special-interest groups have more *clout* (power, money, and influence) than others. But all groups, in their own ways, try to influence senators and representatives to introduce or vote for laws that are to the groups' benefit.

For example, you might be asked to sign a petition for or against a law or program. When enough people have signed it, this petition is sent to members of Congress. Other groups urge their members and friends to send letters or telegrams to their senators and representatives. It is hoped that, if enough letters are received, Congress will be convinced that the majority of the people feel the way the letter writers say they feel about an issue. These special-interest groups may hire people to lobby for them. (To lobby is to attempt to convince the members of Congress that your special interest is a good one.) They advertise, and, except for unions and big business, are permitted to give financial support to candidates who favor their interests. Lobbying and campaign contributions are regulated by strict laws.

Special-interest groups often do not agree with each other. For example, the Arab nations are supported by oil companies in the United States,

These students are signing a petition to save an endangered species

while Israel has the support of America's Jewish citizens (and many Americans who are not Jewish). Each special-interest group exerts all the influence it can to shape America's foreign policy in the Middle East.

THE POLITICAL PROCESS   The American public, therefore, is the ultimate source of America's foreign policy. The public elects Congress and the President. The voting public makes up the public local-interest and special-interest groups that influence congressional decisions. Almost everybody elected to public office is a member of one of the two political parties—Democratic or Republican. Political parties are the framework within which political action takes place. All people have the chance to participate in these activities by working with a local branch of the party they choose. Most Americans, however, do not become active in politics until they are aroused by a specific issue.

THE ROLE OF THE MEDIA   The media (newspapers, books, magazines, radio, and television) make information available to the American public. The public bases its opinions and feelings on the information it receives from the media. A free press tries to uncover the truth, no matter how long it has been hidden, and make it known to the American people.

Sometimes the press exaggerates or even falsifies the news, however. In 1898, for example, newspaper stories of Spanish atrocities in Cuba and the report of the sinking of the battleship *Maine* stirred up much anti-Spanish feeling. The papers were largely responsible for America's going to war with Spain in 1898. This newspaper activity was known as "yellow journalism."

On the other hand, the American press in the 1960s challenged official government reports about what was really happening in Vietnam. A continuous flow of information from the free press was largely responsible for changing the views of the American people. The American people exerted pressure on the Congress, and thus on the President, to end the war in Vietnam.

Summary   The American citizen, if kept informed by a free press, can exert influence on our country's foreign policy. The citizen exerts influence through special-interest groups, by participating in political parties, and through the election process. Although it is the President who makes foreign policy for the country, he must be concerned about the wishes of the Congress and the people. The President needs the support of the Congress and the American people if his foreign policy is going to be successful. Therefore, even though one citizen alone cannot do much, one citizen acting together with other citizens with similar interests *can* do a great deal.

EXERCISES

MATCHING QUESTIONS   Match each term in Column A with its definition in Column B.

Column A

1. draft evader
2. appropriated
3. special-interest groups
4. electoral district
5. legislative branch
6. lobby
7. executive branch

Column B

(a) the area of a state that elects one member of the House of Representatives
(b) set aside from tax money
(c) Congress
(d) some examples are labor unions, business associations, veterans, and farmers groups
(e) the President and his Cabinet
(f) to try to influence the voting of legislators
(g) someone who does not report for military service

UNDERSTANDING WHAT YOU HAVE READ Using the information you learned in the chapter, complete the following statements.

1. The major forces that influence American foreign policy are the world situation and _____.
2. The President's Cabinet is part of the _____ branch of government.
3. One way that Congress may influence the President in the making of foreign policy is through Congress's power to _____.
4. One way that the American public can influence Congress is through

   _____.
5. Groups that have special interests are allowed to _____ before Congress.
6. The main function of the media is to supply _____ to the public.

MULTIPLE-CHOICE QUESTIONS For each question, write the letter of the best answer.

1. The main idea of this chapter is that (*a*) special-interest groups are bad (*b*) ordinary citizens can influence United States foreign policy (*c*) aircraft workers do not want peace (*d*) Israel and the Arab states should have the support of different special-interest groups.
2. Basic foreign policy decisions in the United States are made by (*a*) the President and his Cabinet (*b*) Congress (*c*) the Supreme Court (*d*) special-interest groups.
3. According to this chapter, even though the President makes foreign policy, the ultimate source of American foreign policy is (*a*) the Supreme Court (*b*) the Republican Party (*c*) newspapers and television (*d*) the American people.
4. Which statement in this chapter would be the most difficult to prove either true or false? (*a*) Three American presidents thought we had to help South Vietnam. (*b*) The President needs the cooperation of Congress. (*c*) Most Americans are not interested in foreign policy. (*d*) There are many special-interest groups in the United States.

INDEX